Foundation

Economic Justice

MORRIS SILVER

Professor of Economics
City College of the City University of New York

Basil Blackwell

Copyright © Morris Silver 1989

First published 1989

Basil Blackwell Ltd
108 Cowley Road, Oxford, OX4 1JF, UK

Basil Blackwell Inc.
432 Park Avenue South, Suite 1503
New York, NY 10016, USA

British Library Cataloguing in Publication Data

Silver, Morris
Foundations of economic justice.
1. Social justice   2. Wealth. Distribution
I. Title
339.2
ISBN 0-631-16748-X

Library of Congress Cataloging in Publication Data

Silver, Morris.
Foundations of economic justice / Morris Silver.
p.   cm.
Bibliography: p.
Includes index.
ISBN 0-631-16748-X
1. Distributive justice.   2. Social justice.   I. Title.

HB523.S55   1989   330.1–dc19
88-31903   CIP

Typeset in 11 on 13pt Baskerville
by Graphicraft Typsetters Limited, Hong Kong

Printed in Great Britain at
The Camelot Press Ltd, Southampton

Contents

Acknowledgments

Many of the ideas about feelings and rights presented here originated in a paper (Silver, 1981) prepared for presentation in 1980 at a Conference on Social Justice sponsored by the City College of New York's Departments of Economics, Philosophy, and Political Science. I would like to take this opportunity to thank Armen Alchian and James M. Buchanan, who participated in the Conference, for their comments on this early version. The inspiration to turn this short paper into a book grew out of a series of formal and informal discussions with a number of colleagues at the City College. Many scholars helped me to formulate my thoughts. I am especially indebted to Walter Block, Gerald Handel, Louis Heller, K. D. Irani, Benjamin Klebaner, Robert McShea, Michael Ruse, and several anonymous referees. Finally I wish to acknowledge my intellectual debt to Richard A. Epstein, Israel Kirzner, and Amartya Sen. My research was greatly facilitated by a grant from a fund created by the will of the late Harry Schwager, a distinguished alumnus of the City College of New York, class of 1911.

Introduction

The problem of economic justice is the problem of the derivation of a rule for evaluating the distribution of desired objects in a society (Runciman, 1978, p. 37). Economic justice, however, is not really a distinct branch of justice, a branch that is or becomes relevant only in complex socioeconomic formations. Justice is justice and the questions it raises are eternal. Rather than being a specific form of justice, economic justice is a perspective or model for the study of justice. The model of economic justice developed in this study, with its stress on the *natural right of producers to their objects*, stands in sharp contrast and, indeed, opposition to humanist, voluntarist, or subjectivist theories maintaining that moral principles are culturally or historically relative or that they may be grounded in personal interest or social utility. "Natural right" is, of course, a loaded phrase. In order to avoid misunderstanding, let me hasten to add that the "natural right" I have in mind is constituted on our common feelings about the objects we produce.

The present model, moreover, runs counter to a virtual consensus among economists that property rights are *conventional* or *special* rights. Thus, at one end of the political–ideological spectrum, Kenneth Arrow (1978, p. 477) remarks that property is only a "social contrivance" and Gunnar Myrdal (1961, pp. 196–8) characterizes property rights as part of the "institutional set-up." At the other end of the spectrum, Milton Friedman (1962, p. 162) sees "property rights as matters of law and social convention" and Harold Demsetz (1979, pp. 101–2) testifies that he does "not believe it is possible to defend effectively a particular property right structure by appealing to some overriding concern for freedom, or for equality, or for 'original ownership' " and, consequently, he stresses the "instrumentalism" of property rights systems. Gene Mumy (1987, p. 276) reflects that "presocially efficacious rights are a myth." Similarly, political economists Geoffrey Brennan and James M. Buchanan (1985, p. 25) visualize an "initial leap from Hobbesian anaychy" resulting from an agreement among individuals to respect one another's goods and persons. Robert Sugden (1986, pp. 70–1, Chapter 8), a Humean economist, sees "conventions of property" as the spontaneous products of social experimentation and learning by experience.

Similar views have been expressed by noneconomists, for example by philosopher John Rawls (1971, pp. 313–14). Another philosopher, Allan Gibbard (1985, p. 23), while recognizing that "we are apt in careless moments, to think of a person's property as a part of his person, like an arm or leg," maintains nevertheless that "the first step in thinking about property rights is to realize that property is a matter of complex human contrivance, custom, and convention." Sociologist Derek Phillips (1979, p. 196) and social critic Ralph Nader (Nader et al., 1976, p. 424) also assert the conventionality of property. This is likewise the view of lawyers trained by advocates of the legal–realist view of law (see Paul 1987, pp. 194–5). Legal scholar Lawrence Tribe (1985, p. 165) even warns of the "tilt against redistribution" evident in doctrines of rights treating "patterns and distributions of capital ... [as reflecting] something decreed and indeed sanctified by nature rather than something chosen by the polity." And Roberto Unger (1986, p. 32) speaking on behalf of critical legal studies asserts that: "The prevailing institutional form of the market in *rich Western countries* works through the *assignment* of more or less absolute claims to divisible portions of *social* capital, claims that can be transmitted in unbroken temporal succession, including inheritance." [italics added]

Only a handful of dissenting voices have been heard. For instance, legal scholar Richard Epstein (1985, pp. 5–6) argues that:

No rights are justified in a normative way simply because the state chooses to protect them as a matter of grace. To use a common example of personal liberty: the state should prohibit murder because it is wrong; murder is not wrong because the state prohibits it. The same applies to property: trespass is not wrong because the state prohibits it, it is wrong because individuals own property. At each critical juncture, therefore, independent rules, typically the rules of acquisition, protection, and disposition specify how property is acquired and what rights its acquisition entails. None of these rules rests entitlements on the state, which only enforces the rights and obligations generated by theories of private entitlement.

But Epstein does not discuss and evaluate these "theories of private entitlement." Indeed he does not really intend to attack conventionalism. Instead in the context of the American constitution, the point is that once a convention is established, as by common law, it cannot be disregarded at will. Michael Sandel (1982, p. 84), a political scientist, asks the rhetorical question: "Is our belief in the validity of the institution of property in no way enhanced by a conviction that robbery and theft are wrong?" Sandel does not, however, explain why our "convictions" about robbery and theft matter.

Perhaps the most powerful contemporary voice raised against the conventional wisdom that property is conventional is philosopher Robert Nozick's in his *Anarchy, State, and Utopia* (1974). However, as Thomas Nagel (1975, p. 137), also a philosopher, has forcefully argued in "Libertarianism Without Foundations," the problem with Nozick's seminal analysis is that he *begins* with "the unargued premise that individuals have certain inviolable rights" including, of course, property rights. However: "To present a serious challenge to other views, a discussion of libertarianism would have to explore the foundations of individual rights and the reasons for and against different conceptions of the relation between these rights and other values that the state may be in a position to promote" (Nagel 1975, p. 137). Economist Scott Gordon (1976, pp. 581–2) also recognizes that Nozick's

analysis "is empty without a theory of what legitimately constitutes 'ones' own.' To fill this need, a theory of 'entitlement,' that
is, a theory of property rights is required. At this point Nozick's
elegant structure crumbles." Indeed Nozick never really tells us
what a "right" is. *The objective of the present study is precisely to provide
a foundation for property rights and, hence, for economic justice itself by
undertaking the required substantive analysis.*

It should immediately be clear to the reader that the chosen
task of this research is very different from that of the property
rights approach in the economics of law literature (see, for
example, Kuperberg and Beitz, 1983). This literature is concerned primarily with the relationship between property assign-
ments and the efficient allocation of scarce resources. The present
goal, however, is not to explicate the instrumental role of property
rights in promoting economic growth and raising living standards, although this is touched upon. Rather its purpose is to
demonstrate that property rights are an ultimate value. As
Calabresi and Melamed (1983, p. 57) well note, moral considerations "though possibly linked to efficiency have now a life of their
own."

The theory developed in the body of this work places *feelings*
and indeed *emotions* of property approval and theft disapproval at
center stage in an *objective* moral order. Moral goodness is seen
as objective not in the projectivist sense that it is external to us –
this is the viewpoint of false consciousness wearing philosophical
clothing – but rather as a natural property of our feelings.
Needless to say this emphasis does not conform to the standard
welfare economics framework in which pride of place is given to
the logic of choice and "preferences" or "tastes" are relegated to
the status of a (given) "black-box". The inversion of his accustomed time-tested priorities will understandably be deemed
awkward and even annoying by the economist and decision
theorist. Sadly, the economist who wishes to take into account the
unruly contents of the black-box of preferences cannot expect the
applause of his colleagues. His analysis will not *look* "scientific".
Therefore, purists, die-hard defenders of *homo economicus*, and
(most annoying personally) academic yuppies are likely to agree

with Paul Samuelson's (1985, p. 172) characterization of these "first explorations" as both crude and pretentious. The scholar determined to explore this rough terrain must find solace in the opportunity to make progress toward the solution of the hitherto intractable problem of economic justice.

Note, in this connection, economist Gerald O'Driscoll's (1980, p. 363) timely warning that "having undertaken the study of phenomena in the interstices of academic disciplines" the economist "can no longer be agnostic with respect to preferences, although this also means one cannot remain within the domain of pure economics." Pure economists and decision theorists who discuss "social choice," "fairness," "rights," and other essentially moral issues while ignoring the structure of moral preferences are, as legal scholar Charles Fried (1980, p. 352) points out, taking "a worm's-eye view of the subject matter; they are deliberately acting like the observer at the mathematical congress who does not understand mathematics." Indeed the complaint that preferences are not the economist's "turf", suggests Amitai Etzioni (1986, p. 165), "is but one more reason for a paradigm change, to combine economics with psychology and sociology, to develop a socioeconomics . . ." Morality is simply too large a subject to fit within the domain of rational choice. Economists who are understandably discomforted by the interdisciplinary heat need not take up residence in the social justice kitchen!

It will not do, any longer, to deny the reality of the problem by proclaiming a "world without innate preferences" and to dismiss innate preferences as a "nineteenth century" prejudice dispelled by "modern sociology and psychology", as does economist Lester Thurow (1975, p. 35). In fact, Thurow's anti-human nature perspective, partially under the impetus of sociobiology, has been losing ground not only in the disciplines he names but in anthropology, philosophy, and even economics. Thus economist Jack Hirshleifer (1978, pp. 335–6) recommends that:

The economist's working hypothesis should be not that preferences are arbitrary, but that beneath the ephemeral surface phenomena men's wants have certain analyzable characteristics, which came about because they are adaptive or at least *were* adaptive in the evolutionary past – to his form of life. Of course man as a rational animal can, to a degree, oppose these inbuilt drives – sometimes to his advantage sometimes not – but never without difficulty.

The points made by O'Driscoll, Fried, and Hirshleifer need to be reinforced. The field of moral preferences lies in the virtually untilled territory between economics and biology. Consequently, the welfare economist who disdains evidence made available by sister disciplines, however qualitative and anecdotal, and, most importantly, by introspection runs the risk that his proposals will be obnoxious, his arguments beside the point, and his groundings erroneous. The first penalty is well illustrated by Henry Sidgwick's suggestion that the best way to serve the goals of the utilitarian theory of economic justice would be to keep the doctrine a secret from the public (cited by Dworkin, 1977, p. 175). The second penalty applies to much of the elegant discussion concerning libertarian conflicts in social choice. The third penalty is exemplified in economist Andrew Schotter's (1985, p. 18) excellent little book about *Free Market Economics* by his entirely mistaken assertion that:

> Although it seems quite natural to most Americans, the notion that the individual and not the group should be the basic repository of rights and obligations is neither old nor universally accepted. In primitive cultures there is very little sense of individual property. Property far from being private, is held in common and all individual rights are subservient to those of the village chief.

If the reader will forgive yet another metaphor, the economist interested in social justice should not emulate cartoonist Ham Fisher's Jeff who dropped a coin in a dark place and then searched for it beneath a street lamp where, as he explained, "There is more light." The rigor and tractability of models must not be purchased at the expense of understanding ethical behavior.

A feelings-centered approach to the problem of economic justice also clashes violently with the traditional philosophic framework in which the intellectualist component stands on a pedestal and emotions are obstacles to understanding. I emphatically do not, like an Immanuel Kant (1724–1804) or an Alan Gewirth (1978) or a David Gauthier (1986), seek to discover rationally justifiable moral rules. Neither do I, like an R. M. Hare (1952, pp. 56–78), strain to demonstrate that moral rules are in the final analysis "decisions of principle." The theory developed below will, however, strike a familiar chord among philosophers familiar with the work on "secondary qualities" of P. F. Strawson (1974), Colin McGinn (1983), John McDowell (1985), and John L. Pollock (1986) and, less rigorously, among "moral sense" and other philosophers who test ethical theories by confronting them with their ethical intuitions.[1] Thus, for example, John Rawls (1971, p. 46) has proposed that as a first approximation "one may regard a theory of justice as describing our sense of justice."[2] However, in line with social psychologist Robert Plutchik's (1980, p. 12) position that "cognitions have largely evolved in the service of emotions," the present study does not emulate Rawls in seeking to improve upon our sense of justice. In refusing to attempt the philosophic equivalent of squaring the circle, this analysis insures itself against the inevitable cyclic recoil to a position of skeptical denial that circles really exist (see recently Frey, 1980, Chapter 1).

By this time it should be obvious that it is no more possible to explain the nature of justice, or of the just society, from the disciplinary perspective of philosophy than it is to explain economic development and economic decline from the perspective of pure economics. Within an interdisciplinary perspective it is possible to begin to construct a plausible synthesis of the empirical and the normative. It becomes realistic to think with sociobiologists Ruse and Wilson (1986, p. 191) of laying the foundations for an "applied science" of moral reasoning.

Following a basic examination of ethical words and feelings, Chapter 1 defines a property right as a complex of feelings of legitimate entitlement with respect to an object and distinguishes between a property right and a power (legal or otherwise) over an object. This is followed by an exploration of the nature of theft and its implications for government regulation of the economy, redistributive taxation, free-riding behavior, and several other important policy questions. The focus of Chapter 2 is on productive effort as the major stimulus capable of triggering or eliciting property feelings (feelings of legitimate entitlement) for objects, including natural objects. Due account is taken here of cultural factors. As exchange requires the expenditure of effort in plan formulation and execution it is plausibly understood and, more importantly, subjectively experienced as a component of the production process. In short Chapter 3 argues that exchange is production. Objections to production-based object powers are considered in Chapter 4, most importantly Rawls' argument that producers cannot deserve their objects because they do not deserve their productive attributes. Critical attention is also directed to the view that individuals owe society something for their participation in it and to the "desert principle" requiring entrepreneurs to pay compensation to those participants in the economy who are harmed by their activities. Chapter 4 considers as well the problems of inheritance and employment discrimination, reaching rather unorthodox conclusions. The central argument of Chapter 5 is that *right makes might* – that is, the underlying emotional responses give producers an advantage in their rivalry with thieves. Chapter 5 includes a survey of the historical and ethnographic evidence relating to the ubiquity of the property institution. The ability of social ideas to precipitate behavior apparently contrary to our innate property feelings is illustrated by Marx's theory of the exploitation of labor. Next, after tentatively suggesting that our property feelings are the outcome of biological evolution, Chapter 6 summarizes some of the evidence of property-like behavior among nonhuman animals. Chapter 6 also discusses philosopher Colin McGinn's (1979) argument that as morality induces us to behave in a manner contrary to our interests, it cannot be a product of natural selection. The chapter concludes with a rejection of economist Harold Demsetz's (1979) argument that natural science and nature itself do not distinguish between moral and immoral forms of competition.

Building upon the preceding analysis, Chapter 7 proposes that property rights elicited by production are natural rights. A rights principle is stated and grounded in values characteristic of the human species. This rights principle is found to satisfy the universalizability criterion and to have additional useful philosophic properties. At the same time, the stated rights principle is immune to the challenge of the so-called "naturalistic fallacy" and "is-ought problem." Chapter 8 begins by putting forward a congruence rule for economic justice: the distribution of produced objects is just to the extent that power over objects is congruent with property rights. The succeeding sections discuss and evaluate competing rules of economic justice. The analysis of utilitarian justice begins with the positions of Bentham and Mill and goes on to consider the views of leading contemporary welfare economists including Frank Hahn, Amartya Sen, J. A. Mirrlees, and John Harsanyi. Legal scholar Richard Posner's wealth maximization rule is considered next. Then attention is directed to the fairness or envy-free justice theory developed by economists William Baumol and Hal Varian, among others. The discussion of John Rawls' theory of justice examines his specification of the "veil of ignorance" and notes the malleability of hypothetical or implicit contracts. Chapter 9 takes up the feelings-grounded theory of blame-free justice advanced by economist Andrew Schotter. In the course of the discussion, attention is given to the more general problem of catastrophic allocations of objects requiring the rights of producers (and the rules of justice) to be overriden. The study concludes with a summary and some caveats.

Notes

1 See, for example, Brandt (1979, pp. 16–23), Gutmann (1980, pp. 167–9), and Lyons (1975, pp. 145–9).
2 See Sencerz (1986) for a recent critique of appeals to moral intuitions which, for the *n*th time, returns the philosophical discussion of justice to square one.

1

Property Rights, Object Powers, and the Problem of Theft

1.1 PROLOGUE: ETHICAL WORDS AND FEELINGS

Words pertaining to feelings are comprehended by recalling characteristic feelings. Therefore, we may speak in this connection of *feelings memory*.[1] This brief, boldly stated psychological proposition underlies much of the present chapter and indeed the entire volume. Although the postulated role of feelings memory is easily confirmed by introspection, it is, on a more scientific plane, also consistent with John Stuart Mill's (1806–73) two general "laws of the mind." These laws have been compactly stated by Fred Berger (1984, p. 10) in the following terms:

1. Once a state of consciousness has occurred, it can be reproduced in the mind without the presence of the original cause. Citing Hume, he [Mill] wrote: "Every mental *impression* has its *idea*."
2. Ideas are caused to occur in the mind by other ideas or impressions according to certain laws of association.

If "every mental impression has its idea," it may perhaps be added that: every *idea* has its *word*. This is not to say, however, that the words are specialized to the extent that they convey only feelings.

Naturally the question arises of how the appropriate words for feelings are learned when, obviously, we cannot be instructed by being shown external correlates. For the purposes of the present study it is sufficient to reply that we *do* understand "anger," "pain," "choice," and "infinite," for example, as well as "tree." However, with respect to the learning process, Goldstein (1985, p. 337) explains:

> We normally learn words for kinds of experience from a process that may be called "linguistic inference." By linguistic inference I mean the process of inferring a word's meaning from hearing (or reading) remarks in which the word appears ... As the words "God" and "electron" can be learned without the aid of references to observable signs such as lightning and thunderbolts, or streaks in cloud chambers, so the word "dreaming" can be learned without a reference to some external sign such as tossing and turning in one's sleep. A crucial part of understanding the word "dreaming," obviously, is that one knows the word refers to experience had *while asleep*. This fact about the meaning of "dreaming" can be inferred from the way people talk about "dreaming." We talk about "dreaming" as an experience had while asleep, i.e., while not conscious of one's surroundings. (One needs to have the concept of being asleep before one can understand the word "dreaming.") Central to understanding the word "pain," in the primary sense of this word, is knowing that it refers to something bad, something localized in some part of the body. This is apparent in the way people talk about "pain." We ask, for instance, "Does it feel better now?" or "Where does it hurt?" (See also Denzin, 1984, p. 54)

In short, private events are communicable and we communicate them all the time. Of course, it is true that the private (and cross-cultural counterpart) of "pleasure" is somewhat idiosyncratic, but, then, this is also true of "chair." The discrepancy is a matter of degree, not of kind. Society is workable and so necessarily is the assumption of intersubjectivity.

"Right" and other moral or ethical terms belong to a family of what might be called feelings words. The emotive meaning of feelings words is covered by the rules or conventions of language. For instance, the meaning of the word "right" is comprehended by recalling a kind of feeling of approval. This feeling of approval is the common core meaning of "right." The reader who demands a more precise definition is urged to consider that as feelings have no physical description, this is the best that can be done.[2] The point is well illustrated by some remarks of Adam Ferguson (1966, p. 34) who wrote in 1767:

> Every peasant will tell us that a man has his rights; and that to trespass on those rights is injustice. If we ask him further, what he means by the term right? we probably force him to substitute a less significant, or less proper term, in place of this; or require him to account for what is an original mode of his mind, and a sentiment to which he ultimately refers, when he would explain himself upon any particular application of his language.

Similarly, in explaining his theory of moral sentiments, J. S. Mill wrote that when a person expresses a moral sentiment by saying that something ought to be done, "the word ought means, that if they act otherwise, they shall be punished by ... [an] internal and perfectly disinterested feeling [of pain]" (quoted in Berger, 1984, p. 24).

An implication of the perspective outlined above is that ethical naturalism, the philosophic view that ethical words refer to empirical characteristics, is scientifically tenable provided that feelings are recognized as empirical phenomena, as indeed they are. Ethical feelings constitute an objective ethical reality. Moreover, as will be discussed shortly (in Section 1.3), there are environmental scenarios which, more or less regularly, trigger or elicit the specific feelings to which ethical words refer. Perhaps it is possible to speak with biologists Lumsden and Wilson (1983, pp. 70–1) of an epigenetic rule – namely ethical vocabulary emerges from the systematic interaction of the genes prescribing feelings with recurring features of the external environment. Moral judgments are consequently *objective* in the sense that there is intersubjectivity not only with respect to the ethical feelings themselves, but with respect to the environmental stimuli capable of triggering them (see Lorenz, 1987, pp. 84, 95–6). Thus it is surely misleading to characterize ethical words as "merely" or "nothing but" expressions of the speaker's preferences. I fully agree with Sugden's (1986, p. 154) suggestion that "a moral judgement is a statement of *approval* or *disapproval*, and this is not the same thing as a like or dislike."[3] None of this is to deny that ethical words may be misused in a manipulative manner to gain support for a particular interest or policy favored by the speaker.[4] This problem will be taken up later in the discussions of Marx's theory of the exploitation of labor (in Chapter 4, Section 4.3) and Baumol's theory of fairness (in Chapter 8, Section 8.5).

1.2 PROPERTY RIGHTS AND PROPERTY DEFINED

Property rights (and rights generally) are usually left undefined or, what comes to the same thing, they are "defined" by synonyms (for example, "claims," "that which is due to someone") or according to category (for example, "moral," "utilitarian," or "legal"). However, for an analysis of economic justice to make progress, it is essential to begin by taking the unprecedented step of defining property rights in a manner focusing attention on their emotive dimension. Fundamentally, *a property right is a complex of feelings of approval with respect to an object*. In this study the term "object" is understood in a maximally general sense, including not only physical objects, animate or inanimate, but incorporeal objects such as leisure, effort, information, ideas, liberty, and reputation.

The first requirement for an individual i (the holder or subject of the right) in society s at time t to have a right to object X is that:

1 i must have a feeling of legitimate entitlement (or possession approval) with respect to X.

Interestingly, Kant (1952, Section 7, p. 407) recognized the centrality of mental phenomena in the structure of rights when he visualized a subject's right to an object ("external right") as involving, or derived from, "a specially juridical connection of the will of the subject with that object." Of course, for Kant, moral judgments were directed by the subject's "will" or reason, not his feelings. Note further that unlike standard, especially consequentialist, formulations, condition 1 does not (misleadingly) focus on ownership of X as an aspect of i's *well-being* or *interest* (see Raz, 1986, pp. 165–6). Ownership is a value in itself, not merely a *means* to the end of well-being or whatever (compare Lomasky, 1987, pp. 120–1, and Sen, 1985c, p. 28). Or as Fried (1978, p. 85) aptly puts it: "The assertion of a right is categorical. Thus a right is not the same as an interest, though there is an interest behind every right." More recently, Sen (1987, p. 43) noted in discussing the problem of agency versus well-being that "the point at issue is not the plausibility of their *independence*, but the sustainability and relevance of the *distinction*."

Condition 1 provides necessary but not sufficient conditions for a property right. As sociologist Emile Durkheim (1958, p. 159) pointed out: "Property is property only if it is respected." That is to say, the feelings of other members of society must also be taken into account. Rights must be construed internally *and* externally. Specifically:

2a the other individuals in s must feel that i is legitimately entitled to X; or alternatively,

2b the other individuals in s must have no feeling with respect to i's entitlement to X.

If 2a applies we say that subject i has a *strong* right to X. If 2b then the subject has a *weak* right to the object. It is possible to visualize the strength of i's right to X as increasing with the proportion of individuals feeling that he is legitimately entitled to (or approving his possession of) the object. The purport of this strong-weak right terminology is more or less the same as philosopher David Lyon's (1982, p. 138, n. 6): " 'Strong' rights provide obstacles to the justification of others interference, while 'weak' rights provide justification for one's own behavior." Weak rights, like the Hobbesian "right of nature" (Hobbes, 1962, Part I, Chapter 14), do not include duties upon others.

An object X is the *property* of individual i if conditions 1 and either 2a or 2b apply. If, however:

2c   the other individuals in s, or some fraction of them, feel that i is *not* legitimately entitled to X,

we say that i has *disputed* (or ambiguous) right. What is here at issue between the subject and others is experienced as a matter of truth, not a mere difference in culture, taste, or opinion (Hudson, 1980, p. 27: compare McGinn, 1983, pp. 9–10). Rights are native to the individual and conferred by outsiders. Consequently, when the underlying pattern of feelings is contradictory, so necessarily is the structure of property rights. The subject has and yet does not have a right to the object.

At least in principle a consideration of *evidence* is capable of permitting an *emotional repatterning* and, hence, an untangling of the rights structure. To adopt Pollock's (1986, p. 51) terminology, evidence about who produced an object, for instance, is a *defeater* of "I (or he) has a right to object X." The subject of a defeated right may well be ashamed of his mistaken behavior. Evidence about production of an object plays the same role in the correction of "moral mistakes" as does measurement of (say) size in the settlement of a dispute concerning whether a primary quantity is instantiated in a particular object. The evidential approach is well illustrated by the Roman *legis actio sacramento in rem*. As is well known, to initiate the action the plaintiff and then the defendant had to swear that he owned the object (Diósdi, 1970, p. 94). When differences in belief about the supernatural are responsible for a disputed right, appeals to evidence are less likely to provide defeaters, although oracles and resort to the liver of a sacrificed ox have been known to be efficacious.

Contrary to the position of philosophers G. E. Moore (1965, pp. 44, 54) and Colin McGinn (1983, pp. 150–1), the play given to contradictory feelings in determining, or rather tangling, the rights structure strengthens rather than invalidates my approach. Of course, Moore (1965, p. 54) is quite correct in saying that a feelings approach requires "an entirely different view of Ethics, so far as it is concerned with right and wrong." In this different perspective we do not need, as McGinn (1983, p. 152) wishes, "to say that one side (at least) must be morally wrong" and, to this end, "to entertain the notion of an ideal moral being, one whose moral reactions may well be superior to our own." As opposed to the sterile, above-the-battle traditional position that rights are external or reaction-independent, that one has a right or one does not, the present perspective is capable of coming to grips with, and even predicting, social conflict. This theme will be explored later on in considering Marxian exploitation (in Chapter 5, Section 5.3). For the present, it is sufficient to refer to philosopher G. A. Cohen's (1986a, p. 319) view that outrage against injustice "was certainly an essential element in the French and Russian revolutions, or, indeed, in any other revolution one might care to think of" and to cite Edward Banfield's (1974, p. 216) conclusion to the effect that: "All the large riots of the nineteenth century in American cities were mainly outbursts of righteous indignation."

1.3 PROPERTY RIGHTS TRIGGERS OR ELICITORS

As we have seen, a property right has a social or relational dimension. That is, not only the subject's property feelings must be taken into account. A property right is nevertheless a fact of individual psychology, a fact grounded on individual feelings of legitimate entitlement or possession approval. The feelings element is sometimes hinted in our legal terminology. Thus, Donahue (1980, p. 31) points out that the English word "property" can be traced back to Latin *proprietas*, meaning "the peculiar nature or quality of a thing" and he adds the significant thought that:

> We would not be far wrong if we suggested that even before
> it comes to be a legal term 'property' is an abstraction of the

idea of what distinguished an individual or a thing from a group or from another. It is the face of one to others, what separates me from thee and yes, what lies in a person's view, what has priority in time.

Whatever the words employed by the "natives" or even if they have no specialized terminology, a society knows property if its members experience feelings of possession approval – that is, they perceive the "peculiar nature of a thing," it has an owner.

The disposition of human beings to experience the sense of personification and separation that I call the property feeling or sense is actualized by various stimuli without reason or forethought. We do not simply choose to have or not to have property feelings in the way we decide whether or not to purchase a can of baked beans. In this respect the feeling of what is *proper* to a person is instinctive. Unfortunately, anthropologists have carried out little if any systematic comparative research bearing on moral feelings (Hatch, 1983, p. 111). Social psychologists, for their part, have made only limited progress in constructing a multi-dimensional model of property feelings (see Leventhal, 1980).[5] Casual observation, upon which I am forced to rely, suggests that a limited number of stimuli are capable of eliciting property feelings. The latter include legal convention (for example, an automobile driver owns a prescribed half of the road), precedent (treating similar cases similarly), custom or habitual usage (for example, of fishing or hunting territories among nonliterate peoples), randomization (for example, toss a coin to decide who receives the larger piece of cake), and, most importantly and most consistently, *the act of production.*

1.4 SCOPE OF PROPERTY RIGHTS

A property right is visualized as a vector of distinct rights over an object including those listed below and perhaps others as well.[6]

1 Right to use in all relevant uses (universality).
2 Right to exclude others from using.

3 Right to benefit from use.
4 Right to physically transform.
5 Right to alienate or transmit.

The legitimate entitlement of an individual to an object does not necessarily include each and every one of these rights. Thus, for example, when several individuals are legitimately entitled to an object, each may have the right to use this common property but not the right to transfer its use to an outsider. Again, in the case where all the individuals in a society are entitled to an object, each may have the right to use this public property, but not to physically transform it. In general, however, as noted by legal scholar John Reid (1970, p. 131), "when tested by the norms of private law, communal property becomes merely an aggregate of personal rights."

1.5 PROPERTY RIGHTS VERSUS OBJECT POWERS

In the interests of "objectivity" and "realism" discussions of property rights usually ignore feelings of legitimate entitlement (for example, Coleman and Kraus, 1986, pp. 1345–6) or, worse, confound them with *power* over objects. Thus, object powers produced by or with the aid of the state are commonly referred to as "legal" or "institutional" rights (which are subdivided in the Hohfeldian analysis). However, if one is to study justice it is essential to distinguish between rights (legitimate entitlements) and powers, legal or otherwise. An individual may have a right to an object over which he has no power and, on the other hand, he may have power over an object to which he has no right (see McMurtry, 1978, pp. 73–4). This usage of the term right is consistent with ordinary *and* legal discourse (see Yablon, 1987, pp. 888–94). A right-holder might be able to exclude others from the use of his object only at a prohibitive cost for (say) lawyers, fences, locks, and sentries. "One might say," with philosopher G. A. Cohen (1978, p. 219), "that the power to X is what you have *in addition* to the right to X when your right is effective."[7] Nonowners might be willing and able to marshal the resources to exclude owners from their objects. Power over an object can grow from the barrel of a gun in an owner's ribs or a threat to harm his loved ones. It may easily transpire that owners must pay non-owners for the use of objects to which they have a right, even a strong right! Indeed, in the limiting case of the Hobbesian war of each against all, the distribution of object power might be entirely determined by such personal characteristics as physical strength, bravado, and ruthlessness. Even in civil society the structure of legal "rights" might be indifferent to or even antagonistic to property rights, that is, to feelings of possession approval.

Effective property rights or powers must in general be "bought" and, in this sense, as Hazard (1965, p. 4) explains: "In the doing of justice, or elsewhere, what can be obtained is limited by what can be funded." The neo-Hobbesians overstate the economic problem, however. It will be argued in Chapter 5 that even in the absence of expenditures to this end there would exist a positive correlation between rights and powers. The source of this fundamental relationship is the moral advantage of right-holders over thieves.

1.6 Theft Defined and Illustrated

A *thief* is one who deliberately violates property rights. More specifically, by thief will be meant anyone who employs *coercion* to obtain (partial or complete) power over an object to which another (the victim) is legitimately entitled. That is, thieves seek power by means of *physical force* or by means whose success rests in the final analysis upon physical force, for example, the *threat* of physical force and *deception* (disguised physical force) including the violation of explicit or implicit contracts. It is appropriate to speak in this connection of "disguised" force because an individual (the victim) would not willingly transfer his object to someone (the thief) who had no intention to perform as agreed. In order to gain power over the victim's object or, in *ex-post* terms, retain power, the unmasked contract violator would have to substitute his fist for his handshake.

One reasonable implication concerning which more will be said shortly is that *offers* are not coercive (compare Hoekema, 1986, Chapter 3, and Mumy, 1987, pp. 299–301). Another point is that while theft is necessarily coercive, not all coercions are acts of theft. The threat of punishment, for example, coerces potential thieves without violating their rights (see further below). Coercion and punishment belong to different realms: coercion is a *physical* fact; punishment (like a right) is a *moral* fact (see Mumy, 1987, pp. 297–8). Even more basically, the distinguishing feature of theft is not the *harm* done to the victim, but the violation of his rights. Not all harmful acts are theft and not all harmful actors are thieves (or even coercers). Philosopher Michael Davis (1987, pp. 578–9) maintains, however, that: "To 'steal' my [worthless] scribbles (e.g., by reproducing them) may do me harm (e.g., by causing embarrassment), but the harm done is not theft" and he goes on to ask, rhetorically, "What theft leaves its victim with the same objects and economic resources as before?" If Davis really means "steal" then his own example of stealing worthless scribbles provides a convenient vantage point for answering his question. Our property feelings leave no doubt that an individual's worthless scribbles are *his* and that someone who utilizes coercive techniques to gain power over them (if only to reproduce them) has robbed the individual (see Thomson, 1986a). Similarly, contrary to Gauthier's (1986, p. 210) position, if Joanna "takes" produce from my garden "for which I could find no use whatsoever" and the "taking" is by *force* – that is, I have neither given her to understand that she might take it nor deserted the produce (see Chapter 2, Section 2.2) – then Joanna is a thief. Sen's (1987, p. 60, fn. 2) profound remarks on *freedom* help to place the arguments of Davis and Gauthier in perspective:

> Choosing *x* when *y* is available may be seen as different from choosing *x* when *y* is not available. The language commonly used sometimes does, in fact, take a 'refined' form, e.g. 'fasting' is not just starving, but doing so despite having the option not to starve. Fasting may well be assessed differently from other types of starving precisely because of the 'choice' element implicit in the 'refined' description.

Thievery, of course, takes many forms ranging from the opportunistic transactor who abides by the terms of his contracts only when it suits him to, to the confidence man who sells something over which he does not have power, to the factory owner who gives free reign to his noxious fumes,[8] to the short-changer, to the pick-pocket, to the stick-up man who offers you a choice between "*Your* money or *your* life," to his sophisticated relative, the extortioner, who proposes to charge you a fee for something you do not wish to purchase or that you already own.[9]

The perpetrators of theft may be individuals or groups and, in the case of extortion, may include government officials, even those who faithfully carry out the duties assigned to them. Thus a government that charges an individual for objects he did not agree to purchase at all or at the proffered tax-price is guilty of extortion. That government is offering the individual the choice between "*Your* money or *your* freedom from serving time" (or other punitive action). But only the individual owns his money and his services, not government officials or those they represent.

Economist Robert Frank (1985, pp. 119–20) believes, however, that when the object "sold" by the government is "redistributive taxation":

> *there will obviously be costs on groups that object.* Yet the completely reciprocal nature of the problem means that the alternative is to impose costs on those who want redistributive tax structures namely, the *wastefully high social fragmentation that results when we do not redistribute.* The *essential question,* then, is whether one set of costs is more important to escape than the other ... *To affirm the right to keep the full fruits of one's labor is to deny the right of others who desire redistributive taxation.* Both rights cannot be upheld simultaneously. So a decision must be made as to which of these rights is to be sacrificed. [Italics added]

Let us put aside the problem that Frank makes neither a theoretical nor an empirical case for his proposition that "high social fragmentation" (obviously a bad outcome) will result from a failure to redistribute income. Let us also ignore the fact that redistribution is not necessarily an all or none proposition: those who wish to improve the status of the poor may voluntarily make a contribution to the government for this purpose, as was true, for example, in classical Athens and sixteenth-century England (see Silver, 1980, pp. 30–1). It is, of course, not impossible that the objecting individuals prefer to "waste" their (potential) gains from redistribution just as a person who spends $250 on a suit of clothes prefers to "waste" the benefit from consuming $250 worth of something else. But let us not dwell on this either. And let us dismiss out of hand the street thug's (possibly accurate) claim that you are "wasting" your income, that he will make better use of your wallet's contents than you. Then Frank's "essential" proposition apparently reduces to this: If your action *harms* me I have a *right* to employ coercion to alter your behavior. Or possibly: If your action harms me in a manner that is both "wasteful" and "high" (as when you refuse to redistribute your income!) I have the *right* to employ coercion to alter your behavior.[10] I submit that Frank's proposition is utterly without foundation, and, indeed, is incoherent. No one has a right (feeling of legitimate entitlement) in a particular structure of society and, hence, no one can morally employ force to veto the choices of another person merely because they reduce his welfare (see further Chapter 4, Section 4.3 on "Harms and Rights").

Governments imposing wage and price controls (and many other regulations) are guilty of extorting a restrictive covenant. Here the individual is offered a choice between his services (his freedom from serving time) and using his object in the way he wishes to.[11] An individual who chooses to pay the price charged by the government to maintain power over his services has not consented to the transaction either explicitly or implicitly. He has no feeling of having agreed, of having consented to the transaction "in his heart".[12] The individual feels that he has been robbed just as surely as the individual who hands his wallet to the stick-up man to save his life.[13] As Hayek (1960, p. 134) points out: "Though the coerced still chooses, the alternatives are determined for him by the coercer so that he will choose what the coercer wants." The point is that coercion and choice are not mutually exclusive. Epstein (1985, p. 99) sharpens the focus by noting that: "The thief's threat of force transforms [the victim's] giving into taking." Force transforms consensual transactions into coercive transactions.

None of the above argumentation is meant to exclude the possibility that individuals will *agree* to have the government force them to pay for an object they desire, be it order (Auster and Silver, 1979, Chapter 1), a bomber, or food for a hungry child (see J. M. Buchanan, 1977, pp. 162–4). In order to economize on decision-making costs or to secure a consensus on behalf of the objects they most desire, individuals may agree to simple majority rule or agree to a comprehensive package of objects (see Frank, 1985, p. 119). In the event of a "voluntary coercion contract" in which individuals agree to pool their resources, it is the reneging tax-delinquent who is the thief. (See the discussion of contractual reliance in Chapter 3, Section 3.3.) Similarly, if individuals agree among themselves not to organize monopolies, the individual who subsequently violates his promise and behaves as a monopolist is a thief. To use Davis's (1986) terminology the promise-breaker has taken "unfair advantage" of the other social cooperators and, in legal terms, he is guilty of "unjust enrichment" and must make "restitution." The same point applies to any agreed restriction on the use of objects. *Agreements must be real and not merely assumed, however*. The author has no feeling or awareness of having agreed to pay for government-imposed racial quotas or interest-rate ceilings or censorship of literature or mandatory seatbelts, for example. Neither does he feel that he has agreed to pay for a package including these objects or to a constitutional scheme under which he can be taxed to pay for them. Instead the author feels that he bears significant (external) costs because he has been coerced into purchasing and consuming these objects. The reader is invited to make up his own list of the goods (controversial goods, merit or demerit goods, or simply low-valued goods) whose provision he is *forced* to subsidize by the government. (See further the discussion of hypothetical or implicit contracts in Chapter 8, Section 8.6). Also the free-rider, one who willingly consumes an object *after* having refused to contribute to its cost of production a proportionate tax-price no greater than *his own* full (all-or-none) valuation of the object is clearly a thief (compare A. Buchanan, 1987, pp. 562–6, 586–94).

Punishment is the process whereby a thief is made to suffer by depriving him of otherwise rightfully possessed objects. As mentioned earlier, punishment coerces criminals without violating their rights. The underlying psychological fact is that the other individuals in society feel that the thief is no longer entitled to his objects, or to some portion thereof. That is, the act of theft extinguishes and reverses the complex of feelings termed a strong right. Even the weak right of the thief may be terminated: not uncommonly, the thief himself no longer has a feeling of possession approval with respect to the objects he controls. At best, then, the thief retains a disputed right to this object. (See further the remarks in Chapter 5, Section 5.2.) Thieves may be punished in various ways including fines, confiscation, deportation, incarceration, beatings, execution, and revolution.[14] Needless to add, the circumstances of a theft may be more or less extenuating and, consequently, the punishment more or less severe (see the discussion of catastrophic allocations in Chapter 9).

Notes

1 See Blanshard (1966, Chapter 8), Brandt (1979, pp. 168–71). Locke (1959, Book 4, Chapter 4, Section 9), Rawls (1971, pp. 479–84), Westermarck (1932, pp. 60–3), and Wierzbicka (1986).

2 Note Lorenz's (1987, p. 85) observation that, "The more decisively one defines human perception and cognition as that which is capable of being expressed in words, that much clearer it becomes how many essentially fundamental phenomena cannot be expressed directly in words."

3 Sugden seems unaware of an earlier paper (Silver, 1981) in which rights are grounded on feelings of legitimate entitlement and aversion.

4 For useful discussions of many of the issues raised in this section, see J. S. Mill (1951, p. 51), Pollock (1986), Stevenson (1944), Sugden (1986, pp. 154–5), Urmson (1968), and Wellman (1961).

5 On anthropologists and universal moral principles, see Renteln (1988). J. Greenberg (1984, pp. 178–9) summarizes experimental research indicating that people prefer productivity-based distribution when they believe performance is due to factors under individual control (for example, rapidly adding up columns of numbers) and equality when they believe outcomes depend on chance (for example, high rolls of the dice).

6 See Alchian (1979, pp. 237–40), Becker (1977, pp. 18–20), Baechler (1980, p. 237), and Nozick (1974, Chapter 7, Section 1).

7 See also Hägerström (1953, pp. 350–1), Lemos (1986, p. 99), and McMurtry (1978, p. 75).

8 See Epstein (1985, pp. 115–21) on the physical invasion test for nuisances.

9 For discussions of the curious legal crime of blackmail, see Block (1987) and Davis (1986, pp. 242–3). Thomson (1986a, pp. 129–30) tells the following story:

> Suppose I find out by entirely legitimate means ... that you keep a pornographic picture in your wall-safe, and suppose that, though I know it will cause you distress, I print the information in a box on the front page of my newspaper, thinking it newsworthy ... Do I violate your right of privacy? I am, myself, inclined to think not.

I agree. But what if I inform you that I will not print this embarrassing but newsworthy information if you agree to pay me a sum of $10,000. Is this a case of theft? With Walter Block I would agree that it is not.

10 Frank (1985, p. 123) goes on to put forward a rather interesting illustration:

> Some people undoubtedly would claim that to witness an interracial couple holding hands in public causes them great anguish ... Why is the right to hold hands more worthy of our moral respect than the right to be free from sights that cause discomfort? The answer is surely at least partly rooted in very deep beliefs we hold about the sorts of adjustments people are capable of making. Granted, the racist might honestly feel profound discomfort today at the sight of the interracial couple. Still, we feel strongly that it is much more within his

power to adjust than it would be for people to adjust to being told they are not allowed to hold hands in public.

In other words: If I am the bad guy and you are the good guy, I should not be permitted to use force against you. All of this has a rather Orwellian flavor.

11 Richard Epstein (1985, p. 74) points out that the use of, or threat of, force to interfere with the transfer of property "constitutes an interference with prospective advantage, long recognized as a private tort." See Perlman (1982) for a far-ranging legal analysis.

12 See Coleman and Kraus (1986, pp. 1359–60) on the spurious "compensation-as-consent" argument.

13 Legal scholar A. Kronman (1980a, pp. 477–8), noting the choice made by the victim but not its extortionate aspect, mistakenly classifies robbery as a consensual transaction. Economist K. Basu errs in the opposite direction. Recognizing that once a victim has encountered a stick-up man he can no longer return to his "normal level of happiness," Basu (1986, p. 275) concludes incorrectly that if a person's level of utility is lowered by an "exchange viewed in its entirety," he has been coerced. Thus, suppose that exposure to the goods of individual 2 ("civilized man") lowers the utility level of individual 1 ("tribal man"), then, according to Basu, individual 3 ("merchant man") who sold the advanced goods to individual 2 has thereby coerced individual 1 into purchasing them. The underlying psychological postulate of Basu's illustration seems to be something like: "If others do not have a toothache, your own toothache hurts even more."

14 For an illuminating discussion of these issues, see J. M. Buchanan (1977, especially Chapter 3).

2

Production and Property Rights

2.1 PRODUCTION AND PROPERTY FEELINGS

As noted in Chapter 1, various stimuli are capable of triggering the complex of feelings called a property right. Some of these stimuli are effective primarily for objects that are nonproduced, or seem to be. As Nozick (1974, p. 160) aptly puts it, they apply to objects that appear "from nowhere, out of nothing" (see also Steiner, 1977, pp. 48–9). Since the expulsion from the Garden of Eden our wealth has owed its existence primarily to the sweat of our brows, however. Indeed, my Indo-Europeanist colleague Louis Heller informs me that Latin *proprietas*, from which our word "property" can be traced, is semantically linked to *per*, the *e*-grade root of "to produce." (He adds that the *pauper* is the producer of "few things.") This study focuses on the act of production not because it is the only elicitor of property feelings, obviously it isn't, but rather because it is the most economically important stimulus and, at the same time, is supportive of the most powerful and most widely held moral convictions.

It must be insisted at the outset that the causal relationship between object creation and property rights is a matter of feelings, not of logic. A hint of the role of feelings can be detected in economist Robert Sugden's (1986, pp. 96, 103) vague remarks about the "*natural* prominence" [italics added] of the relationship between objects and their producers. But there are indefinitely many relationships between an object and its environment and

Sugden fails to see that the object–producer relationship is perceived as the "prominent" one because the underlying natural feelings are so strong, not because of some kind of pseudo-geography. Even so profound a student of society as Durkheim (1958, p. 215) stressed logic and reason to such an extent that he completely overlooked the crucial feelings dimension:

> We are not going to say that property derives from labor, as if there were a kind of *logical necessity* for a thing to be attributed to the one who labored to make it, as if labor and property were one and the same. There is nothing about the bond linking the thing with the person ... that can be *analyzed*; there is nothing about labor that compels us to infer that the thing to which this labor has been applied derives from the workman. We have already shown all the *unreason* of such a deduction. It is the society that makes the synthesis of these two heterogeneous terms, property and labor. [Italics added]

Karl Marx (1965, p. 89), on the other hand, in an early work about *Precapitalist Economic Formations* (1857–8), seems to have recognized "property" as the object of feelings triggered by productive activity: "Thus originally *property* means no more than man's attitude to his natural conditions of production as belonging to him, as the *prerequisites of his own existence*; his attitude to them as *natural prerequisites* of himself, which constitute as it were, a prolongation of his body" [italics in original]. Marx's point, and my own, is nicely illustrated in the ethnographic literature by the Tikopia of Polynesia who habitually use possessives to convey the idea of productive activity. Thus anthropologist Raymond Firth (1965, p. 257) recalls: "In Tikopia a pole has been pointed out to me by the lakeside as we were passing in a canoe with the words '*Aku ne ta.*' This translated literally is 'Mine, did cut.' This might mean 'It is mine because I cut it' ... But in fact it means 'I cut it.'" Firth (1965, p. 258) goes on to note the use of the term *tau*, literally "linked," to express ownership of, for instance, a canoe.

None of this is meant to deny that sometimes the connection between productive activity and property rights is ambivalent or uncertain. Thus, with respect to intellectual production the French patent law of 1791, for example, explicitly affirmed that individuals owned ideas. On the other hand, in 1848 a leading academic patent lawyer, William Hindmarch, put his finger on a key moral difficulty: "No inventor can, in fact, have any natural right to prevent any other person from making and using the same or a similar invention" (quoted in Dutton 1984, p. 18). Imitation without compensation is theft; independent discovery is productive activity.[1] Our biological offspring raise even more difficult questions than our ideas (see Becker, 1977, pp. 38–9, and Lomasky 1987, Chapter 7). Is the progenitive act of the parents experienced by them as an act of production? Do parents have property rights – feelings of legitimate entitlement – in their children? If so, what are the characteristics of the rights vector? Is it possible to disentangle the underlying web of feelings including not only of property but of love and duty? (See Epstein, 1980, p. 673.) Questions are abundant, but, unfortunately, answers are scarce.

We do know that in Near Eastern antiquity parents not uncommonly sold their children into slavery without manifesting guilt, at least so far as we know (see Silver, 1983, pp. 68–9). Significantly, I believe, Berlev (1987, p. 153, n. 57) has detected several connections within the language of ancient Egypt between terms relating to childbearing on the one hand and terms for production, work, and property on the other. He points, for instance, to the apparent connection of *bk3* "to be pregnant" with *b3kt* "job, task." (During the Persian and Saite periods *b3k* meant "slave.") Again, the Egyptian word *msjt* means "birth" or "manufacture." We, of course, call the efforts of childbirth "labor." The productivity–virility connection is also found among the early Romans. Puhvel (1987, p. 150) explains that:

> *Quirīnus* was the divine embodiment of the Romans (*Quirītes*) at peace, reflecting **co-virinos* (altered by analogy of *virilis*), even as the collective noun **co-viriā* yielded *curia* 'assembly'

> ... He was the patron of men as producers, as progenitors, which is a sense that Indo-European **wiro-* tends to have when juxtaposed to the quasi-synonym **wer-*, as in Vedic *virákarma-* 'doing a man's work' = 'penis'.

More concretely, Latin *pariō* means "to give birth to, bear children," "produce," and "aquisitions, gains, savings" (see also Chapter 3, Section 3.3). A similar range of meanings is attested for Hebrew *qānītī* and, indeed, this ambiguity permits an amusing word play on the name Cain (*qayin*) in Genesis 4:1. Also the Greek word *poieō* means "produce, manufacture" and "conceive children."

However, it seems that Western producers (parents) voluntarily surrender all or some of their legitimate powers with respect to the human objects they have produced (parented). Rather than spending valuable space and intellectual energy to deal with this thorny and marginal problem, I will stipulate that my production-based theory fails to determine the rights structure of our biological products. As will be seen shortly (in Section 2.4), this theory also fails when confronted by truly novel nonhuman objects. Our property feelings are not as well-behaved and predictable as the theorist would like. Indeed, they sometimes appear to manifest themselves irrationally as for example when we feel it is *wrong* to violate the wishes of deceased producers (see Chapter 4, Section 4.7).

Moreover, what counts as production (that is, elicits property feelings) differs from one society to another. Only the crude biological determinist fails to see that culture matters. Among the Piaroa of the Orinoco basin, the *ruwang* (shaman) controls the "mystical means of production" and consequently deserves a share of the community's game: "This is ... thought of as an exchange, for the *ruwang* transforms the dangerous animal nature of meat into a nutritious vegetable nature" (Santos Granero, 1986, p. 664). For the previously mentioned Tikopia, the ritual-integrating term "work of the gods" stands in part for the expenditure of goods and effort required for proper worship (Firth, 1967, p. 27). Wyatt (1988, p. 119) notes the common etymology of "cultivate" and "cult" and adds that in the Bible the word *'bd* means "cultivation" of the soil (Genesis 2:25) and performance of cult (Exodus 3:12, Numbers 18:7, Deuteronomy 4:19). In many historical societies the priest who prays for rain triggers a right to a portion of the crop. As J. Miller (1985, pp. 209–11) explains, the Vedic sacrifice is regarded as a "work" (*apas*) calling for the "toil" or "sweat" of the priest in carrying fuel, kindling the fire, and "heating" his head (that is, meditating). Consequently, it is not really strange, as Neale (1985, p. 955) believes, to say that the Brahman priest has a property right in the harvest. In his discussion of the Tikopia, Firth (1965, p. 185) makes the more general point that: "granted the present techniques and knowledge of resources, the ritual system is a positive factor in the situation of production, contributing directly to the organization and indirectly affecting the output. In this sense it might be classified as part of the technique of production, being one of the given factors in the total situation. In our own society, of course, what my colleague K. Irani calls "trans-natural technology" is seldom viewed as efficacious (productive). The cultural diversity in productive activity is nicely illustrated by missionary Samuel Alles' reaction to the practice of the Pawnees of the Great Plains of rewarding their priests for conducting ceremonies regulating the natural rhythms. Alles noted with annoyance that even in times of dearth "if there was anything to eat in the villages the old imposters got it" (quoted in White, 1983, p. 176).

In all societies, however, production is a broader activity than manufacturing or transformative processes generally. It is difficult to overestimate the importance of human psychology in this connection. To take a commonplace but striking example, in a supermarket parking lot the driver who has waited for a specific spot to be vacated feels, and there is no better way to describe the feeling, that he has produced that spot. (Compare Sugden's (1986, pp. 94–5) discussion of conventions favoring first claimants.) Indeed, the presence of unexpectedly powerful property feelings should be regarded as a clue, a signal to the social scientist that he should undertake an intellectual reappraisal of the activity in question. Such a reappraisal is long overdue with respect to ownership of natural objects.

2.2 Natural Objects and Productive Activity

Upon reflection it becomes clear that natural objects can be transformed into property by means of *occupation* (or possession) and *improvement*. To begin simply, the forager who picks up an acorn, the hunter who kills a deer, and the miner who extracts a nugget of gold, trigger property rights in their respective natural objects. Olivecrona's (1974, p.27; see also Davis, 1987, pp. 578–9) objection that picking up an acorn (occupation) does not increase its value is certainly mistaken. John Locke (1952, Section 28, p. 18), whose argument Olivecrona is criticizing, had explained rather vaguely that picking up acorns "added something more to them than nature . . . had done." (Elsewhere Locke (1952, Section 40, p. 24) maintained that "labor puts the difference in value on everything.") To put Locke's insight less mysteriously, a *taken* acorn, deer, or nugget is more valuable than the *opportunity to take* them. (As Davis (1987) might put it, picking up an acorn produces a more *convenient* acorn.) However, the natural object itself, not merely the apparent inrease in its value, becomes the property of its occupier-improver. It would appear that in the case of unowned natural objects (about which more shortly), no value is assigned to the opportunity to occupy. Notwithstanding the fact that there has been no physical change in the material of which it is made, the person who picks up an acorn is felt to have produced a new object (see Kirzner 1979, chaps. 11, 12 and Paul 1987, pp. 230–32). His effort has transformed an object in the *natural* order into property in the *social* order, and this is what counts. It is this psychological transformation that underlies Nozick's (1974, p. 174) peculiar proposition that "things come into the world already attached to people having entitlements over them." G. A. Cohen (1986a, p. 119) misses the point when he objects that "people create nothing ex nihilo, and all external [why not internal as well?] private property either is or was made of something that was once no one's private property, either in fact or morally . . ."

In Davis's (1987, p. 578) terminology, "finding" an object fits into the category of producing an "intangible." Ingold (1987,

p. 105) correctly finds "the essence of hunting, or more generally of the production of subsistence from an unmodified environment, as *the subjection of an extractive process to intentional control*" [italics added]. Contrary to the position of legal scholar Richard Epstein (1979, p. 1230), there is indeed a way in which an "individual act can account for a claim of right against the world." Picking up an acorn triggers for the occupier a complex of feelings called a strong property right, precisely "a claim against the world." The appropriator's possession of the acorn is neither "arbitrary" nor "undeserved," as philosopher Loren Lomasky (1987, pp. 115, 129–30) supposes. Of course, if the taker tosses his acorn away or otherwise terminates occupation, the acorn reverts to its original unimproved (natural) state, or, better, in psychological terms, to a state of *nonexistence*.

Note further that the application of effort is a necessary, but not a sufficient, condition for the activation of property feelings. The effort of the acorn thief, no matter how strenuous, is not felt by human beings to have created a new object. Hence, it triggers no claim for the perpetrator (see Lemos, 1986, p. 101, and compare Schmid, 1978, pp. 24–5). An occupied acorn is incapable of being improved by an outsider! Only the first claimant produces the acorn. In the event that the thief makes the stolen acorn more valuable by processing it, my intuition is that he would at best trigger a disputed or ambiguous right to the transformed acorn. Davis (1987, p. 583) proposes that after making compensation and having been punished, the thief might be entitled to compensation for increasing the value of the object. He seems to be thinking here of possible provisions of positive law rather than of rights (feelings), however.

The human nature of land ownership is especially interesting because of its durability and because, contrary to the example of the acorn, occupation and improvement do not completely overlap. The psychological importance of occupation, of a *sense of boundary*, is well illustrated by the fact that with the mere erection of a fence dividing one field from another the so-called legal right of "accession" ceases to be applicable (see further Section 2.3). Surely law follows psychology in this instance. Similarly, in

Roman law the thief may be killed with impunity only if he is captured within an enclosure, be it home, barn, or corral (Watkins, 1970, p. 338). As law professor Carol Rose (1985, pp. 78–9) discovered in studying "Possession as the Origin of Property:" "Possession now begins to look even more like something that requires a kind of communication, and the original claim to the property looks like a kind of speech, with the audience composed of all others who might be interested in claiming the object in question."

Philospher William Galston (1980, p. 23) also calls attention to the "language" of occupation and then turns to the problem of improvement:

> Occupation is in many respects a provisional claim. If we, for example, occupy a plot of land but never live on it or make any effort to improve it, our title becomes suspect ... Occupation gives us the right to use, but if we do not exercise that right, it atrophies ... Usually, the establishment of occupation requires physical proximity and some specific gesture or sign: we must drive the stake, build the fence, raise the flag ... As ordinarily understood, then, occupation requires a certain degree of transformative effort.

Animals, of course, have been observed to demarcate (communicate) their territories to conspecifics by means of scent-or-sound signals whose comprehension is fixed in the genes (see Chapter 6, Section 6.2). Locke's (1952, Section 27, p. 17) peculiar proposition that people acquire property rights in natural objects by "mixing" their labor with them serves to call attention to the improvement dimension of human ownership. Taking triggers lasting property rights to land only if appropriate signals of transformative effort or *labor signals* are forthcoming.[2] Whether a labor signal is appropriate is a question to be answered by the evidence, not by abstract reasoning.

In the American West in the 1870s the rush for claims under the Homestead Act "was so heavy that it was wise for a claimant on the praries to plow a few furrows, start to dig a well, or lay four poles in the shape of a pen to make a show of occupancy and to warn others away while he went to enter his land" (Dick, 1970, p. 141). Again in the West, an agriculturalist might gain owner-ship of a stream by diverting the water from its natural course (but see further Epstein, 1979, pp. 1232–6). W. Robertson Smith (1956, p. 96) adds that: "Originally ... private rights over land are a mere consequence of rights over what is produced by private labor upon the land. The ideas of building and cultivation are clearly connected – the Arabic *'amara*, like the German *bauen*, covers both – and the word for house or homestead is extended to include the dependent fields or territory." Smith's point is illustrated among the Tswana, a contemporary herding people of South Africa, by the ability of an individual to transform a temporary cattlepost into permanent property by erecting a hut or a sturdy corral (Herskovits, 1952, p. 344). It appears, on the other hand, that the early Roman *usus auctoritas* and the classical *uscapio* are legal forms linking land ownership merely with a lengthy term of possession. The appearance is misleading, as Diósdi (1970, p. 92) explains:

> The two years' period [of possession] ... shows that *uscapio* was closely connected with cultivation. With respect to crop-rotation two years were needed for it to become apparent who was the actual cultivator of a plot of land ... [In the early agricultural Roman society] *cultivators take possession of agricultural land by the very fact of cultivation*. [Italics added]

In Papua New Guinea's highlands the villagers plant trees around the borders of their gardens to signal the continuity of occupation during the long fallow period (Grossman, 1984, p. 100). The Tikopia utilize trees, hedges, and paths to demarcate their orchards and gardens (Firth, 1965, p. 269).

2.3 SETTLERS AND INDIANS IN NEW ENGLAND: A CASE STUDY

The behavior of English settlers and Indians in New England is relatively well documented and quite informative. Note first of all that the English settlers did not intrude upon the land cleared and currently cultivated by Indian women. The labor signal of cultivation was easily comprehended by the Europeans and triggered a strong right for the Indian farmers. Obviously, the Indians also had strong rights to the game they took from the wilderness (see Ingold, 1980, p. 155, and Reid 1970, pp. 133–4). The colonists did intrude as farmers upon the land exploited by the Indians as foragers and predators. This intrusion is understandable and predictable. The wilderness showed neither signs of occupation nor of improvement and, consequently, it was unowned. Historian William Cronon (1983, pp. 52, 57) is inclined to dismiss the colonists' interpretation of property and the respect they showed for the Indians' agricultural land as "an ideology of conquest conveniently available to justify the occupation of another people's lands." Perhaps. Cronon fails to explain, however, why the English conquerors needed to bother themselves about an "ideology."

More basically, Cronon takes as self-evident that the hunting grounds were "another people's lands." This is not in the least obvious. Cronon (1983, p. 158) admits that "we have little direct evidence in colonial records of the New England Indians' conception of property." Nevertheless, it is reasonable to assume that in their land-and-game-rich environment, the Indians saw no profit in improving their hunting grounds and therefore chose not to make the effort. Consistently with this assumption, Cronon (1983, p. 62) reports that the Indian families of southern New England abandoned even their planting fields "after a number of years. Once abandoned a field returned to brush until it was recleared by someone else, and no effort was made to set permanent boundaries around it that would hold it indefinitely for a single person." Quite probably the Indians did not have feelings of legitimate entitlement (property rights) with respect to the land they hunted. There is reason to believe, then, that the land the English settlers took did not belong to "another people."[3]

To adopt Rose's (1985, p. 83) terminology, it is difficult sometimes to devise "texts" of ownership capable of being read by outsiders. An appreciation of this problem can be gained by first noting that by clearing fields the Indians created "openings in the forest that provided the diversity of landscape and the proliferation of edge habitats the deer needed to obtain the variety of food necessary for their well-being" (White, 1983, p. 2). Suppose, counterfactually, that the Indians had deliberately speeded up the tedious process of land clearing and abandonment in order to increase the deer population. How would the Indians have signaled their improvement of the hunting ground to the English? Certainly, the wilderness, despite the abundance of game, would not have emitted comprehensible signals. Unable to transmit a convincing signal of ownership, the rights of the Indians would be disputed (see Chapter 1, Section 1.2). Cronon (1983, p. 57) puts basically the same point in a negative light: "Few Europeans were willing to recognize that the way the Indians inhabited New England ecosystems were as legitimate as the way the Europeans *intended* to inhabit them." Climbing down from the pedestal of historical hindsight it is well to ask why the colonists should have recognized this alleged "equal legitimacy?"[4] Despite the fact that Indians and settlers shared the *same property feelings*, recall the respect shown by both groups for cultivated land, the fate of the hunting grounds could hardly have been different.[5]

2.4 LOCKE'S MIXING METAPHOR AND PROVISO

The problem of communicating productive activity is also raised by Nozick's (1974, pp. 174–5) attempt to cast doubt on the explanatory value of Locke's mixing metaphor:

> But why isn't mixing what I own [my labor] with what I don't own a way of losing what I own rather than a way of gaining what I don't? If I own a can of tomato juice and spill it into the sea so that its molecules (made radioactive, so I can check this) mingle evenly throughout the sea, do I thereby come to own the sea, or have I foolishly dissipated my tomato juice?

The first difficulty with Nozick's example is that the sea might already be owned. (As will be noted shortly, occupation-improvement is not the only mode of acquiring ownership of natural objects.) The second problem is that a sea into which tomato juice had been poured would not be regarded as an improved sea. However, it must be admitted that even if the sea were unowned and improved by the juice, comprehensible signals of occupation would not be forthcoming. In the absence of the required signals, property feelings would not be elicited. The basic problem raised by Nozick's and similar extreme examples is that they fall outside the range of human experience and, hence, of an appropriate emotional response. The dissemination of information about the productive contribution of the tomato juice pourer would help, of course. The underlying problem raised in the previous section by the supposed attempt of the Indians to improve their hunting ground and by Nozick's more extreme example remains, however. For the truly novel product, legal or social convention might turn out to be the only stimulus capable of eliciting or completing determinate property feelings. This counts as a demerit against my production-based theory but in no way does it justify a *wholly* negative verdict.

This problem is placed in perspective by Lomasky's (1987, p. 189) remarks concerning thought experiments and their philosophical implications:

> What many of these virtuoso philosophical conjurings presuppose is that moral principles, and most especially principles grounding basic rights, must be true across all possible worlds to be true in any. Their status is like that of mathematical truths. It is this appraisal of the logical status of moral judgments that is being denied. Because morality is to a considerable extent a function of contingent social phenomena, thought experiments have limited utility within normative ethics. Moral demarcations not only fail to characterize all works, they have limited currency even in the actual world.

Neatly demarcated moral boundaries are hardly to be expected when emotional reactions to productive activity are so little determined by rational calculation and so largely shaped by cultural variables and even more, I believe, by biological evolution (see Chapter 6). Thought experiments including Nozick's pouring of tomato juice into the sea are so far removed from the central issues of evolutionary survival that they provide little guidance to the moral theorist (see Epstein, 1980, p. 676).

The argument that people obtain ownership of natural objects by means of occupation-improvement runs counter to the frequently encountered assertion that in the "state of nature" these objects *necessarily*, virtually as a matter of definition, belong to the "public" – that is, to "everyone" (in the entire world? including even the unborn?). It is incumbent upon a serious proponent of this position to point to a stimulus capable of triggering in the normally formed human being the required feelings of legitimate entitlement. In the absence of an elicitor no one is entitled to an unimproved acorn and, hence, no one needs to be asked for permission to take it.[6] Locke's (1952, Section 28, Section 30, p. 18; Section 35, p. 21) state of nature, like Kant's (1952, Section 6, pp. 405–6) is explicitly a state of *no-ownership*. It is a state in which the rule of occupation or capture prevails (compare G. A. Cohen, 1986b, p. 112). Fressola (1981, p. 322) speaks in this context of a "natural privilege of using ... unproduced resources as are unclaimed by anyone else, and a claim to noninterference with ongoing use of the things which one is at liberty to use." E. F. Paul (1987, p. 236) deduces "rights of motility" from the "conditions of man's survival on earth." More simply, the individual who, for his own reasons, occupies and improves a natural object triggers a property right where previously there had been none.[7]

The above conclusion holds despite what has been described as a "loss of competitive equality" and a violation of a so-called "no-loss requirement" with respect to "natural means of production" (Becker, 1977, pp. 41–3). Realistically, of course, it is difficult to conceive of an act of production, including the scholarly creation of ideas, which does not impose a "loss" on (present and future) others in the sense of their being excluded from a specific set of opportunities. At the very least, others will find that the foreclosure of these opportunities has marginally increased their own expected costs of production. What then, it may be asked of Locke's (1952, Section 27, p. 17) famous proviso that individuals may take ownership of natural objects only "where there is enough and as good left in common for others?" Putting aside extremist examples and postponing discussion of catastrophic allocations until Chapter 9, the appropriate reply to all those scholars who, in one or another version, embrace Locke's proviso is that it is completely besides the property feelings point.[8] That is, the taking of natural objects triggers (guilt-free) strong property rights without reference to the magnitude of the residual pool of natural objects or to the worsening of the positions of others.

At the same time, Locke's proviso is of no practical importance, at least in its standard explications. The number of income-earning opportunities is effectively infinite. It is indeed quite possible to live luxuriously without owning even one natural means of production. (The ancient world even knew wealthy slaves.) Moreover, despite the solemnly intoned platitude that "literally and figuratively we are running out of room," it is quite possible to augment the stock of "natural means of production," including land, by expending effort and other resources. If he is so inclined a person may also offer income in return for ownership of a portion of the existing supply of natural means. On the grander scale the process of discovering income-earning opportunities and removing them from their "naturally" common state in the economy is called entrepreneurship. Although this is in no way essential to our argument it is worth noticing that the gains from innovation and the resulting economic growth normally accrue not only to the opportunity foreclosers themselves, but to the foreclosed general public.

2.5 SOCIAL CONTRACTS AND NATURAL OBJECTS

Some additional remarks are necessary in the interest of complete-ness and to forestall possible misunderstanding. Although the facts are not entirely clear, it appears that individuals or groups may secure a right to forage or hunt or fish within a given area by means of mutual agreement (see Durrenberger and Pálsson, 1987, and Ingold, 1980, pp. 152–5). Usually the evidence for this process is indirect and circumstantial. For example, hunters have been heard to refer to "my path" and fisherman to "my creek" (Ingold, 1980, pp. 152–5).[9] Scholars have, however, also detected instances in which common hunting areas were *deliberately* transformed into exclusive property. The objective of this change in status was to encourage conservation. Mature and consequently more valuable animals were in this way reserved for those who took the trouble to preserve them in their immature state. Thus, for example, when the steep expansion of the European beaver trade resulted in rising prices and overhunting, the Montagnais and Ojibwa Indians of the Canadian Labrador Peninsula divided their traditional hunting ground into individually owned parcels.[10]

Well and good. Outsiders, however, would not detect psychologically meaningful signals of occupation and improvement and, hence, would not feel bound by agreements in which they did not participate.[11] This limitation on binding force of social contracts with respect to natural objects applies equally to agreements to preserve the hunting ground or other natural objects in an undeveloped form. An invading people would not feel that the natives were legitimately entitled to their hunting grounds and nature preserves and, for their part, the natives probably would not feel the invaders were entitled to the improvements they made in the wilderness. The problem of disputed rights is, of course, obviated when there are no outsiders, as is presumably the case with respect to the ongoing negotiations with respect to the sea and outer space. "Presumably" because these agreements might not be binding on future generations.

In conclusion, it goes without saying that hunting grounds and other unowned objects may be valued so highly that peoples are willing to kill their neighbors to keep them or to take power over them (see Reid, 1970, pp. 133–4). Recent scholarship has confirmed, for example, that in the seventeenth century, Indian waged ferocious war against Indian (for example, the Iroquoian

"Beaver Wars") in an attempt to monopolize trade with the English and French markets (Jennings, 1984, pp. 68–9, 84–112).

Notes

1 Presumably basic knowledge in mathematics and science is non-patentable at least in part because it is not feasible to distinguish between imitation (theft) and independent discovery (production).

2 Kant (1952, Section 10) also deserves credit for understanding that labor legitimizes the possession of land.

3 The peaceful displacement of the Kalahari Basarwa ("Bushmen") who foraged in the Savannah near the lower Blotletli river by farming peoples points in the same direction. Intruders (Kalangas) interviewed by Cashdan (1986, p. 313) said they "asked the Basarwa for permission to hunt, and that it was never denied . . . Kalangas are of the opinion that if permission is not granted by the Basarwa and one hunts anyway, one will never be able to catch anything." It seems clear that the Kalangas' request for "permission to hunt" is merely a matter of courtesy to the Basarwas, not a matter of their *ownership* of the hunting area. Cashdan (1986, p. 313), like Cronon, takes it as self-evident that the foragers "previously owned the land."

4 It is well to note in this connection that among the Lango of East Africa, according to Herskovits (1952, pp. 345–6), hunters may not deny entry to cultivators.

5 Among the Bushmen of the Kalahari, an individual who discovers a bees' hive or a nest of ostrich eggs may reserve it for future use by driving an arrow into the soil nearby (Forde, 1963, p. 29). The Siriono of Eastern Bolivia reserve a newly found fruit tree by notching it (Holmberg, 1969, p. 44). The person who disregards these signals is regarded as a poacher or trespasser (see Marshall, 1976, p. 311). Outsiders, however, might or might not comprehend and respect these texts of ownership.

6 Does a person feel even the slightest disquiet when he clears and cultivates some ground without having consulted and requested the permission of "mankind at large?" To ask the question is to expose its absurdity.

7 Difficult allocation problems may arise with respect to natural objects as is illustrated by Ackerman's (1980, Chapter 2) parable of

the unexpected discovery of a manna-stocked world by the crew of a spaceship.

8 See Gauthier (1986, pp. 209–11), Gutmann (1980, pp. 159, 167–8), Lemos (1986, pp. 107–13), and Nozick (1974, pp. 78–82, 180). G. A. Cohen (1986b, pp. 118–30) and Reeve (1986, pp. 131–6) provide perceptive discussions of Locke's proviso.

9 Service (1979, p. 23) suggests that in hunting and gathering societies "the most common instance of apparent restriction on common rights to resources occurs with respect to nut- or fruit-trees" which "are *allocated* to individual families" [italics added]. Does "allocated' imply a distribution of the commons by mutual agreement? Or, alternatively, had the "allocated" trees previously been discovered by their present owners? Or, like the coconut trees of Tongareva Polynesia, had they actually been planted and tended by the present owners?

10 See Bishop (1974, p. 12), Demsetz (1967, pp. 351–3), and Harper-Fender (1981, p. 70). Ault and Rutman (1979) provide additional examples.

11 See Durrenberger and Pálsson (1987, pp. 514–15) on the conflict between Karen villagers and swidden cultivators in northern Thailand. See Epstein (1980, pp. 680–1) on possible conflicts between efficiency and common law.

3

Exchange as Production

The exchange of objects raises more difficult problems than their manufacture or occupation-improvement. In general terms the question at issue is the extension of the producer ethic from the isolated, autarkic individual of the frontier to the complex nexus of exchange economies. What do our property feelings tell us about objects acquired by means of exchange? About objects which are jointly produced and, hence, not automatically allocated in a precisely determinate manner among cooperating producers? Without in any way meaning to underestimate the difficulties and the ambiguities, this chapter puts forward two interconnected hypotheses about the relevant (empirical) property feelings:

1 individuals feel that they have produced the objects they acquire by means of exchange; and
2 with respect to cooperative production, individuals feel that they have produced the objects they agreed to accept in return for their services.[1]

Before developing the arguments and evidence in support of these propositions, however, the positions of Nozick and Durkheim will be discussed.

3.1 NOZICK AND DURKHEIM ON EXCHANGE

Nozick has worked out a two-step solution to the problem of the ethics of exchange. First he puts forward a "principle of justice in transfer" requiring transactors to desist from using force and to fulfill their contractual obligations. "Some people steal from others, or defraud them, or enslave them, seizing their product and preventing them from living as they choose, or forcibly exclude others from competing in exchanges. None of these are permissable modes of transition from one situation to another (Nozick, 1974, p. 152). Nozick's (1974, p. 151) second step is to build the "principle of justice in transfer" into the following proposition: "A person who acquires a holding in accordance with the principle of justice in transfer from someone else entitled to the holding is entitled to the holding."[2] Sen (1985a, p. 4) reminds us that Nozick's approach

> involves the rejection of the way economists – the pro-
> fessional group most immediately concerned with the assess-
> ment of the role of markets – have typically examined the
> case for and against the market. In the economist's picture of
> "social welfare," rights are seen as purely institutional
> (typically legal) artifacts, without any importance of their
> own: rights are judged – in the typical welfare economics
> framework – in terms of how they fulfill or thwart people's
> interests.

Nozick's departure from the economist's paradigm viewing rights as "purely institutional artifacts" deserves applause, not least from economists.

It is clear, then, that Nozick's entitlements to objects acquired by exchange are not mere institutional artifacts. But what precisely are they? The answer seems to be that Nozick's rights are artifacts of a process of logical inference. The question of whether a person is legitimately entitled to an object, however it may have been acquired, is, as has been argued at length above, a question of *feelings*, not of the rules of recursive systems (compare Nagel, 1975, p. 141).[3] Arguably it is a more prudent strategy for researchers on the uncharted sea of legitimate entitlements to objects obtained via exchange, to keep the shore of feelings as much as possible in sight and not to rely on the uncertain winds of logical inference. This is not in the least to deny that logic and, hence, predictability are valuable features of a legal code. Indeed, they may, like works of art, be appreciated for their own sake.

Durkheim (1958, pp. 148–9) came close to the feelings mark when he noted the "contagiousness" of the right to property: "It tends always to pass from the objects in which it resides to all those objects that come into contact with them" (see also in this connection Sugden's (1986, pp. 93–7) remarks on "natural prominence" and possession). Moreover:

> The existence of this singular capacity is confirmed by a whole collection of juridical principles which the legal experts have often found disconcerting: these are the principles that decide what is called the "right of accession." The idea may be expressed in this way: anything to which another of less importance is added ... communicates to it its own status in law. An ownership that comprises the first is extended *ipso facto* to the second and comprises it in turn ... The proof that this is a matter of contagion by contact is, that where there is separation, when a boundary is made to a field and it is thus detached in law and *psychologically* from its surroundings, the right of accession does not arise. (Durkheim, 1958, pp. 148–9) [Italics added]

Interestingly, the "right of accession" is illustrated in the "primitive" society of Tikopia by the rule that a tree planted by one person on the land of another belongs to the landowner (Firth, 1965, p. 263). However, Durkheim (1958, pp. 123, 173–4) lost his chance to capitalize on this psychological insight when he asserted without qualification that "*Exchange is not labor*" [italics added]. More recently, Christman (1986, p. 164) similarly asserted that "transfers are not themselves instruments of labor, nor can it plausibly be claimed that a person's 'labor' extends into the future to include sales of the object." What then is "labor?"

3.2 PRODUCTIVE ACTIVITY AND EXCHANGE

Labor or production is the channeling of effort, including not only of "raw" labor-power, but that of directing and supervising it, to create (in the future) a new object. Consequently, labor includes, in addition to manufacturing, such activities as storage, transport, exploration, and, sometimes, ritual incantations. Exchange is an activity requiring a person to expend effort in plan formulation and execution. It is therefore predictable that producers (and third parties) would experience the manufacture of object X and its exchange as steps, or operations, in the creation of a new object Y. (Manufacture of X and exchange are arguments in the individual's production function for object Y.) The newness of Y is, of course, a psychological rather than a physical property. Introspection and casual observation of people's behavior do seem to indicate that, generally speaking, a property right triggered by manufacture or occupation-improvement is shifted to objects the producer acquires (produces) in exchange for his objects (compare Goodin, 1985, p. 176). One implication of this is that there is no psychological problem of "alienation" inherent in the process of exchange.

A producer is entitled to the fruit of his labor including whatever he might be able to sell his object for on the market. It follows rather obviously that no one may rightfully pay less than this "market value" simply by seizing the object and compensating the owner for his cost of production and foregone consumption of the object, leaving the owner with no net loss in *utility*. (See Chapter 9, note 2, on "property rules" versus "liability rules.") Only thieves hunt bargains with shotguns. The owner would be within his rights to retake his object and keep the so-called "full compensation" as the first installment of the thief's punishment. (The inadequacy of the utility measure is considered at length in Chapter 8, Section 8.3.) On the other hand, a right to the fruit of one's labor is *not* a right to receive more than the owner is capable of realizing on the market. Rights are not income guarantees. For the elicitation of stable property feelings it is not required that trading parties or third parties enjoying the advantage of hindsight should assess the objects exchanged to be of comparable value. Neither must an individual who knows that he is capable of making more productive use of an object than its present owner desist from consummating a trade until he has raised the present owner's productivity by giving him information, training, or other assistance.[4] No one has a duty to improve his trading partner's bargaining power. We may be angry with ourselves for making a "bad deal." We may even harbor ill-will against the trader who "took advantage." But uncharitable acts are not experienced emotionally as acts of theft. As we do not feel legitimately entitled to the charity of our trading partner, we do not, I submit, feel that the ungenerous terms of trade to which we have agreed violate our right.

Quite consistently with this line of argument, Locke (1952, Section 28, p. 18) suggested that "the turfs my servant has cut . . . become my property" (see Reeve, 1986, pp. 125–32). At the same time, my intuition is that the wage of the "servant" is rightfully his in return for "cutting the turfs" (that is, his labor-power). Political scientist Jon Elster (1985, p. 226) claims that: "One is not morally entitled to everything one is causally responsible for creating." I am inclined to disagree, but what is it exactly that someone has "created?" Again this is a matter of psychology not of physics. The underlying feelings are, it seems to me, as follows:

1 the entrepreneur is legitimately entitled to no more and no less than the object he has created by bringing together the inputs of his employees and capitalists; and
2 the employees and capitalists are legitimately entitled to no more and no less than the objects they have created (produced), namely the (money or in-kind) wages, interest, and rent they have agreed to take for their services.

In summary, assuming the absence of force or fraud, my conviction is that each cooperator is *felt* to have created and, conse-

quently, to be legitimately entitled to the objects he contracted for
(see further Chapter 4, Section 4.6). I can neither follow the logic
of nor detect a basis in feelings for G. A. Cohen's (1986b, p. 114,
n. 6) proposition that: "The propertyless proletarian who cannot
use the means of production without a capitalist's leave suffers a
... lack of effective self-ownership." Is this not equally true of a
man who cannot place his lips against the lips of a woman he
desires without her permission? It will no doubt be objected that
(current) capitalists "actively erect barriers" to the ownership of
"means of production" by (current) proletarians. To this alleg-
ation it seems to me the appropriate response is the following:
capitalists employing force to erect barriers are thieves and not
entitled to their objects; capitalists erecting barriers without
employing force are not thieves and are entitled to their objects.
(What is the nature of these peacefully erected barriers, I
wonder?) Similarly, of two rivals for the hand of a woman, the one
who seeks to prevent his rival from keeping a date by puncturing
his tires is not entitled; the one who wins by setting out to block
his rival's path by always being more punctual and courteous is
entitled. Some readers may consider these romantic interludes to
be singularly inappropriate or even frivolous. I disagree. One
point in their favor is that they manage to make their point
without resorting to sleight-of-hand: a worker who plays by the
rules and acquires means of production does not count against the
barrier theory because he is, after all, a capitalist, not a worker.
(See further the brief remarks in Chapter 4, Section 4.6 about
"propertylessness" as an adjustment to market incentives.) Of
course, introspection and casual observation must ultimately be
confronted with systematic evidence about property feelings.

If my working hypotheses concerning the content of property
feelings is reasonably accurate, it is not necessary to decompose
the market value of a final product into portions contributed by
each cooperating resource in order to judge whether each has
received its legitimate entitlement. No property right would be
violated by a discrepancy between the reward of a resource and
the exchange value of its contribution. It would not matter
whether the discrepancy was due to monopsonistic exploitation,
lack of information, changes in market conditions, chance, or to

any other cause with the exception of theft (see E. F. Paul, 1987, pp. 234–5). This finding is indeed fortunate, for as Sen (1985b, p. 16) explains, the economist's notion of marginal productivity is of quite limited usefulness in determining who created what:

> In fact, the marginalist calculus is not concerned with finding out who "actually" produced what. Marginal accounting, when consistent, has an important function in decision making regarding the use of resources, suggesting when it would be appropriate to apply an additional unit of resource, and when it would not ... For example, if it turns out that, using the marginalist calculus to evaluate factor contributions, yields the result that 40 percent of the output is due to labor, 40 percent due to machinery, and 20 percent due to management, this just tells us something about the respective values of the marginal contributions multiplied by the total amounts of the respective resources. It would not, of course, follow that any of these three factors of production could produce their respective shares unaided by the others. Indeed, the apportioning is not even one that is done by adding together the marginal contributions of all the respective units one after another but rather goes by weighing the *entire* amount of the resource input by the marginal contribution of the counterfactual additional contribution of that resource *at the point of equilibrium.*

This is not to deny, of course, that factor rewards will approximate the standard marginal productivity imputation in a perfectly competitive economy.

Now we must take care to see that it does not follow from Sen's discussion of the limitations of marginal productivity analysis for determining who produced what, as he seems to believe, that the question of who produced something is of limited ethical significance. Contrary to Sen's (1985b, p. 17) position, the relevance of productive contribution is by no means restricted to cases in which, for example, "we are asked to arbitrate between two children fighting over a wooden toy, which has been made unaided and with free wood by one of them." The preceding analysis of property feelings is in principle capable of handling Sen's example as well as more complex ones in which the participants are consenting adults. To repeat, my considered position is that each cooperator is *felt* to have produced the objects he contracted for.

Admittedly, as James M. Buchanan (1977, p. 56) objects, the principle of reward according to property right is consistent with almost any distribution of the gains from cooperation. Because "end-state results" depend entirely "on the institutions of voluntary exchange that emerge from personal interactions" and, consequently, "no one set of institutions would seem to warrant priority over any other," Buchanan (1977, p. 57) characterizes the "content" of entitlement theory as "minimal." My response is that if socioeconomic reality fails to offer sufficient challenge to the theorist or the social engineer, so be it. The point of social science is to understand the world, not necessarily to change it. In any event, the implications of legitimate entitlement theory for current public policy are hardly minimal.

3.3 EXCHANGE AS PRODUCTION: THE EVIDENCE OF LANGUAGE AND RITUAL

A survey of linguistic evidence offers support for the hypothesis that exchange is *felt* to be of the same genus as production and, hence, triggers strong property rights. Note first that many ancient Near Eastern terms for "purchase" also mean "seize," for example, the Akkadian word *sabatum* (Silver, 1985, p. 90). Benveniste (1973, p. 70) argues that the Latin word *emo* "buy" once meant "take, seize": "The notion of 'purchase' had its origin in the gesture which concluded the purchase (*emo*) and not in the fact of paying over a price, handing over the value of the object." *Mancipatio* (*manu capere*), an ancient Roman ritual of sale, called for the buyer to physically seize the object (Diósdi, 1970, pp. 67–8). Several scholars have conjectured that seizure symbolizes theft. It seems more reasonable that the ritual was somehow

intended to impress the seller and the witnesses with the fact that
the buyer had acquired the object legitimately, not that he had
stolen it. Seizure probably symbolized the buyer's effort (productive activity) and, hence, his legitimate possession of the object.
This point, I suspect, lies behind Gernet's (1981, p. 257, n. 8)
vision of the act of seizure as reflecting the "notion of the 'absolute
beginning' in the actualization of 'ownership'." It may be added
that in the formulaic recitation accompanying the act of seizure
the transferee made mention of the "law of the Quirites ('citizens,'
'Romans')" whose divine embodiment, Quinnus, was the patron
of productive activity (see Puhvel, 1987, p. 150). An effort
symbolism interpretation of *mancipatio* is also consistent with the
fact that Romans might acquire title to an ownerless object by
occupatio, "seizure." Note also, taking a comparative perspective,
S. M. Paul's (1969, p. 73, fn. 3) suggestion that Akkadian *ṣibittu*
"correct behavior" is derived from *ṣabatu* "to seize." And Egyptian hieroglyphic inscriptions of the late third to early second
millenniums BCE announce that the tomb owner had acquired
objects (cattle, ships, grain) legitimately, literally, "by my arm"
(Polotsky, 1930, pp. 194–6). Similarly, the first line and cola of
Psalms 78:52–4 should be translated: "and He led forth like a
flock his people," "whom His right arm had purchased" (Freedman, 1981, p. 25).

Gernet's linkage of seizure with an "absolute beginning" of a
traded object is strongly supported by a recent semantic analysis
of buying and selling terminology. Hawkins and Morpurgo-
Davies (1982, pp. 102–3) notice that verbs of buying (acquiring)
often derive from verbs of producing (making, doing):

> Colloquially we find usages such as Modern Italian *mi faccio
> la macchina*, "I get myself a car," with *faccio fare*, "to make,
> do": German *wir haben neue Möbel angeschafft*, "we acquired
> new furniture" (*anschaffen* vs. *schaffen*, "make, do") ... The
> verbs which indicate trading etc, often derive from spec-
> ialized uses of the verbs for making or doing. The process of
> specialization is much clearer when we consider both the
> verbs and the nouns connected with them; cf. German

geschaft "business", vs. *schaffen*, "make, do"; Italian *affari*, French *affaires*, "business", vs. *fare, faire*, "make, do" . . . Presumably these parallels may help to explain the specialized use of Akkadian *uppušu*, the intensive of *epešu*, "to make", in Middle and Late Assyrian documents [ca. 1600–ca. 600 BCE]. The verb occurs in statements about the purchase and sale of slaves, land, objects . . . , [and] it is normally preceded by the name of the item bought or sold and is followed by the subject, a prepositional phrase which indicates the price and another verbal form for giving and taking.

Along the same line, in the second half of the third millennium BCE, the Egyptian verb *iri*, "make, do" also meant "buy, acquire" (Fischer, 1961a, p. 52, fn. 10). Inscriptions of the era record that an individual "made" his tomb and then go on to list the various objects paid to the artisans who constructed it (Fischer, 1961b, pp. 61–2). Somewhat later, a tomb owner records that he "made" it "with my own copper." No later than the middle of the first millennium BCE the meanings of "property" and "something acquired" came together in the word *nkt* (Berlev, 1987, p. 153, n. 57). Note also the Akkadian expressions *sibûtam kašadu*, "do, make business' and *harranam epēšu*, "make a business trip" and their Hebrew cognates *měṣo ḥepeṣ* (Isaiah 58:3) and *'ăśôt derek* (Fishbane, 1985, p. 304). To illustrate further, Hebrew *qānîtî* means "produce, create, acquire, own, possess, purchase" (for example, Genesis 47:11, purchase of land; Isaiah 1:3, ownership of an ox).

Equally revealing is the fact that the Latin word for *business* activity, *negotium*, is from *nec-otium*, literally "absence of leisure" (Benveniste, 1973, pp. 115–18). Latin *pariō* means "produce" and "settle a debt." The related term *parō* means "produce" and "to acquire at one's own expense, buy." *Prēktēr*, a Greek term for "trader, merchant" also means "doer." Further, the Greek word *poieō* means "produce, manufacture" and "procure, get (money)." Perhaps the most striking piece of evidence for the identification of exchanged objects with produced objects is that the Greek verb *ergazesthai* applies to manual labor of all kinds and to earning interest from capital (Vernant, 1983, p. 248). The absence of special terms for commerce provides a strong and objective indication that, in the beginning, commerce was seen as corresponding to other, more direct, forms of productive activity.

3.4 Exchange as Production: Ethnographic Evidence

The support given by ancient and modern languages to the hypothesis that exchange is emotionally experienced as a component of the production process can be reinforced by several bits of ethnographic evidence.

In the seventeenth century, the era of the great Indian-European fur trade in eastern Canada, a Jesuit missionary overheard the remarks of a Montagnais chief: "The Beaver does everything perfectly well, it makes kettles, hatchets, knives, ...; and, in short, it makes everything" (Martin, 1978, p. 153). The same kind of point is illustrated by the attitudes of the Mbuti (Pygmies), a hunting and gathering people of Zaire's Ituri Forest, who, since the 1950s, have exchanged antelope meat with commercial meat dealers for cassava flour and rice. The Mbuti describe their antelope hunt as a "hunt for cassava flour" (Hart, 1978). In Papua New Guinea the Melanesian concept of *bisnis*

> involves control of a cash-generating enterprise ... In the Highlands, common examples of *bisnis* include coffee production and marketing, trucks for transporting goods and people, trade stores and bars. In other parts of Papua ... different cash crops are included in a list of *bisnis* along with timber and mining operations, carving and home industries, and plumbing and carpentry. (Boyd, 1985, p. 329)

Significantly, Boyd (1985, p. 329) adds that *bisnis* is viewed as a type of work (*wok*) and "is often referred to as *wok bisnis* and is distinguished from *wok mani* (wage labor)."

3.5 EXCHANGE AS PRODUCTION: THE LEGAL TREATMENT OF PROMISES

In support of the exchange is production hypothesis note also the differential legal treatment of promises. In legal systems derived from English common law and in France and Germany, bargained-for or reciprocal promises are contracts – that is, they are legally enforceable.[5] Gratuitous or "naked" promises or unilateral pledges to confer benefits are, on the other hand, generally not legally binding.[6] Barnett (1986, p. 290) is mistaken in suggesting that because it is "exclusively process-based" the bargain theory of consideration "cannot itself explain why certain *kinds* of commitments are not and should not be enforceable." It is quite true that a promisor who refuses to deliver his gift disappoints the promissee, perhaps grievously (Fried, 1981, p. 37). But a promisor who refuses to compensate a promisee who has made the effort required or assumed in their bargain is a thief.[7] Reliance or, more fundamentally, *effort* is the differential moral or feelings element that provides the psychological rationale for the differential legal enforcement of promised object transfers (compare Fried, 1981, p. 29). This point was recognized in 1651 by Thomas Hobbes (1962, Chapter 14, p. 107):

> He that performs first in the case of a contract is said to merit that which he is to receive by the performance of the other; and he has it as his *due*. Also when a prize is propounded to many, which is to be given to him only that wins; or money is thrown amongst many, to be enjoyed by them that catch it; though this be a free gift; yet so to win, or so to catch, is to *merit* and have it as *due*.

The question of whether or not the feelings foundation upon which the common law doctrine of consideration is erected is consistent with the requirements of economic efficiency is fascinating, but beside the point. The object of this study is to explain the pattern of law not the pattern of feelings.

3.6 ANTIQUITY OF EXCHANGE

There is evidence, admittedly indirect and controversial, that the division of labor and exchange are virtually as old as the human race itself. This raises the possibility that the powerful feelings surrounding exchanged objects are not merely parasitic on our feelings about manufactured objects. The late Glynn Ll. Isaac (1978, 1983) reported archaeological evidence from Eastern Africa (the Olduvai Gorge in Tanzania) suggesting that some two million years ago a hominid behavior system was operative in which meat was transported to central locations as part of a food-sharing process. However, another anthropologist, Richard Potts (1984) has put forward an alternative explanation of the data. Potts (1984, p. 346) suggests that early hominids used the Olduvai sites to store stone raw materials and manufactured tools for processing parts of carcasses:

> The use of these sites, the stone caches, primarily as processing areas implies that social activity was not focused there as it is at modern hunter-gatherer campsites. Yet, as to which resources were brought there, these early sites were the *antecedents* to home bases. Later, with the development of home bases, both hominid social activity and resource transport came to focus on the same places. A controlled use of fire and the relatively complete processing of meat and bone would have permitted greater social activity at the sites to which the resources were brought. The development of modern hunter-gatherer campsites was thus made possible.

While it remains for future studies to clarify the issues dividing Isaac and Potts, it is nevertheless suggestive that recent evolutionary hypotheses outlined by Kurland and Beckerman (1985, p. 741) raise the possibility that: "Humans became distinct from pongids when they began to produce and exchange their subsistence" or, alternatively, emphasize "the feedback between the food sharing, home bases, and the labor division generated by tools and carrying equipment." Isaac and Crader (1981, p. 91) explain that:

A social system involving exchange of energy in the form of transported food puts a premium on the ability to exchange information and to make arrangements regarding future movements of group members ... All these influences might be expected to favor the evolutionary development of an effective communication system, such as proto language, and of sharpened intellectual capabilities.

In support of the antiquity of exchange, the phenomenon of "generalized reciprocity" or sharing behavior so characteristic of contemporary hunting societies ought to be noticed (see Chapter 5, Section 5.2). It is, moreover, widely appreciated by scholars that the Indians of Eastern Canada were quick to grasp the opportunity to trade with Europeans. Indeed, we are informed that in 1534 Jacques Cartier was literally mobbed by enthusiastic Indians wishing to trade their furs (Martin, 1978, p. 8). Martin (1978, p. 153) adds that the "Eastern Canadian tribes had bartered with neighbors long before European landfall; the haggling and logistics of trade were hardly introduced *de novo* by whites." The first Cree hunter encountered by Henry Hudson's expedition in the spring of 1611 also showed himself to be familiar with the process of trade and bargaining (Thistle, 1986, pp. 3–4). "Nor," Thistle (1986, p. 5) adds, "was the meeting characterized by the extreme caution of 'silent trade' said to be common in initial contact." Reid (1970, p. 129) offers a similar account of the experience of the Cherokees of the southeast:

In 1756 Raymond Demere, in charge of constructing Fort Loudoun among the Overhills, reported that the Cherokees were "coming to us both by Land and Water with Eatables ... to sell to the People which they do in such Numbers that this Place already begins to have the Appearance of a Market." ... His dispatches to superiors in Charles Town make clear that he dealt with the Cherokees as individual vendors selling privately-owned property, and that most of the sellers were women ... The unmistakable conclusion is that the women, the ones who did the farm work, owned what they raised and could dispose of it as they

pleased – evidence supporting the supposition that the product of labor belonged to the laborer. Another conclusion
seems even more certain: the Cherokees did not learn from
the Europeans the law of barter and sales. From antiquity
they had been a trading people, dealing among themselves
and with other Indian nations, exchanging the steatite
deposits of their country and their skill at manufacturing fine
pipes for seaboard goods and salt, an item they always had in
short supply.

Herskovits (1952, p. 196) presents a variety of ethnographic
evidence in support of his assertion that "it is apparent both from
the achaeological evidence and from the ubiquity of present day
trading practices [in nonliterate societies] the world over that the
passage of goods from one people to another is a phenomenon of
great antiquity." The antiquity of exchange is attested not only in
exchanges between humans but in gifts to the gods – that is,
"sacrifices" – for which the deity later on rewards the donor with
"well-being," "peace," or, as in the case of the Vedic god
Mithras, by "bringing riches." We are really dealing here with
intertemporal barter exchange, as I have noted elsewhere (Silver,
1985, pp. 34–5).

The universal or at least widely observed psychological sense of
indebtedness – that is, the feeling that one is obligated to repay
others for benefits received from them – may also be adduced as
evidence for the proposition that exchange is production. Casual
empiricism in this area finds some support in social psychological
experimental data and the field studies of sociologists and anthropologists (see M. S. Greenberg, 1980, pp. 23–6).

It begins to seem possible, then, that Adam Smith (1976, p. 17)
knew whereof he spoke and was not merely, as Appleby (1978,
p. 279) alleges, reflecting the "restless energy and material
orientation" of his era with its "global dimensions" of trade, when
he asserted:

The division of labor, from which many advantages are
derived, is not originally the effect of any human wisdom

which forsees and intends that general opulence to which it gives occasion. It is the necessary, though very slow and gradual consequence of a certain propensity in human nature which has in view no such extensive utility: the propensity to trade, barter and exchange one thing for another.

Macpherson (1962, pp. 237–8) has discovered a similar conception of market-man in Locke's property theory. The commercial mentality may, however, have much deeper roots than is imagined by Appleby and Macpherson and in stage theories of economic development.

Notes

1 The fuzziness at the limits of hypothesis (2) are illustrated by the following example:

Economists earn more than philosophers on university faculties because their alternative earnings opportunities are greater. But do philosophers feel (empirically) that the economists are "entitled" to their higher earnings?

My intuition is that while philosophers might prefer payment by internal (university) marginal product, they would nevertheless agree that all professors, economists included, were entitled to the reward they had contracted for.

2 For a similar formulation, see J. S. Mill (1965, Book II, pp. 215–17).
3 A related objection may be lodged against Brennan and Buchanan's (1985, pp. 99–100) view that what is crucial for the concept of *desert*

is the legitimacy of the participants' expectations that the rules be followed ... If these expectations truly are legitimate then individuals who base their conduct on them do not desire to have them disappointed. . . . A rule is legitimate and violations of it constitute unjust behavior, when the rule is the object of voluntary consent among participants in the rule-governed order.

Our emotions, however, supply the answer to the question "Why does consent matter?" Sugden (1986, p. 155) comes closer to the feelings mark.

4 Note in connection with informational asymmetry *Pratt Land & Improvement Co. v. McClain* (135 Ala. 452, 456, 33 So. 185, 187 (19022)): "A purchaser [of real estate] though having superior knowledge of values does not commit fraud merely by purchasing without disclosing his knowledge of value" (quoted in Kronman, 1980a, p. 496, fn. 52).

5 Bargained-for promises can be assimilated to the "real" contracts of Roman law formed by the delivery of an object to one's trading partner.

6 Dawson (1980, pp. 221–3), Goetz and Scott (1980, pp. 1261–5), and Goodin (1985, pp. 44–52).

7 In the United States, courts have increasingly demonstrated a willingness to view willful breach of commercial contract as *tortious*: "The imposition of tort liability enables courts to award damages far in excess of those available under traditional contract law, including damages for all proximately caused injury and punitive damages" (Chatorian, 1986, p. 381).

4

Alleged Limits on the Right to Property

4.1 DESERT AND PRODUCTIVE ACTIVITY

According to philosopher Lawrence Becker (1977, p. 55, see also p. 44) a producer *deserves* his object only if his effort has benefited someone else: "Deserving a benefit from producing something from which only you profit is a strange notion." The underlying property feelings suggest otherwise. The producer feels he deserves his object ("I created it") and so do third parties ("He created it"). It is Becker's notion that, to deserve, one must benefit another that is strange, very strange. Morality does not require one to give free rides (see Gauthier, 1986, p. 206).

Another philosopher, John Rawls, launches a more serious assault.

> It seems to be one of the fixed points of our *considered judgments* that no one deserves his place in the distribution of native endowments, any more than one deserves one's initial starting place in society. (Rawls, 1971, p. 104) [Italics added]

> There is no more reason to permit the distribution of income and wealth to be settled by the distribution of natural assets than by historical and social fortune ... Even the willingness to make an effort, to try, and so to be *deserving in the ordinary sense* is itself dependent upon family and social circumstances. (Rawls, 1971, p. 74) [Italics added]

A producer does not deserve his "endowment" of physical characteristics, talent, and motivation and hence, according to our "considered judgments," does not deserve his object. Similar positions have been taken by prominent economists Kenneth Arrow (1973, p. 247) and Jan Tinbergen (1978, p. 37) and also by political scientist Jon Elster (1985, p. 202) and legal philosopher Ronald Dworkin (1985, pp. 195–6). Sociologist Derek Phillips (1986, p. 36), on the other hand, complains that Rawls's argument is too "deterministic." The more strenuous efforts of philosophers Robert Nozick (1974, pp. 214–28), George Sher (1979), and David Gauthier (1986, pp. 219–21) to defend an individualistic position against Rawls must be deemed failures. The reason is that their arguments are not grounded in a theory of property feelings, as is noted by A. Buchanan (1985, p. 71) and Kronman (1981, pp. 64–5). Consequently, Nozick, an important target, is defenseless against mean-spirited attacks. For example, welfare economists Boadway and Bruce (1984, p. 176) who perceive "no reason to postulate that a person who is born with sight and productive capacity is more entitled to consume than a person who is born blind and unproductive" go on to assert that:

> If one begins with a postulate, "Individuals have rights", as Nozick (1974, p. ix) does, and if one defines these rights to include whatever social institutions one seeks to defend (e.g., the distribution of income as determined by the existing system of property rights) then there is little left to say except that one's conclusions follow (trivially) from one's premises (or is it vice versa?).

It follows from Rawls's position that the loser of a foot race can claim that the winner does not deserve first prize because his superior technique and effort are morally arbitrary. The rewards for the peculiar talents of the professional athlete, the entertainment celebrity, the ordinary drudge, and, lest we forget, the brilliant philosopher or political economist, are due to chance and, consequently, undeserved. Even the desire to play one of these roles is morally arbitrary and unworthy of respect.[1] All of this is of course utterly inconsistent with our self-understanding. Despite Rawls's implication that feelings of choice, self-reproach, and pride in achievement are mere illusions, we continue to experience them – strongly. (In a later work discussing freedom, Rawls (1980, p. 543) notices that "citizens think of themselves as self-originating sources of valid claims.") Producers do not *feel* less deserving because their productive attributes are "undeserved." The self is not "bifurcated" with one part setting goals and the other containing the means to realize them (Kronman, 1981, pp. 72–3). The results made possible by *my* attributes are *my* results. This psychological fact (of self-ownership) is in reality the foundation of Hume's (1948, Section 27, p. 17) metaphysical proposition that: "Every man has a property in his own person; this nobody has any right to but himself. The labor of his body and the work of his hands, we may say are properly his." The same psychological fact also lies behind Lomasky's (1987, p. 140) seemingly mystical description of a "robust liberalism:"

> If an end, a talent, a material object happens through a chain of circumstances to become mine, then I have a personal stake in it that I have a unique reason to protect. Successful civility requires that others acknowledge and respect these personal attachments reciprocally with my like recognition of the individuality of others. That which is initially a surd becomes suffused with moral significance once it enters the projects of a person.

Sociologist Charles Cooley (1964, p. 169) penetrated to the heart of such propositions when he wrote in 1902 that the self *is* the "feeling of mineness" or "sense of appropriation."[2]

According to Ronald Cohen (1982, p. 148) the emerging psychological theory of equity "rests partially on the assumption that individuals perceive justice as a correspondence between ratios of characteristics and outcomes. It further assumes that individuals feel it is *both* ethically appropriate *and* possible to determine the extent to which each recipient unit is distinguished by a certain level of a relevant characteristic." This equity theory according to which deserved rewards *vary* with certain individual attributes does not provide comfort for Rawls's position. More concretely, when psychologist Richard Harris (1983, p. 221) asked subjects how four business partners should divide the profits of a business enterprise, "there were only 12 (2.2 percent) reversals of the fundamental criterion" that rewards should increase with contribution. (Harris (1983, p. 22) adds that 11 of the 12 reversals were probably due to errors in arithmetic.) Not in the least surprisingly, when a national probability sample was asked in 1975–7 to characterize a "fair economic system," a large majority of Americans, 78 percent, chose "people with more ability would earn higher salaries," only 7 percent believed "all people would earn about the same," an 15 percent declined to express a preference between the two choices. In 1978–9, 71 percent stated that it was "fair to pay wages according to how they had worked," 6 percent believed it was "fair to pay wages according to economic needs," and 23 percent declined to make a choice (see McCloskey and Zaller, 1984, Table 3–10, p. 84). Similarly, in 1980 when Kluegel and Smith (1986, p. 112) asked a national sample the following question: "Do you think that the income a person receives should be based more on the person's skills and training or more on what their family needs to live decently?," the responses were as follows: skills, 81 percent; family needs, 13 percent; both (volunteered) 6 percent.

It is quite clear that our feelings prohibit expropriating the productive attributes of a person for a common pool.[3] In this connection philosopher Thomas Nagel (1979, p. 37) observes cogently:

> About ourselves we feel pride, shame, guilt, remorse – and agent regret. We do not regard our actions and our characteristics merely as fortunate or unfortunate episodes – though they may also be that. We cannot *simply* take an external evaluative view of ourselves – of what we most essentially are and what we do ... It is this internal view that we extend to others in moral judgment – when we judge *them* rather than their desirability or utility.

Indeed, a person who took seriously Rawls's "considered judgment" that all his actions were predetermined would refuse to act and, hence, would be incapable of survival. Nagel (1979, p. 36) points out that "the self who acts and is the object of moral judgment is threatened with dissolution by the absorption of its acts and impulses into the class of events." Human beings may be intellectually persuaded by deterministic arguments but, as Nagel (1979, p. 33) aptly notes, "they [nondeterministic conceptions] reappear involuntarily as soon as the argument is over." G. A. Cohen (1986b, p. 111) adds that in his experience those "leftists" who disparage the thesis of self-ownership

> do not immediately argue that, were eye transplants easy to achieve, it would be acceptable for the state to conscribe potential eye donors into a lottery whose losers must yield an eye to beneficiaries who would otherwise be not one-eyed but blind ... The fact, in a word, that they are merely lucky to have good eyes does not always convince them that their claim on their own eyes is no stronger than that of some unlucky blind person.

The message is worth repeating: We cannot reason away the physico-chemical events in the brain we call by such names as "choice," "free-will," and "self."[4] All of these are emotive terms whose meaning is comprehended by recalling characteristic feelings (see Chapter 1, Section 1.1).

Rawls and his supporters fail to distinguish between the fact that our actions are caused and the entirely *emotional* question of what we deserve. The problem of the deterministic thesis, as Strawson (1974) has shown, is not falsity but irrelevance. It will be argued in Chapter 7 that a valid theory of economic justice or desert needs to be grounded in feelings. For the present it suffices to characterize Rawls's proposition that people do not deserve the fruits of their productive activity as utopian morality or, better still, as a mere debating point incapable of being taken seriously as an evaluative guide.

4.2 What Does Society Deserve?

Macpherson (1978, p. 206) objects to basing property powers on effort and advocates instead the "right not to be excluded from the use or benefit of those things (including society's productive resources) which are the achievements of the whole society." To begin with, it is not true, as Marx argued and as Macpherson seems to believe, that purchasers of labor-power ("capitalists") systematically rob the sellers (workers) of a portion of the social product (see Chapter 5, Section 5.3). It is, of course, quite true that a portion of the gain realized in a particular transaction is made possible by the broader network of social cooperation in which it is embedded. The importance of economies of scale, division of labor, use of money, and various "externalities" is obvious and undeniable. Yet society is not a single cooperative enterprise. Rather social cooperation is an individually and equally produced object and, hence, is incapable of generating net claims of "society" on any subset of individuals. Each of n cooperating persons produces and therefore is legitimately entitled to $1/n$ of the total cooperation. Thus, if one individual "B" can be said to owe another individual "A" something for "A's" $1/n$ contribution, it is equally true that "A" owes "B" an equal amount for "B's" $1/n$ participation. There is complete implicit in-kind compensation for each of the n cooperators. This holds, it should be noted, whether "B" is already a social cooperator or is about to participate for the first time. As between cooperators the social cooperation books are necessarily balanced and Macpherson's "right not to be excluded" is necessarily honored.[5]

It remains true that a randomly selected producer could not accurately claim that his gains (in terms of income and social status) were entirely his own doing in the sense that his gains would be the same without the cooperation of his fellows. Contrary to what I understand to be economist James M. Buchanan's (1977, p. 62) position, this fact raises no doubts in anyone's mind concerning "What is mine and what is thine?" Each cooperator is felt to be entitled to the objects he freely contracted for (see Chapter 3, Section 3.2). Neither does it, as Gauthier (1982, p. 62) believes, provide a basis for $n - 1$ cooperators, possibly acting through the government, to seize a portion of the *n*th producer's objects (his "rent") in the name of taxation or an immigration fee.[6] (Or, as Frank (1985, p. 124) would prefer, as payment for "high-ranked positions in the income hierarchy.") Many scholars would deem the imposition of a charge for social participation to be a violation of the individual's freedom.[7] In the present analytical framework, to charge a person for participation in society is *extortionate*, as he is the owner of his participation (see Chapter 1, Section 1.6). An individual who chooses to hand over his money in order to preserve his place in society has not implicitly or tacitly consented to this exchange; he has been robbed. In a consensual transaction each party chooses, without coercion, to hand over something he owns in return for something owned by his trading partner.[8] Unfortunately, the argument for imposing a charge for social participation is, as Epstein (1985, p. 15, fn. 20, pp. 310–11) points out citing *Carmichael v. Southern Coal & Coke Co.*: "not just a hypothetical one. All extensions of the power of taxation have rested upon the idea that the simple benefit of living in civilized society is sufficient quid pro quo for whatever tax the government wishes to impose."

The preceding argumentation does not, and is not intended to, make a case for unrestricted immigration or other interaction. My point is that each individual is felt to be entitled to what he agrees to take for his services. At the same time, one individual may legitimately charge another whatever he wishes to for the services he renders to him or withhold his services entirely. Equally one individual may legitimately offer any payment he wishes to for the services of another or abstain from purchases. And unless monopolistic collusion is ruled out by prior agreement (see Chapter 1, Section 1.6), an association of individuals is similarly entitled.

4.3 Harms and Rights

Philosopher Lawrence Becker (1977, pp. 54–5) asserts a "desert principle" requiring entrepreneurs to pay compensation for those of their actions which "reduce total welfare, or opportunities, or which otherwise disadvantage their fellows." The inclination of legal scholar Richard Posner (1985, p. 1196) is similar to Becker's but more practical: he hesitates to impose compensation because for an invention "it would be infeasible to force the inventor to identify and negotiate terms of compensation with all the losers." According to Goodin (1985, p. 118), the entrepreneur owes compensation to those most vulnerable to his actions. The problem with these views should be apparent. As no one has a property right (feeling of legitimate entitlement) in a particular structure of the economy, no one can morally veto or demand compensation for a change on the ground that the change reduces his welfare (see Epstein, 1985, pp. 80–5).[9] Not all harms suffered by a person at the hands of others are violations of rightfully held objects.[10]

Similarly, person "A" cannot morally demand compensation from person "B" solely because "A's" actions have increased "B's" welfare. (See also the remarks on free- riding in Chapter 1, Section 1.6.) An uncompensated conveyance of benefits from "A" to "B" does not necessarily violate "A's" rightfully held objects. More specifically, contrary to Frank's (1985) position, "B" is not morally indebted to "A" for the "*positional benefit*" he (allegedly) receives *merely* because "A's" income is lower than his own. "A" does not own "society" and cannot legitimately charge "B" for his place in it (see Chapter 1, Section 1.6). Neither may any individual or group morally veto economic change on the ground that: "I (we) find the widening income gap between members of the community unacceptable" or on the ground that "Your success displeases me (us)." "Robin Hood" altruism and envy are or may be strong feelings but they are not moral feelings (on envy, see Rawls, 1971, p. 533).

4.4 Private Property versus Personal Property

It is reasonably clear that the Marxist analytical distinction, as stated for example by anthropologist Elman Service (1979, pp. 22–4), between *private* property meaning objects used for the "profit" of their owner and *personal* property meaning objects which are directly consumed by their owner, has no foundation in people's property feelings. David Selbourne (1984, p. 54) notes cogently in his *Against Socialist Illusion*:

> In fact, the entitlements to ownership are seen, by the light of the ideological consensus, to attach equally to a mansion or a council house, to a pair of old boots or a boot factory; to retain their legitimacy whether exercised by their owners or conferred (in any way they choose) on others; and to be an equally-shared cross-class right, however unequal the appropriations. It is almost exactly as Locke but not Marx, as the Declaration of the Rights of Man but not the *Communist Manifesto* intended.

Selbourne (1984, p. 55) adds that Marx failed "to forsee that the legitimacy ... of personal appropriation ... would come to attach to *all* forms of appropriation, both personal and private, as the capitalist mode of production extended its purchase, and as the notion of community of property became culturally more marginal than ever." I would only add that Selbourne's all too common assumption, that private property is part of an "ideological consensus" manifested only with the emergence and spread of the "capitalist mode of production" and that "community of property" was at one time the dominant form, is just one more "socialist illusion" (see Silver, 1985, pp. 99–102).

4.5 EMPLOYMENT DISCRIMINATION

The legitimate entitlements of producers are violated when they are required to exchange their objects for labor-power according to externally imposed, so-called just rules of preferential hiring (see Thomson, 1973). (It is important in this connection to distinguish between the rights of owners, including taxpayers, legislatures, and boards of trustees, with the powers of their agents, for example presidents of public universities and government bureaucrats.) This proposition holds also against "utilitarian" rules requiring employers to desist from "capricious discrimination" or to discriminate in favor of competence, as proposed by philosopher Alan Goldman (1979, Chapter 2), and against "egalitarian" rules requiring employers to give preference to characteristics unrelated to productivity, for example the race, sex, or religion of the applicant. An applicant who is denied a position solely because his color is the "wrong" one may understandably be angered and saddened by the insult and injury. Nevertheless, no right of his has been violated. Provided, that is, there had been no prior agreement or understanding between employer and prospective applicants, the latter have neither a right to equal nor to unequal treatment. If, however, an employer advertised that "only merit counts" or "only minorities need apply" and then goes ahead and hires his favorite nephew or a nonminority, that employer is a thief. He has stolen the effort of the applicants or at least of the applicants who would not have bothered to apply were it not for the employer's fraudulent advertising.

It is helpful in this connection to consider a scenario described by philosopher A. I. Melden (1977, p. 91):

> If I have a dozen candies and proceed to distribute them among the dozen street urchins clamoring for them, but give one of them two candies leaving none for the last member of the group, he has a right to complain that I am unfair, but not a right to complain that I had violated his right to one of the candies. He has no such right. My action may be arbitrary, inconsiderate, wrong, or unfair but hardly a case of violating his right. And to say that he has a right to complain is only to say that he is justified or has sufficient warrant for complaining.

Well and good. However, if I *invited* the same dozen youngsters to a party and then gave nothing to one of the group, he would indeed be justified in complaining that I had violated his right to some of the candy. In our society an invitation to a party is universally understood to include a guarantee of reasonably equal treatment by the host. The thrust of this example is quite consistent with the legal fact that reasonable reliance is often a ground for complaint, even where there is no explicit promise. In the job market, however, discrimination is an accepted fact of life. Unless applicants are explicitly informed to the contrary, they do not assume that employers will be fair to them in some well-defined manner.

What matters for property rights is not the content of a preference or its "relevance" or "irrelevance" in utility terms or its "fairness," but only whether or not it is the producer's preference. The moral issues are often obfuscated by a tendency to ignore the supply side and to conceptualize the problem as one of "awarding scarce positions" or in terms of a "game" with "prizes." Perhaps it is difficult for noneconomists to realize that "positions" are scarce only because someone must take the trouble to produce them. We find, for example, even so perceptive a commentator as philosopher Thomas Nagel (1979, p. 95) declaring: "Certain abilities may be relevant for filling a job from the point of view of efficiency but they are not relevant from the point of view of justice, because they provide no indication that one deserves the rewards that go with the job." Nagel here not only ignores the right of the producer to dispose of *his* position as he chooses to but denies the right of the employee to the wage he contracted for.

4.6 ILLICIT WEALTH AND ORIGINAL SIN

Historical events raise the possibility that feelings of legitimate entitlement atrophy once a person's wealth crosses some threshold. Perhaps the underlying objection is of unequal bargaining power, a theme familiar in the social critiques of populist philosophers, for instance Reiman (1981) and R. W. Miller (1981). The *logical* problem with their arguments is that large accumulations of wealth do not necessarily entail monopoly power. Monopoly power results from a limitation on the number of possible trading partners. In any case the dependence on the market of the "masses" or of the "workers" – that is, those persons whose sole or primary investments are in human capital – as well as of "capitalists" – those persons whose primary investments are in material capital – are more or less voluntary adjustments to the market institution. Autarchy (and hierarchy) are always available as alternatives to market participation in the long run.

It seems reasonable to assume, therefore, that the real, if unstated, objection is that it is not really possible to accumulate great wealth by legitimate means. Witness the so-called "robber barons." There is evidence that by the third generation the children of the very rich do not feel legitimately entitled to their wealth (see further below). Is this because they have come to believe that the wealth they have inherited was "stolen" by their great-grandparents? Just this kind of assumption of illegitimate acquisition, it seems to me, underlies philosopher Kai Nielson's (1982, p. 272) desire to expropriate the latifundists of Latin America. Certainly Nielson provides no evidence, theoretical or empirical, in support of his claim that the Latifundia system is "highly inefficient." The same can be said of Elster's (1985, p. 517) uncharitable attribution of "bad faith" to anyone who would presume to "argue that the differences in endowments [in present day capitalism] are largely due to voluntary choices to invest rather than to consume." (This charge of "bad faith" also serves as a form of intellectual intimidation.) Marx's theory of "primitive accumulation" is a monument to the popularity of the illicit wealth-acquisition assumption and simultaneously its most important intellectual pillar. In the classical Marxist view the stage is set for capitalism by the *forcible* separation of the workers from their means of production (see, for example, G. A. Cohen, 1986b, p. 116). The theory trades on an oversimplified view of the English experience in which the importance of enclosure is exaggerated and voluntary shifts of farmers into household and urban industry are underestimated. An original sin origin for *all* current accumulations of wealth is created by universalizing this distorted view of the earlier history of English capitalism. My considered opinion is that the only primitive accumulation firmly grounded in evidence is Stalin's collectivization of Russian agriculture in the 1930s.

A non-Marxian version of the original sin argument has been put forward by philosopher Loren Lomasky (1987, pp. 115–16):

> Whether or not some Neanderthal man established just title to an expanse of land millennia ago bears not at all on the propriety of present ownership relations. We can be sure as one can be about such matters that there exists no unbroken chain of just transfers leading up to the present and thus no legitimate holding based on just initial acquisition . . . These considerations further reinforce the view that property relations are morally up in the air and that allocation *de novo* according to a morally grounded program cannot be in violation of anyone's rights.

Several comments are in order. First, having no "primitive accumulation" on which to hang his redistributive hat, Lomasky suggests, or so it seems to me, that a *single* unjust transfer at any moment in the time span between Neanderthal man and the present is sufficient to compromise the current distribution of objects (compare, however, Lomasky's remarks on pages 145–6). Second, Lomasky can confidently assert that "allocation *de novo* . . . cannot be in violation of anyone's rights" only by ignoring people's rights – that is, their feelings of legitimate entitlement with respect to current holdings (for a similar objection, see Harsanyi, 1987, p. 350). (Elsewhere Lomasky (1987, p. 130) maintains that: "*What is in fact the case* carries moral weight." Why?) Third, and most basically, let us assume for the sake of analysis that our property feelings were consulted and rendered a verdict of "unjust" – that is, seriously and irremediably tainted by countless thefts over the millennia – against the "present ownership relations." Suppose further that in line with the verdict it was agreed to build a Just New World by reallocating all objects, or some subset of objects (for example, "natural" resources), according to a "morally grounded program" (for example, equal shares for all). The adoption of this grand design would of course guarantee the justice of the *current* distribution of objects and the problem requiring solution would become the proper moral rule for evaluating *future* object distributions (see G. A. Cohen 1986b, pp. 116–17). The position argued for in this work is that the appropriate rule is that of *congruence*: The distribution of power over objects in society is just to the extent that it is congruent with property rights (see Chapter 8, Section 8.2).

Taking a quite different line, economist Arthur Okun (1975, p. 35) suggested that production-based rights lose their meaning "in a modern industrial society that rests heavily on wealth in the form of paper claims to assets that owners do not use directly." Anthropologist Tim Ingold (1987, pp. 224–5) adds that:

> It has also to be admitted that in our own 'modern' society, where manufactured commodities epitomize the category of wealth in general ..., the extreme development of the concept of private property has gone hand in hand with the reduction of the bond between producer and product to a bare minimum ... Most of what we own we have not produced ourselves. A moment's reflection shows that the hunter-gatherer's 'private ownership' of tools and our 'private ownership' of commodities represent diametrically opposed situations.

Perhaps the perspectives of Okun and Ingold have merit. It is not enough, however, merely to invoke terms like "paper economy" and "modern division of labor" and walk away as if this solved the problem. My position is that exchange is experienced as productive activity. Moreover, I find it to be self-evident that the assembly-line worker feels as strongly about the financial assets or consumer durables he has purchased with his wages as does the hunter about his deer or the cobbler about his pair of shoes. Would the critics of the production-based theory deny this evaluation? If not, where does this leave the so-called "paper economy?" Is it possible that the critics of production-based entitlements are really saying that in "our" complex, modern society people's property feelings *should not* matter?

In a spirit similar to Okun's, economist Paul Samuelson (1957, p. 209) argues:

> Suppose my reactions are not better than those of other speculators but just one second quicker ... I make my fortune – not once, but every day that important events happen. Would anyone be foolish enough to argue that in my absence the equilibrium pattern would fail to be reestablished? By hypothesis, my sole contribution is to have it established one second sooner than otherwise ... The worth of this one-second's lead time to society is perhaps $5, and if we ... accept a Clarkian naive productivity theory of ethical deservingness, we may say I truly deserve $5. Actually, however, I get a fortune.

The reader will I trust recall that in Chapter 3, Section 3.2 the marginal productivity theory of desert was explicitly rejected. Each cooperator is *felt* to have produced what he contracted for, however great or small. On the intellectual plane, Samuelson's line of argument was anticipated by the English philosopher Francis Hutcheson (1694–1746) who explained that while being the first to take advantage of an opportunity might be a trifling difference, it is a trifle capable of determining the right of one party when there is no right to weigh against it on the other side (cited in Forbes, 1975, p. 35).

4.7 Gifts and Bequests

Difficult problems of evaluation are raised by gifts or one-way transfers from a donor to a recipient. Possibly the recipient of a gift may thereby acquire a property right to the object. Against this stands the widely held attitude that gifts are different from wealth acquired by means of productive activity (including exchange). Greene (1973, pp. 418–19) explains:

Envy may often be generated by the belief that others possess something not possessed by oneself and for which the other individual has done nothing which has not also been done by oneself. If the other had performed some action interpreted as meriting differential reward, envy is less likely to be generated. The neighbors on either side of one's house may display precisely the same material comforts. The one on the east, however, may have let it slip that dad had left a considerable trust fund. Feelings about that third car may be considerably more antagonistic.

These remarks are quite realistic. But would anyone insist that your neighbor's dad had no right to give him a trust fund? Is giving itself morally wrong? Hardly. In the case of gifts, the donor (producer) maintains his right to the object and, as economist Kenneth Boulding (1973, p. 3) reminds us, "may even regard the assets of the recipient as a part of his own asset structure, so that the gift is more like a rearrangement of assets among the parts of a single organization than it is a true transfer." Consistently with Boulding's position, in the Melanesian Kula certain gifts termed *kitoum* remain the property of the producer (*gamag*) despite their physical separation from him. Damon (1980, pp. 282, 284) points out that:

> *kitoums* are brought into the Kula by the labor of specific individuals . . . No matter who holds it [a *kitoum*] as *mwal* or *veigun* ["gift"], it can be claimed by its owner, thus violating the asymmetry of the "opening gift/closing gift" distinction, and destroying, or seriously impairing a relationship. Only a crisis situation would lead them to this event, of course, but good Kula performers must keep this possibility in mind.

Gregory (1980, p. 640) who studied the economy of Papua New Guinea goes so far as to compare a gift to a "tennis ball with an elastic band attached to it. The owner of the ball may lose possession of it for a time, but the ball will spring back to its owner if the elastic band is given a jerk." It would appear that gifts fall into a distinct moral category.

Boulding's insight also seems to find support in object transfer documents of the ancient Near East. The quittance and relinquishment clauses (the seller is "to be far," *rḥq*) found in sale contracts of the fifth century BCE from Elephantine in Egypt and in much earlier Mesopotamian deeds are conspicuous by their absence in gift conveyances (Malul, 1985, p. 72, and Muffs, 1969, p. 26). Gifts are explicitly given in "affection," raising the possibility they will be taken back when affection is no longer felt (Muffs, 1969, pp. 40–3).[11] As the donor retains his right to the object its theft from the approved recipient would outrage the donor and third parties (on outrage, see further Chapter 5, Section 5.1).

Inheritance, the process of succession to the property of a decedent, represents a special case because the donor (producer) of the gift is incapable of having feelings. Accordingly, as Brittain (1978, p. 2) points out: "Although other types of current accumulation, such as capital gains, are appropriately subjected to tax, it is the direct inheritance of material wealth, openly and explicitly creating inequality of 'life chances,' that has been seen as the most defensible basis for wealth taxation." At least this view is commonly held among economists and egalitarians (see, for example, Dworkin, 1985, p. 195). But Brittain himself wonders whether it is shared by the general public, recalling that a "cry of outrage greeted presidential candidate George McGovern's call in 1972 for a very heavy inheritance tax" (Brittain, 1978, p. 2, n. 4).

It would appear that the rights of deceased producers do not lapse (for several generations at least). (Perhaps the weak right terminology of Chapter 1 applies here.) Their wishes and intentions very obviously matter to the living.[12] We feel that it is *wrong* to disregard the testamentary preferences of the the dead. Ernest Partridge (1981), a philosopher, doubts that these peculiar feelings provide an adequate justification for heeding a duty of "posthumous respect." To obtain a proper justification, he suggests, we must assume the perspective of a "moral spectator" who has an interest in respecting the wills of the deceased because he wishes his own will to be respected. Partridge does not really explain why an individual should believe there is a causal connection between his actions today and what the living will decide to do tomorrow, however. The more basic objection is that while 'posthumous respect" can be reinforced by collective actions, it requires no justification outside the "inappropriate" sentiments about the wishes of the deceased all of us have experienced. And, historically speaking, respect for the wishes of the deceased far precedes inheritance laws and other collective attempts to enforce wills.

Callahan (1987, p. 349) nearly hits the nail on the head:

> We need to recognize that the failure of arguments which purport to demonstrate that the dead can be harmed or wronged shows that these intuitions are not to be accounted for philosophically (i.e., brought into reflective equilibrium with some philosophical theory) but are, rather to be accounted for in some other way. That is, I want to suggest that our pretheoretic intuitions regarding harm and wrong to the dead are not genuine moral convictions at all but are, rather, judgments we are inclined to make simply because we *think of* the dead as the persons they were antemortem. They are sentiments which are to be accounted for psychologically.

I say "nearly" because Callahan fails to recognize that "*genuine moral convictions*" are exclusively matters of psychology, that is, of feelings. Partridge's argument and Callahan's dismissal of "our pretheoretic intuitions" as matters for "psychosocial scientists" well illustrate the overly intellectualized approach of contemporary moral philosophy. They also illustrate a temptation even more strongly felt among economists of assuming that only interests are capable of motivating behavior.

Notes

1 It should not, however, be thought that Rawls's constructivist position entirely disregards feelings. He does stress the importance of

"self-respect" in an appropriate conception of justice: "Self-respect is not so much a part of any rational plan of life as the sense that one's plan is worth carrying out. Now our self-respect normally depends on the respect of others" (Rawls, 1971, p. 178; see also pp. 440–2). In view of his deterministic analysis of desert it is appropriate to wonder how and why an empty self, a mere phantom of its own sensations, is worthy of respect (see Lomasky's (1987, pp. 138–41) perceptive comments). To the best of my recollection, Rawls never tells us that the importance of self-respect is one of his "considered judgments."

2 See also Baechler (1980, p. 273) and Denzin (1984, p. 51). Baechler (1980, p. 273) citing English, German, French, Italian, Greek, and Latin, finds it "remarkable that all languages combine the two senses of 'property' as that which is proper to someone or something and as that which pertains to someone."

3 Expropriation is the goal of Rawls's "difference principle" calling upon the state to maximize the welfare of the most disadvantaged persons (see Rawls, 1971, pp. 76–80).

4 On freedom of decision and action, see Thorp (1980); on consciousness, see Schilcher and Tennant (1984, pp. 198–203).

5 An argument functionally equivalent to Rawls's and Macpherson's has been put forward by anthropologist Tim Ingold. Ingold (1987, p. 227) begins with the eminently sensible proposition that people "come into the world as helpless infants, and for a very long period they are wholly or partially nourished by food procured through the labor of others." From this he deduces not merely that parents own their children (or that parents give gifts to their children, or even that children owe something to their parents), but that: "To the extent that people are mutually involved in the production of each others' existence, the products of their respective labors are due to all. Thus what a man appropriates through his labour, he appropriates *on behalf* of the collectivity through which – and only through which – he finds his being" (Ingold, 1987, p. 227). Real people, that is their feelings, are not like that at all.

6 Compare Becker (1977, pp. 82–3), Brennan and Buchanan (1985, pp. 103–4), and J. M. Buchanan (1977, p. 53).

7 See, for example, Fressola's remarks in Chapter 2, Section 2.4.

8 According to Brennan and Buchanan (1985, p. 103), however: "The mere fact of participation obligates each participant, as if by an explicit promise to abide by the rules, provided that the participants

have a *genuine option* not to participate if they so choose" [italics added]. The obligation is clearly applicable to "free immigrants," but for "general citizens voluntariness is not so clear" as "participation amounts to playing the 'only game in town'" (Brennan and Buchanan, 1985, p. 104). However, even for general citizens, Brennan and Buchanan (1985, p. 104) believe, "there is some sense in which violation of the rules is 'unjust' to the other participants ... Does not the mere fact that such rules have prevailed for a long time contribute to [their] legitimacy ...?" See in this connection the useful remarks of Epstein (1985, pp. 99–100).

9　Contrary to what I understand to be the position of Coleman and Kraus (1986, pp. 1353–4), the invasion of a person's interest cannot be (morally) *wrongful* unless that interest is embodied in a right.

10　This line of reasoning is applicable even when the activities of the entrepreneur fail to heed the traditional principle of "equity" calling for "equal treatment of equals." One participant ("equal") is morally permitted to be harmed (benefited) more than another participant ("equal"). Indeed the changes introduced into the economy are morally permitted to contradict the newer principle of "horizontal equity" (or the no-rank-reversal criterion) calling for the preservation of the pre-existing ranking of utility levels of the participants in the economy (see Boadway and Bruce, 1984, p. 187).

According to A. Buchanan (1987, p. 561): "The libertarian can be put on the defensive by one simple but powerful observation about what is at the heart of morality: morality is fundamentally (though not exclusively) concerned with avoiding states of affairs that are harmful for individuals." This assertion is not only incorrect but deserves to be characterized as "paternalism without foundations."

11　Among the Hindus, donors who seek to resume their gifts (*dana*) to Brahmans are subject to supernatural sanctions (Parry, 1986, p. 461).

12　See J. S. Mill (1965, Book II, P. 216) and Tullock (1971, pp. 465–6).

5

Producers versus Thieves

5.1 Right Makes Might

Upon becoming aware that a thief is after the fruits of his labor, the normally-formed producer reacts in rather stereotyped fashion, he experiences the hot surge of anger and assumes a menacing facial expression and stance (see Cheyne, 1977, and Strongman 1978, Chapter 8). In respect of this trait at least it seems plausible to speak of the psychic unity of mankind and even of genetic control. The term "incorporation phenomenon" refers to the producer's feeling of unification with his objects. This psychological principle no doubt lies behind Hegel's (1942, pp. 37–41) metaphorical argument that a person makes an object his own by injecting his will into it. Marx's rather similar insight concerning the objectification of labor is well summarized by Wood (1981, p. 38): "They [men] view the objects they create as a sort of evidence or testimony to the self-actualization of their capacities and the meaningfulness of their lives." No wonder, then, that the producer experiences theft as an attack on his personality (self).[1]

To some extent the producer's emotion of outrage is experienced by normally formed third parties. Note Walter Berns's (1979, p. 16) suggestion that "If men are not angry when a neighbor suffers at the hands of a criminal, the implication is that their moral faculties have been corrupted." On the other side, a normally formed person, upon assuming the role of thief, experiences fear and guilt, that is, a strong aversion or "self-concept distress" (see Walster, Walster, and Berscheid 1978, p. 23).

The phenomenological conceptualization of the emotional pattern of property defense has a great deal in common with a legal trial.[2] Note first that unlike feelings emphasizing "the relation of *a person to his own body*," emotional feelings emphasize "the relationship of *the person to his external physical and social context*" (R. I. Levy, 1984, pp. 220–1).

1 Consideration of the evidence results in the belief that a producer's object is being stolen. Cultural factors may, of course, play an important role in shaping the interpretation of the facts.
2 The producer (and third parties) render a judgment on the theft taking the form of outrage or moral indignation.
3 The sentence meted out takes the form of an inclination on the part of the judges (producer and third parties) to punish (harm) the thief. It is not enough for the thief to make his victim "whole" by restitution or the payment of compensation. The judges feel that the thief *deserves* to forfeit a (variable) portion of his objects.[3]

The producer's property right (complex of property feelings) gives him a significant advantage, a "moral advantage," against the thief. His power is enhanced by his own outrage (and the outrage of third parties). The heightened prowess of a wronged producer corresponds to the Roman *furor*, the Celtic *ferg*, the Germanic *wut*, the Greek *menos*, and the Malay *mengamok*. The thief is weakened by his fear aversion. Apparently the biochemical changes that accompany (are) moral outrage elevate motor performance while fear aversion depresses it. Thus, *ceteris paribus*, an *agression differential*, or in ethological terms the "relative dominance of ownership," favors the producer in his struggle with the thief. *On the average, property right makes might.*

Obviously, physically strong, fearless individuals and those less prone to "conscience decrement," or, as Pollock (1986, p. 516) puts it, more prone to "moral blindness," make more effective thieves just as those producers who are fearful, physically weak, and less prone to angry defense make easier victims. Note here the adage about "the fool and his money." It is, for instance, known that some individuals can defeat the polygraph because they have the ability to lie without emotion. This trait is of course of no small advantage to the criminal. A variety of, as yet, inconclusive research findings hint at the possibility that some individuals are biologically disposed toward criminal activity (Wilson and Herrnstein, 1985, and Cloninger and Gottesman, 1987).

Manifestations of fear aversion and guilt by thieves and, even more, of anger by victimized producers are perhaps so commonplace and obvious that they tend to be overlooked in inventories of social–psychological facts. Only the more striking examples such as brutal peasant rebellions and the lynching of cattle rustlers, seem to find a secure place in the literature. Speaking historically, instances in which outraged bystanders have intervened are not rare. They have collared purse-snatchers, joined posses and vigilante groups, and even volunteered for military service. Truly this is the "stuff from which heroes are made." But the interventions often take more modest forms: contributions of horses, supplies, and information to the avenging posse, even a stout length of rope for the hangman. Unfortunately, we cannot hope for properly standardized data suitable for testing the aggression differential hypothesis or for calculating the relevant probabilities of victory. Some indirect evidence is available, however. Why, if not for the empirical observation that producers usually triumph, have diverse societies thought it fair to rely on trial by battle to resolve disputes over the ownership of objects? For example, as Lowie (1920, pp. 405–6) notes: "Among the Chukchi [of northwestern Siberia] differences are sometimes settled by a wrestling match, there being a firm conviction that a wronged man will be victorious. The same means is used by the Ifugao to ascertain disputed rice-field boundaries."[4] Also the postulated aggression differential among humans appears to have a counterpart among territorial animals in "invincible center" behavior – that is, the observation that residents usually triumph in disputes with intruders (see Chapter 6, Section 6.2).

5.2 Ubiquity of the Property Institution

James M. Buchanan (1975, pp. 8–9), a leading contractarian economist, speaks of the necessity of "allocating or parcelling out 'rights' among individuals" in a world where "there are few 'natural' limits" outside matters of personal life-style. Once equipped with a set of "rights," Buchanan (1975, p. 10) continues, each of us becomes truly an individual "in a position to initiate agreements with other persons, to negotiate trades or, in more general terms, to behave as a free man in a society of men." Buchanan's (1975, p. 23) assumption of a world without production in which goods simply "fall down" is quite appropriate within the context of his Hobbesian model.[5] The fatal weaknesses of this model within its own assumptions have been demonstrated by Gauthier (1986, pp. 193–9). More basically, the model is incapable of comprehending a world, the real world, in which production is the source of wealth and, consequently, powerful emotions give producers an advantage in conflicts with their competitors, the thieves. Similarly, Umbeck's (1981, p. 37) proposition that "all private ownership rights are ultimately founded upon the ability to exclude potential competitors" ignores the fact that producers have more "ability to exclude" than thieves. The "state of nature" is not a state of unlimited predation. Moreover, in a world in which productive activity triggers that complex of feelings of legitimate entitlement we have called strong property rights (see Chapter 1), it is simply not true, as Brennan and Buchanan (1985, p. 3) suggest, that, but for law and custom, every man would seek by means including physical force those changes in power over objects that will improve his welfare. Brennan and Buchanan (1985, p. 26) are mistaken in supposing that: "Political order must ... be antecedent to economic order." Economic order and, more generally, *society* itself, are antecedent to explicit or implicit agreements concerning rules. Indeed it is not at all obvious that an agreement to "parcel out 'rights'" would ever be consummated in a Hobbesian world. As Sugden (1986, p. 167) has forcefully reminded us, a person (possibly the modal person) "who possesses relatively little might be better off taking his chances in a state of nature" (see also Arneson, 1987, pp. 301–2).[6]

Even Gauthier (1986, pp. 193, 268), a self-described Hobbist, who competently, but against all odds, seeks to demonstrate the possibility of "morals by agreement" in the end throws up his hands at this problem: "Fortunately, the prospect of society is realized for us; our concern is then to understand the rationale of the morality that sustains it." In order to "understand" this sustaining "morality" Gauthier (1986, pp. 16–17 and elsewhere) simply *assumes* that individuals "who take no interest in other's interests" *voluntarily* desist from bettering their position through interactions that worsen the position of others. (An interactive context is one in which an individual believes that the way he is dealt with by others depends on his own choices.) Gauthier unduly magnifies the contribution of this assumption by grossly underestimating the importance in society of noninteractive contexts. (In noninteractive contexts an individual believes that the behavior of others toward him does not depend on his own choices.)

I learned a great deal from Gauthier's excellent book about *Morals by Agreement* (1986) and I recommend it to the reader. A few additional critical remarks are necessary, however. Gauthier (1986, pp. 16, 192) maintains that the voluntary abstention of his individuals from "taking advantage" of others is "part of morals by agreement," but "is not the product of rational agreement. Rather, it is a condition that must be accepted [better 'heeded'] by each person for such an agreement to be possible." Understandably, Gauthier is troubled by an assumption that is either incoherent or amounts to incorporating prior moral suppositions into a theory intended to explain the emergence of morality itself (see the comments of Harsanyi, 1987, pp. 342–4). This discomfort, we must suppose, lies behind some rather peculiar assertions:

1 "Only beings whose physical and mental capacities are either roughly equal or mutually complementary can expect to find cooperation beneficial to all" (Gauthier, 1986, p. 17).
2 "Humans benefit from their interaction with horses, but they

do not co-operate with horses and may not benefit them (Gauthier, 1986, p. 17).

3 "Among unequals, one party may benefit most by coercing the other, and on our theory would have no reason to refrain" (Gauthier, 1986, p. 17).

Now either (1) includes everyone and is devoid of content or else it ignores the gains from division of labor and is consequently misleading. With respect to (3), a Hobbesian chestnut intended to enhance the importance of interactive contexts, thieves do not have to be "unequal" to their victims: "You and I are 'equal' in every respect but this gun in my hand makes me 'more equal'." A *rational* individual in a *mass* society has no particular interest in stealing or otherwise discriminating against an *anonymous* individual who has previously stolen. (Neither will a saintly "Kantian" retaliate against a thief (see Arneson, 1987, pp. 311–15).) Equality in and of itself is incapable of transforming noninteractive social contexts into interactive ones and, hence, cannot preclude coercion. What finally is the relevance of the "horses" in (2)? Surely they have nothing to do with the rational persons who will not unilaterally desist from using force! (see Arneson, 1987).

To continue, as the existing distribution conforms rather badly with the (apparent) distribution of ability to use force, it is questionable that either the wealth distribution or the rules of the property institution can be legitimized "*as if*" they emerged from a contract (current or continuously negotiated) among individuals equipped with Hobbesian values (compare Brennan and Buchanan, 1985, p. 22, and Lomasky, 1987, especially Chapter 4). The insights of contractarian theory are undoubted; they are also quite limited in scope. On the other hand, that the property institution,[7] by which is meant a reasonably tight fit between object production and object power, seems to be a common characteristic of societies differing markedly in place, time, and complexity is supportive of the postulated aggression differential in favor of producers (see Herskovits, 1952, pp. 327–9). I say "seems" because to gather a truly convincing standardized body of evidence would take years of research. All that can be accomplished here is to extract a small, hopefully representative sample from the historical and ethnographic literature.

The sale, lease, and inheritance of privately owned fields is observable in Mesopotamian and Egyptian records no later than the middle of the third millennium BCE (Silver, 1985, pp. 92–102). The Bible takes note more than once of privately owned land as do the *Iliad* and the *Odyssey* and Rome's Twelve Tables (ca. 450 BCE).[8] In ancient Rome, according to Coulanges (1980, pp. 59–60):

> Every field had to be surrounded ... by an enclosure, which separated it completely from the domains of other families ... On certain appointed days of each month and year, the father of the family went round his field ... He drove victims before him, sang hymns and offered sacrifices. By this ceremony ... above all, he had marked his right to the property.

Despite endlessly repeated assertions to the effect that private ownership was absent in the East, the available evidence suggests otherwise. Kumar (1985, p. 365), for example, reports that inscriptions dating from the Chola regime of medieval South India make ample reference to private object power including mortgage, sale, and inheritance of land. An articulated private ownership of fields is also found, again contrary to preconceived ideas, in so-called "primitive" or "tribal" societies including the Kapauku, and agricultural people of Western New Guinea (Pospisil, 1963, pp. 130–40), and the pastoral peoples of East Africa (Schneider, 1979, p. 73). Lowie (1920, pp. 210–33) supplies additional examples and also discusses most perceptively the question of "primitive communism" versus "individualism."

The principle that waste or neglected land came under the legal control of those who cleared it was familiar to the Mycenaean Greeks in the second half of the second millennium BCE and to the Romans. Similar practices are revealed in North Africa even under the Vandals in law codes of 494–6 CE. During the Dark Age following the arrival of Germanic peoples in the territory of the

Western Roman Empire, the Bavarian laws and numerous charters leave no room for doubt that a freeman held permanent title to land upon which he or his ancestors had expended labor. Even a slave had heritable property powers over the land he cleared and the house he built. Under Germanic law, a man permitted to settle and cultivate a plot of land for a year and a day thereby acquired protected possession. During the later period of population growth and land reclamation the hard-working pioneer acquired property in what were then called "acquisitions" or "assarts" or, as in Spain, *aprisio* or *presura*.[9]

The practice in India as hinted in the Sanskrit literature by the "Laws of Manu" (ca. 184 BCE to 320 CE) granted title in land to the man who first removed the stumps and put the land to the plough (Baden-Powell, 1899, pp. 1329–31). Saracen views are mirrored in a maxim dating from the economic "golden age" (between 900 CE and 1400 CE): "The servants are the servants of God, and the countries are the countries of God, and he who cultivates waste land, to him it belongs" (Castorina, 1980, p. 123). Indeed, under the law of Islam, unoccupied land acquired an owner by being "quickened" (W. R. Smith, 1956, p. 96).

The Australian root-gatherer "transmits to her daughters the root-patches she has tended and exploited" (Forde, 1963, p. 375). Among the Menabe, a wet-rice cultivating people in Madagascar, the family expending labor to prepare and maintain rice beds and terraces establishes property power (Linton, 1933, p. 129). In the Highlands of Papua New Guinea, according to Grossman (1984, pp. 100–1):

> When a person cuts vegetation to prepare a garden on land that has not been cultivated within memory, he is clearing *araka bata*, or "new land." When the garden is fallowed and vegetation regrowth is well developed on the plot, the site and regrowth together are referred to as *kandu*. This term also signifies proprietary rights established by first cultivation, and these rights pass by inheritance from father to son ... An individual can obtain a proprietary interest in trees

of economic importance such as coffee ... by planting, inheritance, or gift ... Proprietary rights sometimes confer the right of permanent transfer [including sale]: A man may grant these rights in a plot that he cleared first, but cannot do so with such rights obtained by inheritance or transfer.

Quite similar patterns have been observed among the Siriono of Eastern Bolivia, the Navaho and Hopi of the American Southeast, the Indians of Southern New England and Mississippi, Melanesians, Polynesians, the Yoruba, Tallensi, and Ashanti of Western Africa, the Bushmen of the Kalahari, the Karen and Lisu of Thailand and the Semai of Malaya.[10] Among the South African Bushmen, the person who burns a patch of veld owns the wild vegetables whose growth he has encouraged (Herskovits, 1952, p. 340).

In first millennium BCE Israel, Assyria, and Egypt, the digger of a well owned its water. (The Egyptian owner of a well legally owned the land it irrigated.) Ownership of water by the digger is also found in more recent times in nomadic Arabia and Northern Iran and among the herding peoples of South Africa.[11] Glick (1979, p. 97) discovered that in Spain's Duero Valley in early medieval times:

The modalities of appropriation of water rights greatly resembled those of the American West ... Almost all of the documentation indicates that water was subject to *presura* [appropriation] and that prior appropriation ... was the rule of the day. The Fuero of Lograno (1095 CE) contains a perfect expression of this norm: "Whoever can find water for irrigating pastures and vineyards, or for mills and orchards, or whatever they might need, let them take it."

Shares in the ownership and the appurtenances of irrigation systems were bought and sold (Glick, 1979, p. 148). Among the Ifuago of North Luzon, water rights are heritable and transferable, and the first to clear a field below a spring has priority to its water (Hoebel, 1961, p. 108).

According to Lowie (1920, p. 21), in British Columbia an Indian who "constructed a deer-fence or fishing station . . . was entitled to the exclusive use of what his individual efforts had produced and the right descended to his heirs." Herskovits (1952, p. 342) adds that these rights were advertised by means of totem poles. The Eskimo hunter in East Greenland who cut a seal hole was entitled to the seals caught in it. A seal escaping with a harpoon in it belonged to the ultimate killer, but the harpoon head, identifiable by its markings, was to be returned to its manufacturer. The shares of Baffin Islanders who participated in a walrus hunt were tied roughly to the importance of their contribution: "He who first strikes a walrus receives the tusk and one of the forequarters. The person who first comes to his assistance receives the other forequarter; the next man the neck and the head; and each of the next two, one of the hindquarters" (Hoebel, 1961, pp. 79–80; see also Ingold, 1980, pp. 156–7). Similarly, in the cooperative monkey hunt of the Birhars of the Chota Nagpur plateau in central India, the owner of the net in which a monkey was captured received the common share plus the forelegs (Sinha, 1972, p. 389). Harako (1981, pp. 535–6) describes the distribution practices of Zaire's Mbuti:

> Primary ownership of a carcass is determined by involvement in wounding and/or killing the prey . . . Net borrowing is common among the Mbuti, however, and the rule is that the borrower gets one leg and the net owner the rest . . . Another convention is that the person who makes the morning hunting fire . . . before a net hunt gets all the heads of animals captured that day . . . If a dog tracks down prey without human assistance and the first arrow kills it, the carcass belongs to the dog's owner and the archer gets the loins.

In the American Great Plains the Pawnee who killed a buffalo owned it; the man who butchered the animal claimed half of its meat (White, 1983, p. 187). Why did a Choctaw chief keep a significant share of a kill? Jonas Adam, an English trader, explained that it was the chiefs who owned the guns and rented them out to the hunters. Ingold (1980, p. 18) notes that in many cultures the hunter using a borrowed weapon must present his kill to the lender. For the Tikopia the head of the household is the "man linked with canoe" – that is, its owner – as Firth (1965, p. 258) explains: "In concrete terms he is the man who initiated its building, who is acknowledged to have the primary right of disposal of it, who grants the use to others, who is called upon to distribute any catch of fish made from it." When the contributions of the participants in a hunt were indistinguishable, as for instance in a surround, the kill might be turned over to a chief or elder for distribution.[12] This should not be taken to mean, however, that no attention was paid to participation in determining the shares of individuals (see Firth, 1965, pp. 279–87, and Testart, 1987, p. 293).

As the owners of a kill frequently distribute is to a wider community it may mistakenly be supposed that the elaborate rules utilized by many hunting peoples to establish ownership are much ado about nothing. In the first place, as Dowling (1968) and Ingold (1980, pp. 158–9) point out, an able hunter acquires status and a claim to a leadership position in the community. Second, contrary to Ingold (1980, p. 158), the owners may take home an above average portion of meat in terms of size or quality. For example, in the collective bear hunt of the Eskimo of Ammassalik on the coast of Greenland, the individual who first saw the animal "gets the skin, the head, the neck, the forequarters, the vertebral column, and the insides" (Testart, 1987, p. 289 citing the research of Robbe). Among the African Bushmen, owners retain the animal's skin and sinews for making cord (Herskovits, 1952, p. 322). Moreover, the owner of game is often in a position to tilt the distribution in the direction of his relatives (Marshall, 1976, pp. 297–303). Thus, the Ammassalik Eskimo who kills a seal unaided takes it home to his wife who "cuts it up into sixteen pieces which are redivided and distributed between the hunter, his wife, his children, his parents, his parents-in-law, his siblings, his wife's siblings, his first cousins and the village elders" (Testart, 1987, p. 289 citing the research of Robbe). Most importantly, the identification of the owner and the rituals of distribution serve to reinforce the game owner's claim to repayment at a later date and to enhance his reputation as a creditworthy person. It may sometimes be appropriate to speak of repayment systems. For example, some hunting societies give relatively large shares to the old men – that is, the former hunters – and in others the hunter is prohibited from consuming his own game (Testart, 1987).

With respect to repayment systems it must be remembered that the returns to hunting are quite variable and, as Dowling (1968, pp. 502–3) explains, "wild game animals are frequently large" and "techniques are seldom available for preserving meat for future use" (or are expensive in terms of resources or produce an unpalatable product). Collectable debts and a good name are, of course, valuable assets. Lastly, the owner of game has the power to deny meat to shirkers and to nonreciprocators (Herskovits, 1952, p. 117, and Ingold, 1980, p. 167).

Lowie (1920, p. 234) suggests that for pastoral peoples: "There is . . . [an] accentuation of the sense of individual property rights, attested by the branding systems current among such tribes as the Chukchi, the Kirgiz, and the Masai. Among peoples who are predominantly stock-breeders individual ownership is often vehemently asserted even against the claim of family ties." Anthropologist John H. Dowling (1968, p. 504) is convinced that property is a cultural universal. The general trend of ownership in nonliterate societies is that people are entitled to what they have produced (see Herskovits, 1952, pp. 375–7, and Linton, 1952, pp. 655–6). The kind of evidence summarized above is usually dismissed by economists as "anecdotes" or, worse, "selective anecdotes" (for example, Samuelson, 1985, p. 168). But anecdotes are at least an antidote to the unfounded assertions to which economists are sometimes prone. For example, according to Schotter (1985, p. 18):

Although it seems quite natural to most Americans, the notion that the individual and not the group should be the basic repository of rights and obligations is neither old nor universally accepted. In primitive cultures there is very little sense of individual identity. Property, far from being private, is held in common and all individual rights are subservient to those of the village chief. Furthermore, goods and services are invariably allocated not by the principle of marginal productivity – that each person gets what he contributes – but by customary rules.

Schotter is not only totally mistaken about property in "primitive cultures," but he also, even more surprisingly, ignores the difficulties raised by *team* production. Recall the difficulties of distribution according to contribution in communal hunts. As explained by Alchian and Demsetz (1972, p. 779):

> There is a source of gain from cooperative activity working as a *team*, wherein individual cooperating inputs do not yield identifiable, separate products which can be *summed* to measure the total output. For this cooperative productive activity, here called "team" production, measuring *marginal* productivity and making payments in accord therewith is more expensive by an order of magnitude than for separable production functions.

Moreover, Schotter's "customary rules" may reflect marginal productivity under a relatively stable technology. And, after all, in modern America where "status" is unimportant and "contract" is supreme, most employees are paid a salary that is, by input, not by piece!

The evidence I have been able to examine also suggests that theft is widely, perhaps universally condemned and punished.[13] To illustrate, Firth (1965, p. 268) reports that among the Tikopia:

> Attempts to alienate land permanently or to abstract equipment or other goods secretly are fiercely resented and are characterized as theft (*te kaia*) . . . The immediate reaction is

usually to shriek loudly in the formal Tikopia prolonged cry of '*Iafu!*' ... The commotion brings up a crowd of people, who inquire the reason, and on hearing it, proffer sympathy and suggestions as to who may have been the culprit.

Clamor, of course, is widely attested in the Indo-European language-speaking world (Watkins, 1970, pp. 339–40). Indeed, theft is so strongly resented that even societies inclined toward the blood feud permit producers to execute thieves caught in the act ("manifest thieves") without fear of retaliation.

It is appropriate to append to these brief remarks concerning crime and punishment a comparison with the thrust of the law-and-economics literature. To begin with, it is of course, quite true that the threat of punishment deters criminal activity. However, the proposition of the law-and-economics literature that society punishes criminals in order to direct transactions into markets utterly fails to recognize the emotional foundations of the punishment institution. It is misleading to this extent at least. Criminal activity extinguishes and reverses (or, possibly, overrides) the complex of feelings termed a strong right with the result that the thief forfeits some of his otherwise rightfully held objects (compare Lemos, 1986, pp. 79–80). Punishment is one of those social practices which, in Strawson's (1974, p. 25) words, "really *are* expressions of our moral attitudes and not merely devices we calculatingly employ for regulative purposes." No appeal to a deterrent effect is necessary to explain or to justify the punishment of criminals, our retributive feelings are necessary and sufficient. Why is it, it may be added, if not for these moral attitudes, that victims and third parties give no weight to the gains made by thieves? The assignment of a zero weight to the injurer's benefits (psychic or wealth) is what distinguishes crimes from torts. "But," as Alvin Klevorick (1985, p. 918) points out, "such a distinction cannot be derived from the standard law-and-economics approach to explaining the criminal sanction which views criminal law as an extention of tort law." The defects inherent in the economics of law literature's functional view of legal rules are well summarized by Klevorick (1985, p. 909):

The need to answer questions about legitimation of the transaction structure to explain the existence of the criminal category implies that *although our explanation of why society invokes the criminal sanction can be stated in economic terms, that vocabulary and mode of analysis do not provide a complete substantive understanding.* To the contrary, a coherent explanation of the criminal category necessitates answers to noneconomic questions about political legitimacy and authority, about the rights of individuals and the power of the state, about the political, moral and legal constraints in the exercise of rights and powers. [Italics added]

Psychologists Hogan and Emler (1981, pp. 132, 140–1) provide building blocks for a more complete theory of punishment taking moral culpability into account by maintaining that the punishment of thieves is a cultural universal and suggesting: "Indeed, one might even argue that the urge to retaliation must be a part of one's nature if one is to survive."

5.3 Employer as Thief

The acceptance of certain ideas about the nature of social relations may precipitate behavior appearing on the surface to deny the existence or importance of property feelings. Upon further examination, however, it is revealed that these ideas trade on the very feelings they seem to subvert. Marxist economic analysis provides an instructive example of the power of social ideas and of the importance of false consciousness in social life.

In 1840 the French socialist Proudhon discovered that "Property is Theft" (Gide and Rist, 1913, pp. 299–300). But Marx demonstrated his mastery of the sources and revolutionary potentialities of moral indignation in his theory that the discrepancy ("surplus value") between the value of a worker's labor-power (his wage) and the value of his labor (his output) accrues to the employer as an unearned or exploitative income. Concretely, the employer compensates the worker for only a portion of his working day (total effort) notwithstanding his *promise* to pay the worker a specified wage for each and every hour of effort. Marx's economic analysis is not valid,[14] but his psychological insight is profound. Workers who believe they have been defrauded by the system are more likely to support or engage in revolutionary activities. Their thought process might be reconstructed as follows: "You tricked me Mr. Capitalist. First you gave me to understand that you would compensate me for my entire effort and then, greedily, you turned around an paid me for a portion of my effort. Now Mr. Moneybags the time has come to eliminate you and your lying system." Marx spoke frequently of the sale of labor-power without an equivalent ("unpaid labor"), but *with the semblance of an equivalent* (Elster, 1985, p. 223).

Contrary to the position of philosopher Allen Buchanan (1987, p. 130), there is no "mystery" about the "moral wrongness" of traditional Marxian exploitation. Moreover, as political scientist Kenneth Minogue (1985, p. 110) suggests, Marx's theory of surplus value

> has been believed in no hypothetical spirit at all. It has rather been taken as a dogma, and the motive power of revolutions has been *moral indignation* rather than scientific curiosity, or even the technological quest for efficiency. Further both the tone and the context of the theory of surplus value suggest that it is hardly at all the answer to a scientific question; *it is rather a translation into structural terms of that increasing hatred of any people who might be construed as social parasites*, with spread over Europe towards the end of the eighteenth century. [Italics added]

Thus, the young Marx wrote in 1843 that: "criticism is no passion of the head, it is the head of passion ... Criticism appears no longer as an *end in itself*, but only as a *means*. Its essential sentiment is *indignation*, its essential activity is *denunciation*" (quoted in Minogue, 1985, p. 41). Marx's meaning is clear enough.

Once the surplus value-unpaid effort ideology spreads a market-oriented society becomes increasingly unstable and prone to the phenomenon termed "legitimation crisis" by Jürgen

Habermas (1975, see also G. A. Cohen, 1986a, pp. 317–20). Not surprisingly, Marx wrote in the *Grundrisse* that the proletariat's realization of its exploitation was the "knell of its [capitalism's] doom":

> The recognition by labor of the products as its own, and the judgment that its separation from the conditions of its realization is improper (*ungehörig* [elsewhere replaced by *ein Unrecht*, "an injustice"]) – forcibly imposed – is an enormous awareness (*enormes Bewusstsein*), itself the product of the mode of production resting on capital and as much the knell to its doom as, with the slave's awareness that he *cannot be the property of another*, with his consciousness of himself as a person, the existence of slavery becomes a merely vegetative existence and ceases to be able to prevail on the basis of production. (Quoted in Elster, 1985, p. 106; see also Lukes, 1985, p. 51, fn. 1)

Here we find the solution to resolving the paradox that Marxism, as Lukes (1985, p. 25) aptly puts it, "has remained, in its distinctive and curious way, both anti-moral and moral."[15]

Nevertheless, William Baumol (1983a, p. 306) employing surprisingly polemical terminology for a deservedly respected mainstream economist suggests that only "vulgar Marxists and vulgar opponents" believe that Marx taught that the wage was equal to the value of labor-power and that "wages under capitalism were immoral and constitute grounds for revolution." This "Marxism," Baumol (1983a, p. 307) maintains, is but a "popular legend" that is easily demolished by Marx's denunciation of the "romantic" socialist views of Lassalle and Proudhon and his tenet that "there is no such thing as an absolute standard of morality." Another economist, Edmund Phelps (1973, p. 26), explains more realistically:

> Marx himself did not criticize capitalism for being unjust. He did not specify a particular set of ethical preferences, such as utilitarianism, in terms of which to make that claim.

Presumably he believed that his condemnation of capitalism
was robust enough not to depend upon forseeable vicissi-
tudes in morality, was not so delicate as to need a *special moral
theory.* [Italics added]

In short, Marx the objective scientist did not need to create a
"special" moral theory because he relied on something much
more powerful, the innate property feelings of workers and third
parties. Note, however, that in his *Critique of the Gotha Program,*
Marx explicitly recognized these feelings (how else can his
position be explained?) when he put forward for the coming
"lower" or "early" communist society (Lenin's "socialism") the
following principle of economic justice: "The right of the producers is proportional to the labor they supply. The same amount
of labor which he [the producer] has given to society in one form
he receives back in another" (quoted in Husami, 1978, p. 41).
Consistently with Phelp's position, in 1906 the Austro-Marxist
Otto Bauer rejected the ongoing attempts to supplement Marx
with Kant in the following terms: "Without ever having heard of
Kant's categorical imperative, he [the objective third party] will
immediately judge the maxims flowing from the class interest of
the proletariat differently from those of the classes defending their
property" (quoted in Lukes, 1985, p. 16). Marxism did not and
does not need the help of Kantian philosophy to convince the
undecided individual that exploitative property relations are unjust property relations.

   And if, as Baumol would have us believe, Marx's intentions
were not polemical, why his value-laden nomenclature of exploitation (*ausnützen*), his comparisons of wage labor to slavery, and his
characterization of surplus product as "stolen" (*entwandt*) and
"booty" (*beute*)? Beyond this there is ample reason to believe that
Marx sought to reinforce his incendiary "employer as thief" with
the much older and more potent slander "Jew as thief." As
Gouldner (1985, p. 83) explains, the "association of commerce
with Jewry (*Judentum*) reciprocally intensified a hostility toward
commerce engendered for other reasons, inflaming popular sentiments activated by the recent disruptive growth of capitalist
commerce with two thousand years of incendiary religious bigo-

try." Baumol's remarks about the views of so-called "romantic" socialists reveals a total lack of comprehension of the role of Marx's scientific pretensions and differentiated intellectual product in the no-holds-barred battle for intellectual leadership of the socialist movement. "Fighting," Engel's recalled, "was his [Marx's] element" (quoted in Lukes, 1985, p. 27). Van der Veer (1973, p. 374) reports more concretely:

> Marx was so deceitful and vicious in his relations with others that he early became known as the "calf-biter" ... When any other figure threatened to displace him as the leading socialist he did not hesitate to engage in character assassination and smear tactics. Thus, he spoke of Lassalle as "the little Jew," and "a Jewish nigger."

Lassalle, in addition to being a Jew, of course, had the termerity to found the Universal Working Men's Union at about the same time as Marx organized the First International. As Lenin and Stalin were to do later, Marx frequently denounced views that he later incorporated into his intellectual arsenal (see Husami, 1978, p. 61, and Lukes, 1985, pp. 37–40). Marx's flirtation even with social Darwinism is attested in a letter he wrote in 1861 to Lassalle stating that "Darwin's book is very important and serves me as the basis in natural science of the class struggle in history" (quoted in Gouldner, 1985, p. 72). In his book titled *Why Marxism?: The Continuing Success of a Failed Theory*, political scientist Robert Wesson (1976, pp. 29–30) puts his finger on the essence of Marx's Marxism:

> Proudhon, a more moderate man, once exhorted Marx, "Let us not conduct ourselves like apostles of a new religion." But Marx, ... was fervently intolerant, and this was his strength. He may be seen as the founder of a new type of Christianity. Marx gave the Word for salvation: as he said, "the philosophers have only *interpreted* the world in various ways; the point, however, is to *change* it." *Capital* became a bible, no more read than the Scriptures, used for apt quotations and left to the interpretation of scholars, but important because it was there, a massive testimony to the

revelation that labor is presently exploited but will be victorious in the future ... Although he scornfully rejected utopianism, Marx was, like many a communistic-chiliastic prophet, the greatest of utopians. Looking backward to a simpler age as well as forward to a brave new world, he heralded with difficult syllogism and arcane language the chastisement of sinners and the inevitable consummation of good.

In recent years several descriptive or sanitized versions of surplus value have been put forward, for example, Green's (1981, pp. 224–5) theoretically unsubstantiated reference to an economic "surplus" and Roemer's (1982) lame suggestion that workers somehow own a share of "society's alienable assets." However, the strength of Marx's theory of exploitation relative to "opportunistic-revisionist" versions is, as J. C. Scott (1976, p. 159) suggests, that it provides a "conceptual link between an *a priori* notion of exploitation and the *subjective feelings of the exploited*" [italics added]. Elster (1985, p. 204) cautions the revisionists that the labor theory of exploitation "remains a useful, although special case on which we can test some of our ethical intuitions." Bertill Ollman has stated the issue more bluntly: "The labor theory of value forces the capitalist to justify his role and the benefits he receives in a context where no justification is possible. It puts him in a corner from which there is no escape other than the practical one of keeping the workers from realizing their situation" (quoted by Minogue, 1985, p. 57). Once the capitalist class and its hired intellectual lackeys cease to fool the workers and they realize that they are being robbed, the awesome power of (misguided) property feelings is unleashed against the market system.

Notes

1 For philosopher Allan Gibbard (1985, p. 23) these feelings are merely a "primitive fetish" from which "we must wrench our minds free," if we wish to defend property rights. As if we had a choice about whether to have these feelings!

2 I rely here on Averill (1982), Irani (1983), R. I. Levy (1984), W. Lyons (1980), Plutchik (1980, pp. 12–18; 1983), Solomon (1976), and Strongman (1978, Chapter 5). See further the discussion of "secondary qualities" in Chapter 7, note 1.

3 See Coleman and Kraus (1986, pp. 1356–65) on the difference between the "takings or conditional liability view of torts" and the "rights view of torts."

4 In England trial by battle became obsolete only in the fifteenth century and was formally abolished in 1819 (Painter, 1951, p. 60, and Simpson, 1961, p. 26).

5 This assumption also underlies Sugden's (1986, pp. 58–62) discussion of symmetrical "hawk-dove games;" see further, Chapter 6, Section 6.1.

6 It simply does not follow, as Lomasky (1987, p. 130) believes, that "A has reason to acknowledge and respect B's having [an object] I* conditional upon B recognizing and respecting A's special interest in [object] I." Indeed moral considerations aside, even a wealthy B might find it in his interest to use strength or guile and appropriate objects possessed by others.

7 According to philosopher J. L. Mackie (1977, pp. 80–1):

> Any institution is constituted by many people behaving in fairly regular ways, with relations between them which transmit and encourage and perhaps enforce those ways of behaving. An institution will have rules or principles of action, or both, which the participants in the institution will formulate fairly explicitly, allow to guide their own actions, and infringments of which they will discourage and condemn. They will use concepts closely associated with these rules and principles which cannot be fully explained without reference to these rules and principles; and the rules and principles in turn will usually be formulated partly in terms of those concepts ... An institution ... does not need to be instituted. It need not be an artificial creation.

8 Sources: Silver (1983, pp. 73–4), Andreades (1933, pp. 15–16), Diósdi (1970, pp. 30, 40), and Palmer (1963, p. 186).

9 Sources: Boissonade (1964, pp. 80–1), Glick (1979, pp. 88–9), Herlihy (1960, pp. 86–9), and E. Levy (1951, pp 191–2).

10 Sources: Ashanti: Hoebel (1961, pp. 226–7) and Forde (1963, pp. 389–90); Yoruba, Tallensi, and Ibo: Herskovits (1952, pp. 340, 352–3); Bushmen: Cashdan (1983, p. 53); Melanesians and Poly-

nesians: Herskovits (1952, p. 360); Karen and Lisu: Durrenberger and Pálsson (1987); Semai: Dentan (1968, p. 43); and American Indians: Cronon (1983, p. 62), Herskovits (1952, p. 362), and White (1983, p. 20).

11 Sources: Antiquity: Gardiner (1933, p. 20), Silver (1985, pp. 96–7); Arabia and Iran: Tapper (1979, pp. 3–4) and W. R. Smith (1956, p. 104); Africa: Herskovits (1952, pp. 343–5).

12 See White (1983, p. 4), Ingold (1980, pp. 157–8), and Dowling (1968, p. 506), and compare Testart (1987, pp. 292–4).

13 See Beaglehole (1932, pp. 211–12), Linton (1952, pp. 656–7), and Westermarck (1926, pp. 35–43).

14 See Silver (1984).

15 Elster (1985, p. 216) suggests that: "A worker is *forced to sell his labor-power* if he would be unacceptably worse off were he to withdraw with his own means of production." The implication of this definition is that if an "industrial revolution" permits self-sufficient producers to significantly improve their living standards by selling their labor-power, then they are *forced* to sell it. They are forced to do what they wish to do and to become much better off! Elster's definition once again illustrates the remarkable skill of neo-Marxists in portraying mutually beneficial transactions in a sinister light. My example about the industrial revolution is not so far fetched as some readers might imagine. Two economic historians who have recently studied the Industrial Revolution, Lindert and Williamson (1983, pp. 23–4), report as follows:

> Our tentative findings can be summarized most easily by focusing on the relatively data-rich [English] Industrial Revolution era from 1781 to 1851. Table 7 which collects our best estimates with our "best-guess" real wage trends and proceeding through several long-needed adjustments ... suggests impressive net gains in the standard of life: over 60 per cent for farm laborers, over 86 per cent for blue-collar workers, and over 140 per cent for all workers. The hardships faced by workers at the end of the Industrial Revolution cannot have been nearly so great as those of their grandparents.

Note also that worker's specialized "means of production" reflect choices in order to take advantage of market opportunities.

6

Biology, Ethology, and Property

6.1 Evolution of Property Feelings

The property feelings of normally formed persons lay the foundation for an aggression differential favoring producers in their rivalry with thieves (see Chapter 5, Section 5.1). It does not seem unreasonable to postulate an evolutionary origin for these feelings. Certainly individuals with the gene or gene complexes coding the appropriate enzymes for outraged defense of the fruits of their labor would, *ceteris paribus*, enjoy a distinct reproductive advantage relative to individuals not so equipped. I find it difficult to conceive of beings whose moral reactions would depart radically from this pattern. Even the guilt experienced by the thief may well have an evolutionary origin. Within the *small groups* in which *Homo sapiens* presumably evolved, a "convicted" thief would naturally be denied opportunities to participate in cooperative ventures promising significant pay-offs (see Alexander, 1987, pp. 93–5 on "indirect reciprocity"). Indeed the rejection of the criminal by his peer group would place his very survival in doubt. Thus, as Trivers (1985, p. 389) suggests: "It seems plausible that the emotion of guilt has been selected for in humans partly in order to motivate the cheater to compensate for misdeeds and to behave reciprocally in the future, thus preventing the rupture of reciprocal relationships." The memory of unpleasant guilt feelings experienced in the past (see Chapter 1, Section 1.1) operates to deter criminal behavior and possible ostracism in the present. On the other hand, and much more importantly, the possession of a *conscience* operates to increase an individual's expected opportunities and gains from cooperation. As Frank (1987, p. 594) points out: "Numerous opportunities exist in which it is possible to increase output through cooperation. Unfortunately, performance in many such ventures is either impossible or prohibitively costly to monitor. It follows that a tendency to cheat when there is no possibility of punishment will often eliminate opportunities for gain." It follows from this, as Frank further explains, that the individual whom potential trading partners believe would suffer from strong guilt feelings upon the commission of a theft (including the breaking of a bargained-for promise (see Chapter 3, Section 3.5) makes a relatively attractive candidate for commitment devices. To be honest because it makes one feel badly to cheat is, *ceteris paribus*, the best policy!

The possession of an object may best be understood as being determined by what biologists and game theorists call an asymmetrical "hawk-dove game" or "bourgeois strategy." To see this, let us, with Sugden (1986, p. 70), assume a "labelling asymmetry between the roles of the players in each instance of the hawk-dove game, so that the game can be described as one between A and B." More specifically, let us label producers A and nonproducers B. Then the rules of the game are quite simple: Attack, that is, play the "hawk" role if you are A (the producer); run, play the "dove" role, if you are B (the nonproducer). As Sugden (1986, p. 70) explains:

> If a player is confident that his opponent's strategy is "If A play 'hawk'; if B, play 'dove,'" the best he can do is to adopt the same strategy himself. This equilibrium amounts to a rudimentary system of *de facto* property rights, in which rights [better holdings of] disputed resources are vested in A-players. To say that this equilibrium is stable is to say that these rules of property are self-enforcing.

Given an appropriate biological asymmetry, namely the aggression differential, the property institution develops spontaneously. Indeed, it is difficult to think of an alternative or mutant strategy capable of making its adherents fitter than defending producers and retreating nonproducers.[1] At the same time, unlike other potentially helpful mutations, for example ones enabling humans to fly or breath underwater, the biological costs of providing individuals with theft-triggered feelings of moral indignation seem modest, at least to this layman. Admittedly this explanation of genetic property feelings in terms of evolutionary adaptiveness is at best suggestive. As a nonbiologist it is not clear to me how it might be improved upon.

Perhaps the strongest evidence favoring an evolutionary origin for and genetic control of property feelings is the detection of property-like behavior among nonhuman animals. To begin with there are, after all, numerous similarities between humans and other animals. The nervous systems of all higher vertebrates are fundamentally similar and there are many similarities between humans and apes at the molecular level (Tanner, 1981, pp. 27–35). Also the feeling of outrage which occupies center stage in the study of the property institution is apparently one of the simplest emotions (J. P. Scott, 1958, pp. 54–7). And the ability to socially transmit learned behavior, that is, culture, is not a monopoly of human beings, as van den Berghe (1975, p. 30) shows: "Swimming and face washing . . . have been observed to spread "culturally" through a troupe of Japanese macaques. Chimpanzees pick up and throw sticks to scare away predators; they strip twigs of leaves to use as poles with which to extract termites from hills; and they chew on leaves to make water-absorbing sponges." Box (1984, pp. 199–243) and Tanner (1981, pp 69–75) provide additional examples and discussion.

When we observe object defense behavior in human societies, it is difficult to be sure whether this reflects learning or innate motivation. But, as Pugh (1977, p. 177) notes, "the fact that apes and other nonhumans do not use a symbolic language limits the complexity of concepts that can be assumed to influence their behavior," consequently, "when we see the same basic behavior in the social life of nonhuman primates, then it seems very likely the motivations are innate." Why should we assume, as Sugden (1986, p. 102) does that the property "conventions" of animals are genetically determined while ours are merely "conventional"?

Before turning to the evidence, it is well to repeat anthropologist Lionel Tiger's (1975, p. 115) warning that social scientists and others who insist on ignoring the immense data base provided by ethologists "will be made scientifically obsolete by their commitment to work with an unnecessary 'black box' assumption about human biology and 'human nature'."

6.2 PROPERTY-LIKE BEHAVIOR AMONG NONHUMAN ANIMALS

In 1900 Charles Letourneau (1900, pp. 364–5) published speculations concerning the "biological origins of the taste for property." Seventy-eight years later, sociobiologist Edward Wilson (1978, p. 109) noted how easily "the biological formula for territorialism translates ... into the rituals of modern property ownership." Territorial behavior is widespread in the animal world.[2] This behavior involves an animal's defense of the space in which it carries out such activities as mating, nesting, and foraging. Even the chimpanzee, once lauded by pacifists as the "peaceful primate," is now known to defend a territory. Briefly stated, territoriality is site-related aggression directed by incumbents against intruders of the same species and sex. Typically a territory is defended by an individual male, but sometimes females and even entire communities participate. Among some species (for example, dwarf mongoose, anemone fish, pied kingfisher) individuals unrelated to the owner of a territory help to feed his young, perhaps as a sort of payment for permission to utilize the resources of a rich territory or, alternatively, they may be investing in the opportunity to assume the role of breeder when one of the residents of the territory dies. The defenders of a territory turn a wide variety of "weapons" on intruders, ranging from odors (pheromones), songs, croaks, threat displays, and chest-thumping, to physical assault. Zoologist J. Bruce Falls (1977, pp. 74, 85) reports that among birds:

> The rapidity with which males that are removed from their territories are replaced (a few hours to a few days) suggests that other birds monitor singing and notice if it stops ... These observations suggest that song alone may be *sufficient*

to repel intruders ... Song is a signal communicating mild aggression to other males – foretelling a tendency to chase intruders.[3]

Apropos of our discussion of the aggression differential and asymmetrical "hawk-dove games", J. P. Scott (1958, p. 82) reports that an intruding red-winged blackbird will retreat in the face of the occupant, "but as soon as the line is crossed into his own territory he becomes the pursuer." Lesser black-backed gulls also exhibit this behavior and, according to Yasukawa (1984, p. 182): "this 'resident-wins' phenomenon can override differences in actual fighting ability. Even when the intruder is an adult and the resident is only a juvenile, the young resident wins." Similarly, if one stickleback is placed in the territory of another it seeks to flee (Parringham, 1982, p. 301). Among crabs and spiders the larger individual usually wins the fight for a burrow or a web. However, when the rivals are of equal size the owner usually prevails (Krebs and Davies, 1981, p. 107). Hapgood (1979, pp. 97–8) describes a species of sand bee whose males hatch first and then dig down to the still-buried females. On the average the excavation through the hard, sun-baked surface to the female takes six minutes. Copulation takes place when the male reaches the female. The digging males are often challenged by other males seeking to supplant them. But in 393 such attempts at 50 observed sites the first-digger was displaced in only 51 instances (13 percent). This remarkable pattern leads Edward Wilson (1978, p. 82) to generalize: "The resident animal defends the territory far more vigorously than the intruder who attempts to usurp it, and as a result the defender usually wins."

The behavior manifested by chimpanzees with respect to freshly killed carcasses is not unlike that observed in human hunters. Teleki (1975, p. 150) notes that:

As chimpanzees often pursue and capture prey collectively, captives may be divided among several individuals who manage to get one or both hands on the prey shortly after acquisition ... *The division procedure itself is characterized by appropriating rather than dispensing actions, these being quite different from the exchanging actions seen later during the consumption stage.* [Italics added]

The participants in the hunt seize the prey and tear portions from the carcass (Teleki, 1973, pp. 135–6; 1975, p. 151). However, once division has been completed by the producers, "other chimpanzees approach and form sharing clusters around those holding major portions" (Teleki, 1975, p. 151). According to Teleki (1973, p. 136): "Those chimpanzees who still lack meat at this point tend – . . . *regardless of social rank* – to respect proprietary rights and to *request* meat from others" [italics added]. The rather ritualized "requests" take the form of vocal and gestural signals (for example, the empty palm) (Teleki, 1973, p. 146). All animals are not, as economist Dennis Mueller (1986, p. 8) asserts, "hedonists of the most base kind."

Some chimps do attempt to steal meat, but significantly, the evidence suggests they fare less well than those who request a share in the proper form: the thieves enjoyed a success rate of only 15 percent (Teleki, 1975, p. 151; 1981, p. 335). Anthropologist Tim Ingold (1987, pp. 114–15) maintains that the sharing behavior that a number of observers "claim" to have witnessed is not really sharing because animals lack "self-consciousness." (How does he know this?) Unlike chimps, baboons have not been observed to share meat extensively. Possibly this is due to their much greater emphasis than chimps on plant collection (Teleki, 1975, pp. 140, 152). Consistently with this line of explanation, Harding (1975, p. 248) reports that:

The newborn antelopes, hares, and other animals that the study group [of baboons] killed and ate were all animals that defend themselves against predators by remaining immobile, using whatever cover is available to conceal themselves. It is not surprising therefore, that most of the baboons' kills were made apparently by chance.

Harding (1975, pp. 48–9) adds that on the less frequent occasions when kills were outcomes of deliberate hunting efforts, there was no indication that the baboons were cooperating with each other. "Carl," the largest male in the observed troop, "was able to add considerably to the amount of meat he ate by confiscating animals killed by other baboons immediately after they had been taken" (Harding, 1975, p. 250). Torii (1975, p. 312) states that "in macaques and baboons who have advanced to the ground and established rigid social structures such as dominance hierarchy, once an individual has food in his hand, it is rarely taken away even by a superior."

It is of interest to note the report that rhesus monkeys, baboons, and chimpanzees are more likely to battle over food when they are fed by humans than when they produce their own. It is predictable, of course, that property feelings would be weakened under "artificial conditions."[4] Barash (1982, p. 213) suspects that this more aggressive behavior pattern may be explained by unusual clumping of animals due to clumping of the food resource at feeding time. This explanation is not entirely convincing, however, because, as noted above, chimps are also clustered in the relatively peaceful sharing clusters following a successful hunt. Light is also cast on the sources of social conflict by a butterfly experiment described by Barash (1982, p. 179) – males of this butterfly species defend small sunlit spots on forest floors to which females are attracted:

> If a male approaches a defending male, a brief, vertical spiraling flight ensues ... In all observed encounters between resident and intruder, the resident always won and without an escalated fight. [However,] by surreptitiously introducing two males onto the same spot it was possible to deceive each into thinking he was the resident. In such cases, the ensuing spiral flights lasted ten times longer than when one contestant "knew" that he was an intruder.

This finding is, of course, quite consistent with our earlier argument (in Chapter 1, Section 1.2) that contradictory property feelings provoke social conflict.

6.3 ANIMAL KINGDOM AND STATELESS SOCIETY

Jack Hirshleifer (1977, p. 46), an economist, denies that animals possess property. He argues as follows: "Territory in Nature is held only as it is continuously and effectively defended by the force of its possessors. Property does sometimes need to be defended by force, but what makes it property is the availability of impersonal enforcement through the law of the community." This is not in the least convincing, however. In the first place not all human societies rely on "impersonal enforcement" of property powers. Second, and perhaps more fundamentally, Hirshleifer does not define "law". Do rules have to be written down or spoken in the King's English to be law? If so, Hirshleifer's claim is unassailable and trivial. As Edward Westermarck (1926, p. 51) pointed out, the legal right of property "is essentially a formulated expression of moral feelings." Along the same line the legal philospher Axel Hägerström (1953, pp. 215–16) explained with greater precision that:

> The maintenance of the legal order presupposes in the first place what is called the social instinct. This expression means that in a certain community the members are inclined, *in general independently of all reflection*, to follow certain rules of action, whereby cooperation at least for maintenance of life and propagation within the group becomes possible. A social instinct in the same sense occurs in animals which form communities.

Elsewhere, Hirshleifer (1978, p. 322) wonders rhetorically what would happen to the property of "an animal who falls ill or otherwise suffers weakened ability to defend his dominion." The problem here is that conspecifics perceive a territory to be unowned if the appropriate signals are not transmitted. When, for whatever reason, the incumbent fails to signal ownership his territory is effectively vacant. The takeover by an intruder resembles a misunderstanding more than a theft. Note that when human settlers fail to emit the appropriate labor signals they also may forfeit ownership. This was true in Plymouth colony, for example (Ward, 1973, p. 115; see also Chapter 2, Section 2.2).

The police do not guard our territories "continuously" any more than blackbirds are always on the alert for intruders. It appears, however, that chimpanzees, macaques, and baboons are not thrown completely on their own resources in defending their objects. Torii (1975, p. 312) observes that: "If a more dominant one [baboon] should try to snatch food, the possessor may scream, struggling against him. *Meanwhile the leader may run to the scene of the dispute and drive away the plunderer*" [italics added]. Kummer (1973, pp. 227–8), citing a communication from Menzel, adds that when dominant chimpanzees tried to steal a toy from a subordinate "they distracted him by playing, then snatched the toy. *Often not only the deprived chimp but others as well pursued and threatened the 'thief'*" [italics added]. Kummer (1980, p. 34) also notes that in quarrels between jackdaws the dominant bird regularly takes the side of the lower-ranking combatant. Whether the "control behavior" manifested by apes and some birds is "impersonal" in Hirshleifer's sense I am not prepared to say. Note, however, in this connection, Ellis's (1986, pp. 65–6) interesting observation that in "small" nonhuman primate groups "the 'control adults' were usually the societal leaders; in larger societies, the 'control adults' were usually closely allied with the societal leader during the leader's troop takeover." The absence of a government in the human state of nature, a state that neverleless knows property, is readily explained by economic theory (see Auster and Silver, 1979). Because the demand for protection and punishment services is so limited in small, cohesive societies, full-time specialization in the performance of these activities is not profitable. In larger, less cohesive societies, the total demand is sufficient to support a specialized service firm, the *state*. Now the state, rather than the victim and his neighbors, wields the club, for a tax-price. Of course, in clubbing, as in most other occupations, the division of labor enhances efficiency. In summary, Hirshleifer's arguments fail to provide a convincing basis for distinguishing between the property of humans and the "property" of other animals.

6.4 HUMAN NATURE AND MORALITY

Admittedly "innateness" remains a suspect concept even among scientific scholars who sometimes dismiss it as a form of proof by assumption: "Innateness converts a problem into a postulate." Noam Chomsky (1980, p. 210) who has put forward the hypothesis that language capabilities have a biological basis retorts that "if this a priori argument were valid, then it would hold as well for the development of physical organs, that is, it would show that the hypothesis that the growth of arms rather than wings is genetically determined makes a postulate out of a problem and guarantees that further inquiry will lead nowhere." Innate mechanisms can, of course, be studied empirically. Chomsky (1980, pp. 210–11) adds that there is no reason to assume that cognitive development, unlike physical development, has no genetic component. The point is I believe equally valid for moral development.

While the theoretical arguments and supporting evidence are far from being conclusive, it does not seem unreasonable as a working hypothesis to think with Plutchik (1983) of a psycho-evolutionary origin for emotions and with Tennant (1983, pp. 290–3) of ethics as a product of evolution. This is emphatically not the same thing as deriving rights and duties from the evolutionary process itself (as, for example, the competitive ethic, the communal ethic, and social Darwinism). Sociobiologist George Pugh (1977, p. 5) puts the issue well when he speaks of our "enduring human values as manifestations of a built-in value system, which is an essential part of evolution's 'design concept' for a biological 'decision system'."

To some extent our moral behavior is undoubtedly determined by "reason" and "critical thinking," and to this extent the views of traditional philosophers – for example, Kant, and Hare (1982, pp. 150–1) – are accurate.[5] However, we would do well to heed Tennant's (1983, p. 298) warning that "moral self-congratulation will never flatten the Gaussian hump of natural behavior."[6] Legal philosopher Charles Fried (1981, p. 15) fails to take this "hump" seriously in his discussion of Hume's proposal regarding promises to the effect that the external sanction of public opprobrium, of loss of reputation for honesty, which society attaches to promise-breaking is internalized, becomes instinctual and accounts for the sense of the moral obligation of promise. Though Hume offers a possible anthropological or psychological account of how people feel about promises, his is not a satisfactory *moral* argument. Assume that I can get away with breaking my promise (the promisee is dead), and I am now asking why I should keep it anyway in the face of personal inconvenience. Hume's account of my obligation is more like an argument *against* my keeping the promise, for it tells me how any feelings of obligation that I may harbor have come to lodge in my psyche and this is the first step toward ridding me of such inconvenient prejudices. [Italics added]

According to Fried, usually a perceptive thinker, the first step in overcoming a moral feeling is to understand why it is that you experience it. But what is the second step? Fried has perhaps overlooked the lesson taught by Dostoevsky's Raskolnikov.[7]

Hutcheson understood that it is not possible to make our moral sense conform to our self-interest. Or as Ruse (1986, p. 104) aptly puts it: "Even though we have insight into our biological nature, it is still our biological nature." The behavioral asymmetry resulting from property feelings, a genus of moral feelings, is not only "relatively unambiguous but also relatively cheatproof," to use Sugden's (1986, p. 99) terms.

Philospopher Colin McGinn (1979, p. 98) has presented a different kind of objection to viewing ethics as a product of biological evolution, namely that "morality is essentially such as to induce us in a direction contrary to that designed by natural selection: it cannot therefore be based upon or derived from such laws." The problem here is first of all that natural selection has not always favored narrow egoistic tendencies. Hirshleifer (1985, p. 65) explains very clearly that

in biology *there are two levels of the self* – the organism and the gene. The gene is a "selfish gene" ... But sometimes it is

profitable for a selfish gene to program its carrier organism
to be benevolent (or malevolent) to other organisms. Non-
self-interested motivations on the level of the organism may
therefore be *functionally* self-interested on the level of the
gene.

Altruism and inhibitions against killing women, children, and
conspecifics generally, are also evolutionary products.[8] McGinn's
central difficulty, it seems to me, is an overly deterministic and
restricted view of genetically mediated tendencies. How would he
explain the existence of the following preachments?

The preservation of physical health is a duty.
Be fruitful and multiply (your genes) but do not commit incest
    (genetic damage).
Revenge is sweet.
Might is right and to the victors belong the spoils.
The better part of valor is discretion.
Nice guys finish last.
Seek your own profit and remember that charity begins at home.
It is not wrong to omit doing for others what others would have
    omitted doing for you, if your positions had been appropriately
    reversed. (This is Michael Slote's (1977, pp. 135–6) "Brazen
    Rule".)

It seems to me that these "selfish" preachments *and* admonitions
not to steal or not to seek revenge or to love one's neighbor serve to
reinforce, broaden, and focus genetically based programs permitting a range of possible realizations. Thus, for example, the norm
of reciprocity clarifies and strengthens the underlying moral
feeling of indebtedness. When changes in social organization and
technology create new problems, the guidance offered by biologically grounded values and inhibitions will sometimes be weak,
ambiguous, or even contradictory. Preachments help us to cope
by providing rules of thumb – that is, low-cost control systems. A
two-sided correction system, to use Donald Campbell's (1976)
helpful term, is appropriate when values are contradictory.

"Don't be too selfish" and "Don't be too altruistic," for example, serve to prevent harmful excesses in either direction.[9] The stress placed on a particular pole may change from one place or era to another. As Lorenz (1987, p. 96) suggests: "We humans possess a fine sense for determining whether, in the society in which we live, a deficiency of a specific [emotionally directed] behavior prevails or if it is being proffered in excess."

Whatever the ultimate value of the above observations for the understanding of ethics generally, it is well to recall that the central thrust of this chapter is the hypothesis that evolution has conditioned humans to experience the emotion of moral indignation or outrage when their possessions are threatened by thieves and to respect the objects of others or, what comes to the same thing, to experience "self-concept distress' when they assume the role of thief. Notwithstanding Thurow's (1973; 1975, p. 35) picture of a "world without innate preferences" and his dismissal of them as no more than a prejudice of the nineteenth century, mankind has a stubborn moral nature with respect at least to property (compare Singer, 1981, pp. 76–7). This "built-in" value system provides, as will be seen in Chapters 7–9, an "Archemedian point" for evaluating the distribution of objects among the individuals in society.[10]

6.5 MORAL AND IMMORAL COMPETITION

According to economist Harold Demsetz (1979, p. 112):

> There are a multitude of methods for competing, ranging from a brick through a rival's place of business to a reduction in price to the introduction of a superior product. All these impose harmful effects on rivals but not all are viewed as equally ethical. *The distinction along the ethical dimension between alternative methods of competing is peculiar to the social sciences and the humanist philosophers. Biologists make no such distinction.* [Italics added]

Demsetz is mistaken. One harm is *not* the same as another, and biologists and, more importantly, biological life itself distinguish between alternative modes of competition along an "ethical" dimension. To see that this is so, consider the remarks of sociobiologist David Barash (1982, pp. 339–40):

> We can identify two basic ways in which individuals compete for ... [scarce] resources, *scramble* and *contest* [or *interference*] *competition*. Scrambles occur when each participant attempts to accumulate and/or utilize as much of the critical resources as it can, without regard to any particular social interaction with its competitors ... Fitness, in this case, has been achieved by simply outreproducing the competition ... In contrast, contest competition is occuring if the participants first argue, fight or somehow dispute among themselves ... *Aggression* is the proximate mechanism of contest competition.

Barash (1982, p. 379) adds that competing species sometimes become more distinct in respect of traits in which they overlap, an evolutionary process called "character displacement." In the animal kingdom, thieving animals trigger outraged behavior on the part of conspecifics. Scramblers, on the other hand, are simply ignored.[11]

Given that *Homo sapiens* evolved in small groups of widely dispersed hunter-gatherers, it is possible to understand why scrambling competition is morally acceptable and, why, indeed, morality does not mandate economic paralysis. Biological considerations may well underlie the peculiar "rules of the free enterprise game" in which "roughly speaking it is illegal for anyone to use goods in ways that have undesired *physical* effects on other people's goods" (Alchian and Allen, 1964, p. 742) [italics added]. Just as for scrambling and character displacement our business competitors are not outraged by the introduction of superior or differentiated products. They are of course outraged by bricks hurled through their windows and other forms of agonistic or interference competition.[12] As noted earlier (in

Chapter 4, Section 4.3), no one has a property right (feeling of legitimate entitlement) in the structure of the economy and, consequently, no one is morally outraged by the innovative (scrambling) activities of his competitors.[13]

Notes

1 See Sugden (1986, Chapter 4) and Barash (1982, pp. 177–8) on "hawk-dove games" and the "bourgeois strategy."
2 Sources on territoriality: Eibl-Eibesfeldt (1979, p. 175), Falls (1977), Fredlund (1976), Klopfer (1969, pp. 82–90), and Krebs and Davies (1981, pp. 179–84).
3 Sources: Barash (1982, p. 213), Lawick-Goodall (1971, pp. 201–2), Pryor (1981, pp. 35, 51–2), and Tanner (1981, pp. 102–3).
4 Among humans, economic trends and policies divorcing individuals or groups from productive activity may precipitate "crime waves." A case in point is provided by anthropologist Colin Turnbull's (1972, pp. 222, 280–2, 289) description of the Ik, a hunting people of northern Uganda. At the end of World War II the Ik were denied access to their main hunting ground and confined to a mountainous region previously utilized by them only as an annual resting place. As described by Turnbull, the Ik were so demoralized by a combination of hunger and famine relief that even in periods of good weather and adequate rainfall they chose to use their time in taking leisure and collecting famine relief rather than caring for their fields. Those individuals assigned to carry famine rations back to the old, ill, and very young in the villages instead gorged themselves on the trail. The transport of food to home bases, it must be understood, is a behavior almost universally observed in ethnography, according to Isaac and Crader (1981, pp. 190–1; see also Chapter 3, Section 3.6). Interestingly, the behavior of the Ik seems to resemble the property behavior, or better lack of it, exhibited by animals in captivity. Note also in the latter connection the comments of Lorenz (1987, pp. 100–3) about the behavior modifications observed in domestic animals.
5 What is a *moral* act? Etzioni (1986, p. 166) answers compactly that "for the purposes at hand it suffices to consider moral acts as those that meet four criteria, each necessary by itself but sufficient only in

conjunction: moral acts reflect an imperative, a generalization, a symmetry when applied to others, and motivate intrinsically."

6 Tennant's point holds despite Rawls's claims that "our natural moral feelings may be in many respects irrational and injurious to our good" (1971, p. 489), that "moral feelings are liable to be unreasonable and capricious" (1971, p. 490), and his appeal for "attitudes that appeal to sound principles of right and justice in their explanation" (1971, pp. 489–90).

7 Note the comments of Lorenz (1987, p. 89): "[Artistic] products put together following commercial prescriptions provide, in a certain sense, especially good points for researching our emotions. These products show us how much the model of a releasing object can be simplified and these simplifications exaggerated without sacrificing any of the object's effect as a releaser. I know many serious and critical people who know very well what, for them, is 'kitsch' and what is 'art' and are still incapable of evading the effect of the most primitive kitsch."

8 Sources: Barash (1982), Dawkins (1976, p. 109), Kummer (1980, p. 34), Pugh (1977, p. 228), and Silver (1980, pp. 3–5).

Altruistic behavior and many other examples contradict the predictions of the economist's rational egoist model. Thus Dennis Mueller (1986, p. 5) noted in his presidential address to the Public Choice Society: "The prisoners' dilemma is a popular analytical tool for analyzing individual behavior because it seems to fit so many everyday situations we confront. *Most of us choose the cooperative strategy most of the time*" [italics added]. Mueller (1986, p. 15) maintains nevertheless that there is no need to drop the postulate that "man is basically base" and postulate a set of biologically-based "ethical" preferences. Why, then, do people so often behave in an altruistic or cooperative manner when they might succeed in getting ahead by behaving as rational egoists? Basically Mueller's (1986, p. 5) explanation is that "we were taught to do so," in the first instance by our parents. This explanation, I believe, only serves to raise a greater mystery. Why do parents condition their children to behave in ways that reduce their chances of getting ahead? As if he were aware of this difficulty, Mueller (1986, p. 17) concedes that: "Social animals may evolve gene structures which facilitate learning cooperative behavior, and which make teaching cooperative behavior to one's offspring a quasi-instinctual act."

9 As my colleague K. Irani points out, in Aristotle and early Persian

moral philosophy the *mean* between the extremes of any attitude is recommended.

10 A genetic origin of the property institution is not inconsistent with the social psychological justice theory whose central elements are stated (somewhat ambiguously) by Lerner (1977, pp. 6–8):

> As social psychologists we can describe [the] sequence whereby the child moves from the "pleasure" to the "reality" principle as the development of the "personal contract." ... The child agrees to give up on doing those things that feel good immediately, on the assumption that if he does what is prescribed and gives up that which is proscribed by his experience with the environment, then a given outcome will eventuate. The child will get what he deserves, is entitled to receive ... The development of the commitment to deserving, the personal contract, appears as a natural consequence of human development ... The underlying motivation is probably the desire to maximize his payoffs over a longer time perspective ... What this implies is virtually the opposite of the more familiar notion, which assumes that the individual's commitment to justice is the socialized or internalized derivative of the "social contract" which is functional to the social system. The alternative offered here is that, given the human potential, the personal contract would develop even in an impersonal environment. It does not depend upon others to inculcate the rules of deserving.

Lerner overestimates the importance of "payoffs" in the "personal contract" but his argument that the "psychology of entitlement" is fundamentally the result of an internal process of human development, not of social indoctrination, is provocative indeed. Lerner (1977, p. 7) adds that this "personal contract" also "creates the basis for the person's motivation to see that others get what they deserve."

11 It is of interest to consider briefly Hirshleifer's (1978, p. 324) assertion that scrambling competition may be wasteful as a result of "resource depletion": "Though less obviously so than in the case of interference competition, scrambling also is socially inefficient in that *effort is being invested to preclusively appropriate resources that would have been socially available even without that effort.*" In the first place, Hirshleifer's claim about inefficiency seems to fall under the heading

of the so-called "grass is greener" fallacy. Compared to what feasible alternative resource-allocating mechanism is scrambling "socially inefficient?" If all other decision-making modes are more wasteful of resources, then scrambling is "efficient." The more fundamental problem is that Hirshleifer simply *assumes* the availability of the resources when, in fact, resources become "socially available" only as a result of scrambling. Ths scrambler produces his natural object (see Chapter 2, Section 2.2).

12 The social psychological literature provides some experimental evidence bearing on this issue, see, for example, Lerner (1977) on "parallel competition."

13 Note in connection with the proposition that not all harms are morally objectionable, Hume's (1948, p. 242) observation that: "When a man denominates another his *enemy*, his *rival*, his antagonist, his *adversary*, he is understood to speak the lanquage of self-love . . . But when he bestows on any man the epithets of *vicious* or *odious* or *depraved*, he then speaks another language, and expresses sentiments in which he expects his audience to concur with him."

A Reconsideration of Natural Rights Theory

7.1 PRODUCER'S RIGHT AS NATURAL RIGHT

The foregoing analysis differs markedly from the traditional philosophic approach in which the feelings side of moral experience is slighted. As a philosopher, Richard Brandt (1979, pp. 171–2), explains:

In the traditional picture the intellectual component is causally primary; conative-emotional phenomena are responses to it . . . For present purposes . . . it is . . . important to notice how unconvincing the intellectualist picture of human conscience is, from a psychological point of view . . . Actually, it seems that what we respond to is primarily the thought that a certain act would be telling a lie or injuring someone. That is what is repugnant, not the thought that the action would be wrong. Or, when we reflect on having injured another person it is the thought of how we injured him that elicits remorse and guilt-feeling; it is not the thought that what we did was wrong. Indeed, 'is wrong' is the same predicate in all situations, and it would seem that if the conative-emotional response is just to that it would be identical in all situations, in fact it appears that the conative-emotional response differs from one case to another, according to the character of the situation . . . *It looks, then, as if the intellectualist tradition had things backwards in viewing moral motivation and guilt feelings and disapproval as parasitic on beliefs or knowledge that acts are or would be wrong, and hence a secondary phenomenon.* [Italics added]

In fact there is ample reason to believe that it is the intellectualist component or "moralized feelings" that is "parasitic" on moral feelings. As another philosopher, P. F. Strawson (1974, p. 23) has emphasized: "The existence of the general framework of attitudes itself is something we are given with the fact of human society. As a whole, it neither calls for, nor permits, an external 'rational justification.' " The problem of moral experience is located within the more general problem of *perception*. Thus, philosopher John L. Pollock (1986, p. 510) asks "How is it possible to become justified in believing an object is red on the basis of its looking red?" His answer is most illuminating:

> Once we have acknowledged the existence of prima facie reasons, the problem has a trivial solution: an object's looking red to me gives me a prima facie reason to think that it is red. This is just part of the conceptual role (and hence analysis) of the concept of a red object. There is nothing else that needs to be said – the problem is solved. The problem of perception seemed difficult only when philosophers thought that concepts had to be characterized exclusively by their entailment relations. This engendered a frantic search for entailments relating *red* and *looking red*, but there were none. (Pollock, 1986, p. 510)

Colin McGinn (1983, pp. 6–7) puts it somewhat differently:

> It is sometimes supposed that the dispositional thesis about (say) colour involves a circularity the exposure of which undermines any significant distinction between primary and secondary qualities ... In the case of 'red' and 'looks red' it seems to me that the alleged circularity is just what we should expect, because we are explaining the instantiation of a quality in terms of the production of experiences with a certain intentional content – and such experiences neces-

sarily consist in representing the world as having certain qualities. We might say that the 'circularity' arises, not because being red is inherently resistant to dispositional analysis, but rather because the analysis is inherently intentional: experiences are distinguished by their representational content, so naturally we shall need to use predicates of the external world in specifying them.

Similarly, it is the feeling of approval that makes it good for a producer to have power over his object. The point of the dispositional thesis is that the ultimate criterion of the goodness of an action is how it feels to perceivers. The presence of the feeling of approval is *constitutive*, to use McGinn's (1983, p. 8) term, of the presence of goodness. Nevertheless, McGinn (1983, pp. 146–7) shrinks from the implications of his analysis and insists that "on any reasonably sane view of ethics the comparison with secondary qualities is unapt."[1] "Reasonably sane" or not, however, there are no entailments relating good and feeling good.[2]

It follows that once philosophic priorities are reversed and emphasis is placed on feelings of approval, disapproval, and fear aversion, where they belong, the stage is set for the demystification of natural rights theory. To state matters bluntly, a property right triggered by production is a *natural right*. This is the case most obviously because the producer's right – that is, the complex of feelings of legitimate entitlement–exists in virtue of his human nature.[3] It is independent of institutional arrangements including so-called "rights making" (actually powers making) practices such as legislation.[4] It is nevertheless useful to demonstrate the generality, simplicity, and power of the analysis by beginning with a somehow discovered "rights principle" or "natural law" and then working backward to the underlying feelings.[5]

Rights principle: Individuals ought to hold the objects they have produced; they ought not to be forcibly deprived of these objects.

This rights principle enunciates a natural right in the sense that it is morally basic, that is, the "ought" is explained by or grounded in no other moral principle in our theory.[6] Indeed it is grounded in or supervenes upon a *species characteristic* or, more specifically, in the following ahistorical, universally shared feelings.

Species characteristic: Each normally formed person feels that a producer is legitimately entitled to an object he has produced and is outraged when a producer is forcibly deprived of his object.

The rights principle is stated in the language of *uncompromised absolutes* so familiar in the moral sphere. Notice especially that it is blind with respect to *interests*. Obviously human beings are not so afflicted. In deciding whether or not to steal an object, an individual weighs one set of feelings against another. On one side of the balance are his moral feelings and on the other his interests, that is, his expected utility from consuming the object and the expected disutility from being punished. That individuals make this kind of choice is undeniable even if the decision-making process is somewhat mysterious, at least to the author (but see also the brief remarks in Chapter 8, Section 8.3). The person who decides to steal feels that he has done *wrong*. His victim feels that he has been *wronged*. And third parties share these feelings. *In this sense* the rights principle is absolute.[7] (The question of whether these feelings are manifested in the case of catastrophic allocations of objects is postponed to Chapter 9.)

As Hutcheson explained, the "moral sense" cannot be masked by self-interest: a wrong act may be performed from motives of self-interest, but these motives "have no more influence upon us to make us approve it than a physician's advice has to make a nauseous potion pleasant to the taste" (cited by Hudson, 1967, p. 19). The moral norms generated by property feelings are so immensely powerful that to the individual (thief or victim) they appear to be things set apart from his own personality and society. They are, in philosophical terms, "deontological duties." We fail to realize that in "discovering" these norms we have, like Baron von Munchausen, pulled ourselves up by our own bootstraps (see Ruse, 1986, p. 103). This is well illustrated in the philosophic literature by "God's will" or by Kant's "collective will" and more generally by ethical intuitionism: basically speaking the view that there exists an *external* or *feelings-independent* good and evil which men *perceive* by means of a "moral sense" or "moral intuition" (see Hudson, 1967, and compare McGinn, 1983, pp. 150–1). In ancient religions, as Durkheim (1958, p. 160) noticed, it is exemplified by the magical transformation of cultivated fields into "sacred divine property put into the hands of men by means of a number of ritual ceremonies." Note also by way of illustration of externalized moral concepts the Hindu *dharma* and the ancient Egyptian *maat* and, closer to the present, the principles of a Liberal Order in the West. Hägerström (1953, pp. 5–6), the founder of the Uppsala school, observed in 1939:

> It seems ... that we mean both by rights of property and rightful claims, actual forces, which exist quite apart from our natural powers; forces which belong to another world than that of nature, and which legislation or other forms of law-giving merely liberate ... So we can understand why one side fights better if one believes that one has right on one's side. We feel that here there are mysterious forces in the background from which we can derive support.

In Marxist terminology the view that rights are external to individuals and society is "false consciousness." It is perhaps best illustrated by what I predict will be the major objection to this study: "A *right* cannot be a *mere* feeling."

7.2 Universalizability and Contractarianism

The rights principle put forward above meets Kant's criterion for a "moral law" or, in Hare's (1981) more recent formulation, the property of "universalizability of value judgments" (see also Sugden, 1986, pp. 154–5). As economist Amartya Sen (1985a, p. 170) points out, universalizability is an information constraint: "The basic form of an informational constraint is that of an invariance requirement: if two objects X and Y belong to the same

isoinformation set I, then they must be treated in the same way *J.*"
Underlying the invariance requirement or universalizability of
my rights principle is the feeling of each individual that I am
entitled to objects I produce and you are similarly entitled.

Arrow (1973, p. 247) has raised a serious question about the
possibility of a theory of justice: "The criterion of universalizability may be impossible to achieve when people are really
different, particularly when different life experiences mean they
can never have the same information." Serious problems do in
fact arise when individuals *disagree* about who produced an object
as noted earlier (in Chapter 1, Section 1.2 and Chapter 5, Section
5.3). The more fundamental point is that in respect to the
property feelings triggered by production, people are very much
the same.[8] Hence, in our theory, universalizability is automatic
rather than problematic.[9] It follows that the theory is not
vulnerable to Norton's (1977, pp. 116–17) valid objection against
Nozick's individualist perspective: "The upshot is that, while
Nozick enunciates the principle of the inviolability of individuals,
no individual has reason to be concerned with anyone's inviolability but his
own. Having precluded utility arguments and universalization
arguments he is left with precious little to forestall predatory
behavior" [italics added]. Moreover, not only does a theory based
on property feelings triggered by productive activity meet the
objections of Arrow and Norton by satisfying the universalizability criterion and forestalling predatory behavior, it avoids the
opposite equally serious, moral error of being *impartial* or even-
handed in the sense of calling for equal consideration of the
competing needs, interests, and capabilities of different individuals (see Lomasky, 1987, pp. 24–5). Contrary, that is, to the
anonymity assumption encountered in the welfare economics literature, the identity of the individual obtaining power over an object
is a crucial consideration in ranking alternative social states (see
further Chapter 8). All interests are *not* equal. The mandate of our
rights principle is unequivocal: "*To each producer his object.*"
Producers are "intrinsically superior" to nonproducers to use
Ackerman's (1980, p. 11) term or to use Lomasky's (1987,
p. 124), they are "favored" over nonproducers. In a world of

produced objects it is also unnecessary to follow Gewirth (1985, p. 10) in making a distinction between *two* valid standards of economic justice:

> This is the distinction between a *formal* or *comparative* view of the meaning of 'justice' and a *substantive* or *noncomparative* view. The formal or comparative concept is found in the traditional definition of justice as *treating similar cases similarly*. The substantive or noncomparative concept is found in the equally traditional definition of justice as *giving to each person his due, or what he has a right to*.

When the objects in question were produced, Gewirth's "comparative" standard of justice is either redundant or mistaken.

Another attractive feature of the rights principle is that it is consistent with and, indeed, provides much needed content for the contractualist account of wrongness advanced by Scanlon (1982, p. 110): "An act would be wrong if its performance under the circumstances would be disallowed by any system of rules for the general regulation of behavior which no one could reasonably reject as a basis for informed, unforced general agreement." Certainly a ("perfectionist") rule permitting producers to keep their objects would easily win general agreement. (Note the prevalence of the property institution.) Similarly, the rights principle is easily brought within James Buchanan's (1977, pp. 128–33) contractarian fairness framework. Reflective persons who were aware of their moral feelings and otherwise behind a "veil of ignorance" would surely agree on a rule calling for producers to have power over their objects. Arguably the perennial appeal of social contract theories stands as an impressive testimony to the direction and importance of property feelings.

7.3 AN OBJECTION TO ETHICAL NATURALISM: THE OPEN QUESTION

The argument put forward above describes and justifies our property feelings. In the context of our analysis, "right" and "good" are the verbal expressions of the natural feeling of approval for the producer having power over his object; "wrong" or "bad" are the verbal expressions of the natural feeling of diapproval for the theft of the producer's object. Keeping these connections in mind, let us now turn to the so-called "open-question argument." Someone seeks to challenge the ground of our rights principle by asking: "Is the feeling of approval good?" As "good" is no less and no more than the lexical definition of the feeling of approval, this challenge fails to provide new insights into the nature of good. "Is the feeling of approval the feeling of approval?" is a meaningless question.

A related and equally ineffectual challenge has been put forward by philosopher R. M. Hare (1975, p. 86) who, consistently with "Hume's Law,"[10] maintains: "But the only 'moral' theories that can be checked against people's actual moral judgments are anthropological theories about what, in general, people *think* one ought to do, not moral theories about what one ought to do." (Once again we have an illustration of the philosophical "false consciousness" engendered by powerful moral feelings.) Brandt (1979, p. 20) similarly rejects the "coherence theory of justification in ethics" that seeks justification in the comparison of theories with feelings. Hare's claim can be reformulated in the following terms: "Is what is approved good?" or, alternatively, "Is there a reason or argument for the feeling of approval?" The first reformulation amounts to the vacuous: "Is what is approved what is approved?" The answer to the second question is, of course, "Yes," but the reason lies outside the realm of goodness in the realm of innateness and the evolutionary process.

Within a naturalistic framework the open question makes sense only if it is understood as expressing doubt that the term "good" is systematically linked to the feeling of approval. This is, of course, an *empirical* question but the linkage is eminently plausible. According to W. D. Hudson (1970, p. 87): "The ethical naturalists set themselves up as able to do two things with the word 'good': viz., (i) to point out that it was used to describe certain natural properties; and (ii) to use it in ethical theory. Moore's

achievement was to see that they could not (logically) do both."
But G. E. Moore's (1965) "naturalistic fallacy" argument does
not apply to the version of ethical naturalism put forward in this
study. (The objections of Hare, Brandt, and Moore do apply to
neuro-scientist Roger Sperry's (1983, pp. 22, 50, 73ff) attempt to
develop a "science of values".) In our analysis: (a) "good" refers
to a natural property, namely the feeling of approval and (b)
people can be told it is good to help a producer defend his objects
against thieves. As political scientist Robert McShea (1978,
p. 148) has reminded us: "We rate moral principles by the
importance of their consequences and the only importance
consequences can have is in relation to our feelings." McShea goes
on to suggest that genetically determined patterns of species can
serve as the basis for making value judgments.

Notes

1 McGinn (1983, p. 149), who seems unaware of my 1981 paper
   (Silver, 1981) defining and grounding rights on *feelings* of legitimate
   entitlement and aversion, maintains correctly that "a reaction of
   moral approval is precisely a judgment (or perhaps feeling) to the
   effect that the presented state of affairs is *good*: moral 'experiences'
   have an intentional content." Surprisingly, however, he maintains
   elsewhere (1983, pp. 146–7) that a comparison of ethics with
   secondary qualities is "unapt" (or even unsane!). A compact
   definition of a secondary quality has been provided by McDowell
   (1985, p. 111):

   > A secondary quality is a property the ascription of which to an
   > object is not adequately understood except as true, if it is true,
   > in virtue of the object's disposition to present a certain sort of
   > perceptual appearance: specifically, an appearance character-
   > izable by using a word for the property itself is to say how the
   > object perceptually appears.

   McGinn's (1983, p. 149) objection is to the (alleged) "subjectivism
   which accompanies the dispositional thesis." Is not "subjectivism"
   present in the dispositional position with respect, for example, to red,
   sweet, beautiful, and fearful? The quantitative importance of "con-

troversy" or "subjectivism" with respect to any secondary quality, value or not – that is, the extent of individual variation in assessment – is an *empirical* question. McGinn is, I submit, inconsistent and mistaken on these matters. For Hare (185, p. 51) the view that goodness is a "secondary quality" is not one that would be maintained by "any penetrating thinker." This, of course, is for the reader to judge.

2 Although there is much to admire in Sugden's diffuse discussion I am unable to follow him when he says that "moral judgments are more than bald statements of sensations" (1986, p. 154) or when he speaks of "independent moral justification" (1986, p. 101). Sugden shifts back and forth between the view that conventions provoke moral judgments and the diametrically opposed view that moral judgments provoke conventions. On the whole, however, he regards convention as the causal variable. See in this connection his discussion of "prominence" (1986, pp. 91–7) and, especially, the following remarks:

> It is in the nature of an established convention that everyone *expects* everyone else to keep it. Is it also in everyone's *interest* that everyone else keeps it? If it is, then we should expect breaches of convention to provoke general resentment and censure; and this will predispose people to the moral judgment that conventions ought to be kept. (Sugden, 1986, p. 155)

> Notice that a convention of property may become a generally accepted norm even though it cannot be justified in terms of any external standard of fairness. Having become a norm, a convention *becomes* a standard of fairness, but, on my account, it does not become a norm because it is seen to be fair. (Sugden, 1986, p. 159)

> It is no part of my argument that the morality that evolves in human society is the morality that we *ought* to follow. I am not presenting a moral argument; I am trying to explain how we come to have some of the moral beliefs we do. (Sugden, 1986, p. 175)

The instability of Sugden's theoretical postition can be traced to his failure to develop a considered position regarding "species characteristics" (about which see already Silver, 1981).

3 It was admitted in Chapter 2 that the production of children (Section 2.1) and of truly novel nonhuman objects (Section 2.4) might fail to elicit determinate property feelings.

4 See Becker (1977, pp. 13, 16), Christman (1986, pp. 57–8), Dworkin (1977, pp. 176–7), Gibbard (1976), Lemos (1986, Chapter 3), and Olivecrona (1974, p. 224). For Sugden (1986, Chapter 8) social conventions – that is, rules or norms that are the spontaneous products of trial and error and learning by experience – are "natural laws." I must admit that I have not been able to reconstruct in my own mind a coherent, step-by-step account of how Sugden's spontaneous process might produce the property institution. Sugden admits that "if a convention is to develop it must first be recognized by people" (1986, p. 91) and he goes on to explain that: "In the early stages of the development of a convention, when only a small proportion are following it, these patterns are likely to be hard to spot. People are more likely to find those patterns that – consciously or unconsciously – they are looking for" (Sugden, 1986, p. 92). Why, then, do people "look for" the property institution? Sugden (1986, p. 93) following Hume finds the answer in the "important truth" that "the rule favoring possessors has a natural prominence." "Prominence," natural or artificial, is, I submit, an incoherent concept. To put Sugden's theoretical problem in another way, "prominence" is too weak a pole to support the required vault from a Hobbesian *symmetrical* hawk-dove game to a Humean *asymmetrical* hawk-dove game (see Chapter 6, Section 6.1). In the end Sugden (1986, p. 177) relies on a virtually naked appeal to the status quo to defend the property institution. Lomasky (1987, pp. 130–1) whose analysis of conventions is not as penetrating as Sugden's arrives at more or less the same destination.

5 See Mackie (1977, Chapter 3) and Sumner (1984).

6 See Becker (1973, pp. 64–5, 71), Bodenheimer (1974, pp. 216–22), Midgley (1979, p. 75), and B. Moore (1978, p. 71). Note also Timmons's (1987) discussion of ethical foundationalism.

7 Note the contrast with Gauthier's (1986) analysis in which (ruling out mistakes), rational social contractors cannot commit immoral acts.

8 Arrow (1973, p. 248) himself provides anecdotal evidence confirming this simililarity in describing his "considerable difficulty in persuading" students in elementary economics courses at Harvard that the proposition that an individual is entitled to what he creates is "not completely self-evident"!

9 See in this connection Pollock's (1986, pp. 512–15) discussion of "ideal observers" and "abstract desires."

10 According to "Hume's Law" (Hume, 1948, Book III, Part I, Section 1, p. 33), "ought" statements cannot logically be derived from "is" statements. According to Epstein (1980, p. 679): "The theory of evolutionary biology may well predict the types of rules that are likely to command general consent. Yet they do not, by the same token, state the rules that necessarily *ought* to command that consent. The ghost of Hume still haunts us." I am convinced, however, that the analysis presented in this study permits Hume to rest in peace.

8

Alternative Economic Justice Rules

8.1 TYPES OF RULES

The problem of economic or distributive justice is the problem of the derivation of a rule for evaluating the distribution of desired objects among the individuals in a society. For some purposes it is useful to classify possible rules as either process oriented (antecedentalist) or end-state oriented (consequentialist) and as either endogenous or exogenous (Schotter, 1985, pp. 89–92). End-state oriented rules render a verdict about economic justice by processing the information in the object distribution matrices. Process-oriented rules render a verdict by comparing the information in the object distribution matrices with the history of the distributional matrices–that is, they are concerned with the way in which individuals gained power over objects. An economic justice rule is endogenous if it is derived from the preferences of the individuals in society; otherwise it is exogenous.

8.2 THE CONGRUENCE RULE

The analysis of property rights has prepared the foundation for an endogenous, process-oriented rule for evaluating the distribution of objects. More specifically, it has been shown that the following rights principle

> Individuals ought to hold the objects they have produced; they ought not to be forcibly deprived of these objects.

may be grounded in species characteristics and taken, therefore, as an ultimate value. The right to the fruit of one's effort is a natural right. (It was noted in Chapter 2 that the production of children and of truly novel nonhuman objects might fail to elicit determinate property feelings.) From these discoveries the following rule of economic justice, the *congruence rule*, may be deduced.

> The distrubution of power over produced objects among individuals in a society is just to the extent that power is congruent with property rights.

Putting aside the sometimes knotty problem of disputes regarding who really produced an object, congruence of property rights and object powers implies that neither unsatisfied, legitimate claims nor unfulfilled responsibilities will be observed.

The proposed congruence rule may discomfort those who automatically condemn inequalities in wealth whatever their source and who therefore, in one guise or another, support the redistribution of objects by *force* (theft). However, forced crossings of the natural boundaries of individuals serve only to increase injustice by widening the gap between object power and right (see Irani, 1981). Theft is the major obstacle to economic justice, not limited economic resources. The congruence rule does not preclude charity, public welfare, and, in an uncertain world, schemes of mutual insurance. Even absolute equality of result is not precluded as an objective.[1] Only coerced (see Chapter 1, Section 1.5), unwilling donations and participation are forbidden in a just society.

The remainder of this chapter is devoted to discussions of the more important competitors of the congruence rule, namely utilitarianism, wealth maximization, fairness, and maximin justice. Schotter's theory of blame-free justice is taken up separately in Chapter 9. The standard for evaluating alternative economic justice rules is whether they, like the congruence rule, respect the natural right of producers to their objects. Harsanyi (utilitarianism) and, perhaps, Rawls (maximin) seem to believe that compliance with their rules would be voluntary once the underlying theories were generally understood. For the other justice theorists the question of implementation simply does not arise. In the absence of plausible evidence to the contrary, it is assumed that redistribution is to be accomplished by force. Kronman's (1980b, p. 498) discussion of "liberal theories of society" bears study in support of this assumption.

8.3 UTILITARIAN JUSTICE

In the standard version of utilitarianism associated with the names of Jeremy Bentham (1748–1832) and John Stuart Mill (1806–73) alternative distributions of objects among individuals are evaluated entirely in terms of the utility or happiness or consumption preferences of the members of the society (Sen, 1985c, pp. 2–3). Sen (1982a, p. 28) refers to this element of the utilitarian moral approach as *welfarism* or *strong neutrality* (see also Gauthier, 1982, pp. 157–8). The rule for economic justice is that: "The distribution of objects among a given set of individuals should be one maximizing total social utility or happiness" (see Lyons, 1982). Maximization of the sum total of happiness requires, of course, comparison and balancing of one person's happiness against another's. This balancing is made possible by appropriate assumptions about the measurability and interpersonal comparability of individual utility functions. (In the welfare economics literature the term "invariance requirements" refers to the kinds of restrictions placed on measurability and interpersonal comparability (Boadway and Bruce, 1984, pp. 143–7).) In the classical or cardinal utility approach, the individual's happiness is taken to be measurable with an absolute scale. It follows from full measurability that levels and increments in utility can be compared for given individuals and among individuals. Typically the realization of the maximum sum-total happiness objective would require a (forced) redistribution of objects and in this process the "planner" or "benevolent despot" pays no attention to property rights. The end of maximum happiness justifies the means.

The "invariance requirement" of classical utilitarianism amounts to treating individuals as if they were happiness plants of a single happiness-producing firm, called society (see Mirrlees, 1982, pp. 70–1). It is not without interest that the underlying moral conception of utilitarianism has certain resemblances to Marx's denigration of rights (of "egoistic man") and his elevation of the collectivity at the expense of the individual (Lukes, 185, pp. 61–6). Indeed as Wood (1981, pp. 145–9) has pointed out, historical materialism is a form of utilitarianism (see further Lukes, 1985, pp. 147–9). In the Marxian scheme no less than in the utilitarian "the human animal is ontologically dissolved into the totality of his social relations," as Femia (1985, p. 308) nicely puts it. (This does not mean that Marx was above relying on "egoistic" property feelings to achieve his vision.)

The utilitarian economic justice rule has been formalized by welfare economists and, indeed, utilitarianism provides the foundation of modern welfare economics. A cardinal social welfare function relates society's happiness (U) to the happiness (U_i) of its individual members, $a, b, \ldots, n$. The happiness of any individual is usually taken to be function only of his own (post-redistribution) consumption of goods and leisure. This assumption means that individuals are not directly concerned with the welfare of others. Envy, altruism, concern for social values and other so-called "externalities" are ignored. (Externalities might, however, play a role in the "solution concept," for example bargaining, by which an equilibrium allocation of objects is achieved.) The Benthamite social welfare function is

$$U = U_a + U_b + \ldots + U_n$$

That is, social happiness is the unweighted sum of individual utilities.

Assuming a society consisting of only two members a and b, the Benthamite social welfare function can be represented in two dimensions $(U_a$ and $U_b)$ by a map or family of social indifference curves (SIC). Each social indifference curve in the figure exhibits the combination of a's happiness and b's happiness which sum to a given level of social happiness. The social welfare contours are negatively-sloped diagonal lines with a slope of -1. That is, if individual a's happiness declines by a given amount then social happiness can remain constant only if individual b's happiness rises by an equal amount.

The utility opportunities of society (individuals a and b) are exhibited in two dimensions (U_a and U_b) by the grand utility possibility curve (GUPC). The GUPC is derived, without going into details, by assuming a given stock of employed productive resources, a given technology, and given consumer tastes and then considering how efficient bundles of (say) two consumer goods X and Y might be efficiently distributed between individuals a and b. (An output bundle is efficient if it is not possible to increase the production of X without reducing the production of Y. A bundle of X and Y is efficiently distributed if it is not possible to increase the hapiness of a without reducing the happiness of b.) Each point on the GUPC in figure 1 is efficient or Pareto-optimal, meaning that it is not possible to increase U_a without reducing U_b. The latter consideration (utility conflict) gives the GUPC its negative slope. The cardinality assumption about the individual's utility functions results in the GUPC being concave to the origin.

The maximum sum total of utility is given by the point b where the GUPC touches the highest attainable SIC. This constrained "bliss point" determines the total output of each good and the way the totals are distributed between the two individuals. A society heeding this bliss point is economically just. It can be shown that a perfectly competitive market economy will attain *some* point on the GUPC – that is, it will have a Pareto-optimal configuration. The particular point on the GUPC is determined by the initial distribution of income among the members of society, however. For each different initial income distribution there is a different Pareto-optimal configuration of the economy. In general, then, the actual Pareto-optimal position of the economy will not correspond to the bliss point. Thus the attainment of economic justice (maximum sum-total happiness) re-

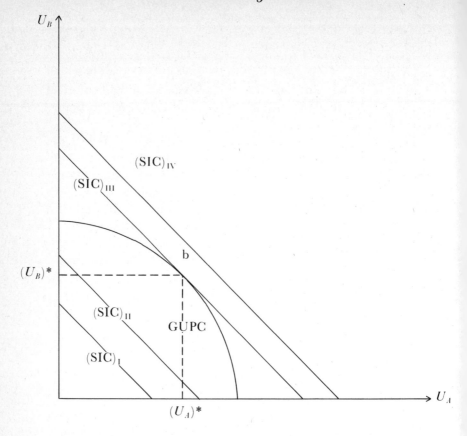

Figure 1   Maximization of social happiness in a two-person
           society

quires (costless, lump-sum) transfers of income from one member
of society to another.

   Obviously a major obstacle to the social applicability of
utilitarian justice (in a market or in a planned economy) is the
difficulty of obtaining meaningful utility information (Sen, 1985a,
p. 174). Additional problems are raised by the cost of implement-
ing available forms of redistributive taxation and the distortions
they introduce in the economy. (Note that any income tax distorts

the choice of individuals between labor and leisure.) The much more fundamental objection to utilitarian justice (or at least to welfarism) is that it is psychologically incomplete. As utilitarianism refuses to consider "action information," that is, the *means* by which redistribution is achieved (by force or voluntarily), it loses sight of relevant, to say the least, "feelings information" (compare Bonner, 1986, p. 182, and Sen 1985c, pp. 181–2). Specifically, in advocating forcible redistribution of objects, utilitarianism fails to consider all the feelings consequences. It ignores the outrage felt by the producers who are robbed of their objects and the guilt felt by the beneficiaries of the stolen goods.

In his perceptive analysis of the utilitarian approach, economist Frank Hahn (1982, p. 189) suggests that public policies themselves "separately from consequences for the allocation of goods, are carriers of utility (or disutility)":

> Let us be a little more precise. Let P be a public policy and
> let C_i (P) be the allocation of goods to agent i under
> this policy ... The welfare economist now write's i's utility
> function as U_i (C_i (P)) ... Hence P affects utilities
> only via its consumption consequences. My examples suggest
> that we should plausibly write the utility function as U_i (P,
> C_i (P)) ... In other words the domain of the utility function
> is the Cartesian product of the goods and policy spaces.

But while Hahn's dual-utility model is a major step forward, it fails to rescue the utilitarian calculus. The reason is that outrage and guilt, the feelings triggered by forcible redistribution, are not different names for the feelings of happiness or unhappiness from consuming the objects in question including the public policy. (Hahn's approach makes sense if "utility" is taken to measure preference not, as in the present discussion, an identifiable mental state, happiness.) Thus even if U_a and U_b are comparable and due account is taken of the happiness resulting from public policies themselves, it is impossible to fit the outrage of robbed producer a on the same scale of measurement as the happiness (and guilt) of theft beneficiary b. Happiness and outrage are qualitatively different feelings and they are consequently incommensurable (see Griffin, 1986, Chapter 5). On the one hand, it is obviously arbitrary for a theory of justice to ignore feelings of outrage and heed only feelings of happiness, as utilitarianism does. A consequentialist moral theory must take *all* the consequences into account. On the other hand, to solve utilitarianism's problem by adding together outrage and happiness is equivalent to adding apples and oranges (see Pugh, 1977, pp. 110–11).

To avoid misunderstanding it should be added that human beings are of course capable of making choices involving incommensurable feelings (see Raz, 1986, Chapter 13). Etzioni (1986, p. 167) explains that:

> Morality affects their choices in two different ways: by providing a sense of an absolute command, and as a source of preferences and a commitment to choose certain means, the moral ones, over others but not at all costs. People first sense an absolute command to act morally, but that does not mean that they will always heed it. That they are less likely to heed it if the costs are high does not indicate that there is no imperative, indeed, all other things being equal, it is what drives up the costs.

John Stuart Mill (1951, pp. 51, 67) was well aware of the incommensurability problem:

> The powerful sentiment, and apparently clear perception which that word [justice] recalls with a rapidity and certainty resembling an instinct, has seemed to the majority of thinkers to point to an inherent quality in things; to show that the Just must have an existence in Nature as something absolute, generically different from every variety of the expedient ... Our notion, therefore, of the claim we have on our fellow creatures to join in making safe for each of us the very groundwork of our existence, gathers feelings around it so much more intense than those concerned in any of the more common cases of utility, that the difference in degree

(as is often the case in psychology) becomes a real difference in kind. The claim assumes that character of absoluteness that apparent infinity, and incommensurability with all other considerations, which constitute the distinction between the feeling of right and wrong and that of ordinary expediency and inexpediency.

In reply to his own towering insight, Mill (1951, pp. 67–8) was able to offer only the weak suggestion that:

> If justice be totally independent of utility, and be a standard *per se*, which the mind can recognize by simple introspection of itself, it is hard to understand why that internal oracle is so ambiguous, and why so many things appear either just or unjust, according to the light in which they are regarded.

But as has been argued at length, and as Mill was no doubt well aware, our "internal oracle" is hardly ambiguous concerning the ownership of produced objects.

If the line of argument I have developed has merit it is difficult to accept Sen's (1984a, p. 283; see also 1987, pp. 74–8) proposal that a

> way of dealing with liberty and other rights in the moral structure is to incorporate them into the outcome morality itself, judging the outcomes in terms of whether people get their entitlements as specified in a system of rights. The 'social ordering' of outcomes, then incorporates attitudes towards the fulfillment or violations of rights, and the actions can be judged taking note of rights even within a consequentialist framework.

The central problem here is the *outrage* or moral indignation a person feels when *his* rights are violated, not "society's" general principles or, as Sen puts it, "attitudes towards the fulfillment or violation of rights." Sen does not explain how he would incorporate the feeling of outrage into the "outcome morality" and, indeed, he does not seem to be aware of this problem of irreducably plural mental states. Hence, despite Sen's (1987, pp. 74–5) explicit assurance to the contrary in a later work, it does not seem that he has fully abandoned the welfarist conception of the self (on this, see Beitz, 1986, p. 285). In Sen's approach the victim's outrage *must be* noninformation and, hence, can find no place in the social ordering of outcomes. Another more familiar way of looking at Sen's dilemma is that the moral rules derived from property feelings are absolute (or at least categorical, as we shall see in Chapter 9). Thus a victim's moral indignation may be viewed as having lexical priority over the pleasure or utility of a rights violator. (In a lexicographic ordering a principle does not apply until those preceding have been satisfied.) This means that if Sen really wishes to incorporate violations of property rights within a consequence-sensitive deontological assessment framework, the outcome is a foregone conclusion. Rights always outrank happiness. Understandably for an economist, Sen (1987, p. 75) suggests that: "What was called the 'engineering' aspect of economics has a parallel within ethics itself. It may not be as central in many ethical problems as it is in mainstream economics, but it can be important enough." It seems to me that once rights are introduced into what purports to be an *ethical* analysis the engineering aspect of economics becomes irrelevant: the intrinsic value, infinite or not, of a right provides sufficient reason for ignoring all instrumental values. Large gains in utility or whatever are incapable of transforming moral wrong into moral right (compare Gordon, 1976, p. 582). In no way does this imply, however, that people will forego large gains in utility so as not to infringe an absolutely inviolable set of private property rights. No doubt there are circumstances in which each of us would choose to do what is wrong. Indeed, wrongdoing is commonplace (see also the discussion in Chapter 7, Section 7.1). So also is the consciousness of having done wrong.

It also follows, contrary to economist J. A. Mirrlees (1982), that the outcome of a forcible redistribution policy cannot be evaluated by summing individual utilities even in a society consisting of isomorphic individuals. (Isomorphic individuals are individuals who, as Mirrlees (1982, p. 72) explains, can be "described in formally identical terms by means of changes in the variables that describe their situations.") Our individuals, then, can be viewed as identical (relevantly isomorphic selves) with the exception that one is the producer of an object and the other is not. If it is true, as Mirrlees (1982, p. 83) maintains, that in a society of isomorphic individuals "everyone ought to agree to have every other individual treated as one of his alternative selves," then forced redistribution should not take place. Mirrlees's (1982, p. 83) conclusion that: "Any acceptable method of moral evaluation should agree with utilitarianism at least in the case of a society consisting of isomorphic individuals" must be rejected. To rob of the fruits of his labor and therefore to morally outrage my "alternative self" is to rob and outrage me. The post-robbery distribution of objects must be judged to be less preferred than the original distribution.

The "mild" and "innocuous" *Pareto principle* holds that: If every individual prefers (in happiness terms) an alternative A_0 to an alternative A_1, the society must prefer A_0 to A_1. *Minimal liberalism* consists of the requirement that: There are certain alternatives over which an individual ought to have a decisive say (a "right") irrespective of the preferences (in happiness terms) of others. Sen's pioneering work in welfare economics includes his demonstration in 1970 that there is no social ordering capable of satisfying both the Pareto principle and Minimal liberalism. This revealing discovery serves to underline the argument of the present study. With respect to produced "alternatives" at least, the preferences (in terms of happiness) of "others" are morally irrelevant. The preferences of producers are decisive.[2] Interestingly Minimal liberalism is concerned with protecting individuals (nonconformists?) from meddling busybodies. Thus the rights it grants to individuals are of a "personal" nature in which the problem of scarcity does not arise. (The meaning of "personal" is apparently taken to be self-evident.) For example, whether I should read a sexy book or what color I should paint the walls of my kitchen. The question of whether I or someone else should be permitted to dwell between the painted walls is a "nonpersonal" choice to be made by society (see Wriglesworth, 1985, and Wolfson 1985, p. 190). "Minimal" is an apt characterization of this liberalism.

Economist John Harsanyi (1982) has tried to humanize utilitarianism by adopting a theory in which the maximum sum-total happiness standard of economic justice is displaced from specific object distributions (act utilitarianism) to the rules or policies for selecting object distributions (rule utilitarianism). "This move," as Sen (1987, p. 88, fn. 27) points out, "has much merit in broadening the scope of utilitarian arguments, and for avoiding some of the special follies of act-based utilitarianism ..." However, this indirect approach does not eliminate the fundamental theoretical flaw of utilitarianism, its psychological incompleteness: feelings of happiness and pleasure are taken into account; feelings of outrage and guilt are ignored. Beyond this, the requirement for rules to maximize utility is far more problematic than the moral intuitions it is designed to evade or supplant. For example, as Sen (1985b, p. 4) points out, "one could have a lively debate" about

> the relative merits of the market mechanism in safeguarding the interests of consumers, or whether, in fact, it is the case that "the freedom to choose" in any substantive sense is better guaranteed by the market mechanism than by some feasible alternative. If it is shown that the empirical relationships on which the consequentialist justifications are erroneous, then the case for the market mechanism, derived from such reasoning, would collapse.

Moreover, for the arena of economic life, notwithstanding the progress of econometrics, "empirical regularities are hard to establish and predictive theories in this field can be extremely flimsy" (Sen, 1985b, p. 5). Harsanyi (1985a, pp. 44, 46) concedes that

> rule utilitarian theory has to assess the social utility of any possible moral code both in terms of the social behavior it would directly prescribe (which may be called observance effects) and in terms of its direct effects on people's expecta-

tions and incentives (which may be called its expectation and its incentive effects) ... As we have seen, one difference between rule utilitarianism and act utilitarianism lies in the fact that the former can and does take full account of the expectation and the incentive effects of alternative moral codes, whereas the latter is logically restricted to considering the expectation and the incentive effects of individual actions.

In the absence of hard or at least of generally accepted evidence about the total utility resulting from alternative rules, the rule utilitarian approach tends to degenerate into a sterile and unnecessary exercise in finding "good utilitarian reasons" and "rational justifications" for the dictates of our conscience.[3,4]

A hint of the problem I have in mind can be detected in the interstices of Harsanyi's innovate and technically brilliant analysis. Harsanyi (1982, p. 40) suggests, like J. S. Mill, that the intuitionist philosophers who opposed the utilitarians "were not particularly troubled by the well-known empirical fact that people's 'moral intuitions' seem to be highly dependent on accidents of their own upbringing and, more fundamentally, on the accident of being raised in one particular society rather than another." Yet only a few pages later Harsanyi (1982, pp. 49–52) defends a "similarity principle" permitting a person to make interpersonal utility comparisons by imagining himself in another's shoes. Then Harsanyi (1982, p. 62) accepts "wholeheartedly the truth that we are not alone in the world but rather share a common human nature with many millions of others" and he is pleased to discover that his "updated version of classical utilitarianism" (1982, p. 61) has something in common with "traditional morality" (1982, pp. 58–9). Harsanyi has, of course, discovered the correspondence by relying on the same "moral intuitions" he previously had characterized as "obscurantism in ethics" (1982, p. 40). As Maher (1986, p. 109) explains:

At times defenders of rule-utilitarianism advance the argument that the point of following rules is that often *we do not know for certain which act will maximize O* [the desired outcome] and that in such circumstances we should follow the conventional rules of society ... But taking rules to mean conventional rules of practice does not show that the purpose of the rules is to maximize *O* – it may well be but equally it may not be, for it could be the case that a particular rule serves to limit *O* because of some other, non-utilitarian value (e.g., fairness).

Another illustration of the malleability of rule utilitarianism and of the correctness of Maher's evaluation is provided by philosopher Alan Ryan's discussion of Nozick's moral rule that if an object *X* would not have existed but for the expenditure of labor, then the producer should determine how *X* is used. For Ryan (1983, p. 226) the argument "on which Nozick trades" exemplifies, in Bentham's terms, the kind of "grandmother egg-sucking instruction" that any "forward-looking" utilitarian would "*invent*" to encourage productive activity in the interest of affluence: Nozick's argument, then, "lends no support to the idea that there is property by natural right" [italics in original]. It becomes abundantly clear that rule utilitarianism can at best provide derived or second-order moral insights not an independent standard of moral appraisal. At worst it serves as a screen for ideology. I would agree with philosopher Carl Wellman's (1985, p. 127) suggestion that "something like Ockham's razor applies here."

A major problem in ethical analysis is that economists and other decision theorists who by training think of themselves as "guardians of rationality," in Arrow's (1974, p. 16) apt phrase, have a vested interest in making the study of ethics an organic part of rational choice theory (Sen's "engineering" aspect of economics). After all, the hedonistic choice theory which reduces all evaluations to a common scale is our stock and trade. Rights, on the other hand, resist quantitative manipulation. This in part may explain why even able welfare economists Boadway and Bruce (1984, p. 177) dispose curtly of entitlement theories of justice and "focus on theories of justice based on social welfare [or utilitarian] philosophy." Note in this connection also Sen's (1987, pp. 47–8) comments on the "lack of interest that welfare economics has had in any kind of complex ethical theory."

It would be grossly inaccurate to portray developments in welfare economics only in a negative light, however. The contributions of Frank Hahn and, especially, Amartya Sen have already been noted. Economists have also made progress toward the scientific study of economic justice by constructing behaviorist or choice models which, despite their superficial resemblance to utilitarianism, avoid the incommensurability problem and are in principle capable of taking due account of property rights. I have in mind franeworks such as Harsanyi's (1976, 1977, 1982; see also Sen 1985a, pp. 187–8) in which the utility numbers assigned by a von Neumann-Morgenstern utility function (about which more shortly) measure *preference* (or desire) with respect to alternative states of the world, not as in utilitarianism a specific mental state, namely pleasure or happiness. This is utilitarianism in name only, as Sen (1985a, p. 193) makes clear in his complaint that the "utility numbers" "are simply accounting values for predicting choice under uncertainty. They need not coincide with any concept of utility that has independent meaning, such as happiness or satisfaction, or desire fulfillment" (see also Sen, 1985c, p. 18). The point of departure for the newer behaviorist or choice models is that individuals considering alternative states of the world (or prospects) in which each person has an *equal chance* of coming out in any one of n positions in a distribution or allocation space would choose the state of the world which maximized their expected behaviorist utility.[5] In maximizing the expected utility number, prudent behaviorist decision makers would, contrary to the assumptions of hedonism, take into account not only the happiness from consumption bundles but their outrage and guilt from violation of property rights. Indeed, if we assume a given total stock of consumer goods, and put aside catastrophic allocations until Chapter 9, then Mirrlees' "isomorphic individuals" or Harsanyi's "sympathetic but impartial observer" would prefer the state of the world in which property rights were respected and there were no forced redistributions. That is, in the event of forced redistributions the utility number assigned to a *given bundle of onsumer goods* would be adjusted downward to take account of feelings of moral indignation and guilt (compare Bonner, 1986, pp. 169–72). Hedonism, of course, has no such implication.

This conclusion can be concretized by means of a simple numerical example assuming risk neutrality. Suppose that a society consists of two relevantly isomorphic individuals (*A* and *B*) each of whom has a 0.5 probability of producing (say) 80 cans of baked beans and a 0.5 probability of producing (say) 20 cans. Then, in a state of the world in which each individual consumes only his own baked beans the utility number depends only on the pleasure from consuming 50 cans, the expected consumption level ((0.5) (80) + (0.5) (20)). Now assume another state of the world in which total production of baked beans is constrained to be 100 cans and there is forced redistribution to secure a consumption level of 50 cans per person. That is, 30 of the 80 cans produced by (say) B would be expropriated and turned over to A, who by assumption had produced only 20 cans in the period. The consumption level of each person remains at 50 cans, but the utility number corresponding to that level of consumption does not remain the same, as hedonism predicts. B will adjust his utility number downward because he is outraged by the theft of 30 cans of his baked beans and A will adjust his utility number downward because he feels guilty about being the recipient of 30 stolen cans.

It is of course doubtful that Harsanyi would approve of this extension of his "preference utilitarianism." This objection would be understandable because to make the extension it is essential to take the unusual step for an economist of penetrating the black box of moral preferences. Frank Hahn (1982, p. 190) aptly explains, however, that: "The utilitarian has no business in prescribing the domain of preferences. Welfare economists for good reasons, have always, however, taken this domain as very narrow: essentially the commodity space. The good reason is tractability. But this may well mean that their prescriptions are not, on a utilitarian valuation, optimal." Hahn's point is, I believe, well illustrated by the work of Mirrlees who has applied his training in mathematics to the problem of economic justice.

Mirrlees (1982, p. 75) derives from a utilitarian analysis the principle: "From each according to his ability, to each according to his need." He claims thereby to have demonstrated that utilitarianism is capable of recommending radical forcible redistribution. Mirrlees (1982, p. 75) insists that it would be wrong "to reject utilitarianism as failing to conform with our moral intuitions ... If utilitarianism is to be a valuable moral theory, one had better be surprised sometimes by its conclusions." But with all due respect for Mirrlees's imagination and technical brilliance, he has fallen into the trap which the rule utilitarians have sought to evade. It is questionable whether an acceptable moral theory, like mathematical analysis (or ideology), should reach surprising conclusions. A utilitarian conclusion that slavery is moral would indeed be surprising but of little value since it fails to take into account our intuitive feelings of outrage (see Herzog, 1985, p. 160).

8.4 Wealth Maximization Justice

Legal scholar Richard Posner (1981, pp. 60–115) has put forward as a rule of economic justice that: "The distibution of objects among the individuals in society should maximize total wealth".[6] For Posner, as for utilitarians, the question of who produced an object is morally irrelevant; objects are treated as a common social pool. Justice, in Posner's view, requires each object to be assigned to the individual placing the highest value on it in terms of effective demand. Insurmountable difficulties arise because the valuations that individuals place on objects are themselves dependent on the initial assignment of objects, that is, on people's initial wealth. Putting this problem aside, it is not difficult to see that Posner's rule clashes with our intuitive moral notions even more than does utilitarianism.

Assuming that transaction costs (all the costs of making exchanges) are zero, the initial assignment of objects is of no consequence for the realization of justice. Exchange will move each object to the user placing the highest value on it. Thus, continuing to ignore wealth effects, if an object is assigned to an outsider its "natural owner" (Posner's term) will repurchase it if he values it more than the outsider. Alternatively, the outsider will retain the object if he values it more than the natural owner. Thus in the first case the producer of an object (its natural owner) has to pay for its return and in the second case he loses it. Nothing in Posner's theory requires the payment of compensation, as total wealth, his maximand, would remain the same if the outsider compensated the natural owner of the object. Thus extortion and theft, provided they are efficient, are intrinsic to Posner's theory of economic justice. Note further that outsiders who are more knowledgeable about technological and business matters and/or less risk averse than natural owners will often place higher values on objects than natural owners and therefore be able to keep objects they did not produce. This implication of Posner's theory holds even for the natural owner's labor-power (see Kronman, 1980a, pp. 240–1). Thus to take a not so far-fetched example, a "moral" woman with zero or little alternative wealth might find herself unable to repurchase her services as a prostitute from the pimp to which her labor-power had been initially assigned. Her loans (if any) would be based on her potential earnings in moral occupations which might be less than in prostitution (see Dworkin, 1980, pp. 208–10). One cannot help wondering if Posner would deem the moral woman deserving of legal punishment if she refused to serve the pimp who placed a higher value on her services than she did and consequently was their just owner (see Fried, 1978, p. 99).

If transaction costs are positive, Posner's "omniscient tyrant" would immediately assign objects to their highest value user in order to economize on scarce resources. Actually, an "omniscient" tyrant is not required. A large computer or even, as Posner (1979, p. 120, n. 10) suggests, a judge can "in many cases anyway ... make a reasonably accurate guess as to the allocation of resources that would maximize wealth." An additional advantage of Posner's approach is that, unlike the case of absolute property rights, even prohibitive transaction costs could not prevent the transfer of an object to an outsider placing a higher value on it than the natural owner.

A theory that objects should be taken by force from those who produced them and assigned to those placing the highest value on them in terms of effective demand teaches us more about injustice than justice. Posner has told us about the advantages of his approach relative to utilitarianism, namely quantifiability, commensurability, even feasibility, but does he really wish to be taken seriously?

8.5 Fairness or Envy-free Justice

According to several economists "the distribution of objects among the members of a society is fair or just if it is envy-free, meaning that no individual prefers another individual's bundle of objects to his own."[7] Hal Varian (1974, p. 64) explains that this basic approach enables us to

> formalize a recurrent theme in ethical thought: namely, considerations of *symmetry* in distributive justice. The equity comparison allows each agent to put himself in the place of each other agent and then forces him to evaluate the other agent's position on the same terms that he judges his own. Thus it allows an interpersonal comparison of a sort, but it restricts the way in which this comparison can be made; in particular there can be no 'double standard' for evaluating others' positions as compared to one's own position.

Baumol (1982, p. 639) adds that in "fairness theory" the basic value judgment is that the desires of the affected individuals, rather than those of some superior arbitrator must count." Similarly, Schotter (1985, p. 91) had characterized this moral theory as "endogenous" because "only individual preferences are consulted and the criterion is unanimity." These assertions are dangerously misleading, however. It is quite true that in fairness theory each individual evaluates the bundles of each other individual in terms of his own preferences. *But these are utilitarian or "welfarist" preferences.* As Thurow (1975, p. 40) properly notes, individuals "have preferences about the rules of the economic game" itself. Our "affected individuals," to use Baumol's term, are emphatically not consulted by fairness theorists concerning the distribution rule. Do the donors believe it is just or fair to transfer their objects to envious individuals? Do the envious recipients believe this is a just or fair process? Would Mirrless's isomorphic individuals prefer (in behaviorist terms) transfers from present owners to the envious? Fairness theory totally ignores these questions. It is reasonable to conclude, therefore, that the economic justice rule calling for an envy-free distribution of objects reflects not, as advertised, the preferences of the "affected individuals" but those of "some superior arbitrator."

In order to explore the issues raised by fairness theory, assume there are two individuals A and B, and two divisible objects, cake (C) an leisure (nonwork) time (L). Suppose also that each individual is endowed with one unit of time so that his leisure time $L = 1 - W$, where W (work) is the fraction of the individual's time spent baking cakes. If both individuals are equally productive bakers, an efficient envy-free distribution will ensue as each individual will choose his most preferred feasible bundle of L and C. Difficulties arise, however, when the two individuals differ in productivity. (Varian (1985, p. 116) speaks of an "original arbitrary distribution of ability".) Suppose that in one unit of time individual A can produce 6 cakes and individual B only 2 cakes. To focus the analysis, assume that both individuals have the same tastes, $L = 2.5C$. (An individual remains equally as well off as before if a unit of leisure is substituted for 2.5 cakes.) Under these assumptions individual A will choose to bake 6 cakes and take no leisure. Individual B will not bake any cakes and will spend his unit of time in leisure. A will not envy the bundle of B, he values it at only 2.5 cakes (A has 6 cakes). B, however, will envy the bundle of A, he values his own bundle (one unit of leisure) at only 2.5 cakes (A has 6 cakes). If 1.75 cakes are taken from A and given to B, neither of the individuals will envy the bundle of the other. The post-transfer bundles are equally preferred, as each individual values a unit of leisure at 2.5 cakes.

The results are more striking if the two individuals have different tastes. Suppose that for individual A, $L = 1.5C$ and for B,

$L = 2.5C$. If 2 of A's 6 cakes are transferred to B, A continues to prefer his post-transfer bundle (he values B's bundle at 3.5 cakes). B, on the other hand, prefers his post-transfer bundle to A's post-transfer bundle (he values his own bundle at 4.5 cakes).

In both of the above numerical examples the post-transfer distribution of cakes and leisure is envy-free. Nevertheless, individual A will be outraged by the expropriation of the cakes he troubled to bake and individual B will feel guilty as the beneficiary of stolen cakes. These feelings cannot be of concern to the envy-free theorist. Indeed several theorists have suggested that the comparison of consumption–leisure bundles is not appropriate because that comparison legitimizes differences in bundles based on differences in productive ability that are after all "arbitrary" (see further Chapter 4, Section 4.1). Pazner and Schmeidler (1972, 1974) have therefore supported an income-equitable or income-fair allocation. This calls for the value of each individual's bundle, including leisure, to be the same. In calculating the value of a bundle, leisure is evaluated at the wage rate associated with the leisure taker's productive ability. Thus an allocation between A and B is envy-free and income-fair, and here I follow Varian (1978, p. 228), if

$$P_C C_A + w_A (1 - W_A) = P_C C_B + w_B (1 - W_B)$$

Where:

P_C is the equilibrium price of cakes,
w_A and w_B are the wage rates of A and B, respectively,
C_A and C_B are the allocations of cakes to A and B, respectively,
W_A and W_B are the fraction of their total time worked by A and B, respectively.

In order to see that income-fair allocations generally exist, divide equally both the total stock of cakes and the total value of leisure between A and B. Thus we begin with an envy-free distribution. With respect to the division of leisure assume, for example, that:

(a) A can bake 2 cakes per hour ($w_B = 2$) and B can bake only a cake per hour ($w_B = 1$); and (b) both individuals take 30 minutes of leisure. It follows that the value of A's leisure is 1 cake and the value of B's leisure is $\frac{1}{2}$ cake. To divide the value of leisure equally between A and B it is necessary to place 10 minutes of A's time at the disposal of B. Individual A gets 20 minutes of leisure with a value of $\frac{2}{3}$ cake and individual B gets 40 minutes (including 10 minutes of A's time) with a total value estimated at B's wage of $\frac{2}{3}$ cake ($\frac{1}{6}$ cake plus $\frac{1}{2}$ cake).

Varian (1978, p. 228) points out that with an even division of the value of leisure and the physical endowments of the economy "each agent will have an identical initial endowment. Suppose we now trade to a Walrasian equilibrium. Agents may sell other agents' labor to whomever wishes to purchase it – firms or the agent in question. In equilibrium it is clear that all agents must hold final bundles of equal value – since the endowments all have equal value." That is, the post-trade distribution is income-fair because it arises or *in principle* could have arisen from an equal and, therefore, envy-free allocation (see Boadway and Bruce, 1984, pp. 171–5). In terms of my simple numerical example, individual B might sell individual A's 10 minutes back to him (trade it for some of A's cakes) or employ it in baking cakes. Thus "asset egalitarianism" or what very much resembles slavery (the forced transfer of an individual's labor-power) plays a key role in making possible what the fairness theorist terms an income-fair distribution. One cannot help being reminded of Posner's rule for economic justice and of Saint-Simon's "utopian" vision of society as a big factory in which idleness is theft.

Holcombe (1983, p. 1153) has strongly criticized Baumol's rather Orwellian application of the word "fair" to an allocation rule that is indifferent to who produced the objects: "The issue is more than just semantic, because the word fair has strong normative connotations, and Baumol's misuse of the term enables him to subtly use these connotations to his advantage (how could anyone object to a fair distribution?), while at the same time eroding some of the precision of the generally accepted definition."[8] Varian (1974, p. 64) is more open about the grave difficulties of envy-freeness as an economic justice rule: "this definition can only be a minimal requirement for fairness" as it fails to take into account a number of considerations including "the history of how each of the agents contributed to the formation of the original bundle." More recently, Varian (1978, p. 228) took note of the possibility that under the income-fair allocation "one might feel that the 'able' are exploited by the 'unable'." Fairness theory is attractive to the economist because it permits the identification of a good allocation without, as in social choice theory, the necessity of an entire ordering of allocations. It is, nevertheless, a repellent theory of economic justice.

8.6 MAXIMIN JUSTICE

John Rawls's celebrated and much debated rule for economic justice can be viewed as a variant of the utilitarian moral approach which drops the maximum sum-total happiness element and pays attention only to the welfare of the worst-off person.[9] "Maximin," the implied rule of economic justice is

$$\text{maximize minimum } (U_a, U_b, \ldots U_n).$$

A just allocation of objects among individuals in society is one maximizing the payoff to its least fortunate member. In his own way Rawls treats wealth as manna but this aspect of his theory is disguised by its social contract superstructure (see Lomasky, 1987, p. 136).

Rawls begins by putting forward the controversial hypothesis that prudent men negotiating in the "original position" under a "veil of ignorance" would choose the maximin rule.[10] H. S. Goldman (1980, pp. 373–4), a philosopher, has summarized a number of objections to Rawls's conclusion, most importantly:

The argument that they [the contracting parties] cannot make ... [probability] estimates relies on the *stipulation* that they possess [in the original position] no knowledge of the course of history or of the frequency with which society assumes various forms. But this stipulation seems to have no independent rationale. Unlike the stipulation that they possess no knowledge of themselves as individuals, it is not needed to prevent them from "tailoring principles to their own circumstances" [Rawls, 1971, p. 139]. Unlike the stipulation that they have no knowledge of the particular details of their own society, it is not needed to secure proper justice between generations [Rawls, 1971, p. 137]. It does not seem necessary to secure unanimous agreement on principles [Rawls, 1971, p. 140]. Thus its *only* apparent role is to prevent them from making probability estimates of the various possible outcomes, despite Rawls' statement that all features of the original postion are to be "natural and plausible" [Rawls, 1971, p. 18]. The same comments apply to the parties' inability to estimate the probability of their turning out to be any given individual in society. The parties' transformation into members of society is not a natural process, a matter of fact about which they could have ordinary evidence. Rather it is a fictitious event whose nature is wholly governed by Rawls' stipulation. His failure to stipulate what these probabilities are, and to allow the parties to know what these probabilities are, needs explanation, and the explanation seems simply to be the desire to secure their selection of his principle of justice.

Rawls has not adequately defended his choice of maximin against other rules consistent with his assumptions. More seriously, as Goldman noted, he has denied information to the contractors that would improve their decisions without compromising their impartiality. First of all, Rawls's contractors are forbidden to know the probability distribution of individual positions in society. Each is also kept in ignorance of his own preferences between leisure and goods, whether he is a hard worker or a shirker and malingerer, and, of course, his moral preferences with respect to these variables. As Melden (1977, p. 114) well notes, "some of the features in respect of which persons differ and which are possible sources of conflict are morally relevant." Rawls, of course, seeks (unsuccessfully) to make plausible his suppression of moral feelings in the original position by asserting that no one deserves his productive attributes and then expropriating the attributes and their fruits for the "common fund" (see Chapter 4, Section 4.1 and Kronman, 1980b, pp. 1493–4). However, as will become evident shortly, in attempting to steer the "veil of ignorance" safely past the Scylla of property feelings, Rawls's "social contract" is inevitably drawn, with no possible escape, into the Charybdis of contested binding force.

Beyond these objections, as Mishan (1981, p. 131) and others have pointed out, maximin is not a moral rule but a maxim of prudent behavior. This aspect of Rawls's model is well explained by Gibbard (1985, p. 22):

> According to Rawls ... our reason for adhering to these principles in the flux of life – our moral reason – is that we would have chosen them from behind the veil of ignorance. We would have chosen them because of their prospective advantages, and these advantages are reckoned in nonmoral terms. Hence, in Rawls' theory, the moral character of the principles of justice rest ultimately on the advantages they offer, and in that sense, Rawls' defense of whatever property rights are sanctioned by his principles of justice is pragmatic.

For Rawls, prudent men are absolute risk averters. But why, it must be asked, would not prudent men constrained by Rawls' veil of ignorance simply agree on a *minimum income* for each individual? Again, why would prudent men choose a lifetime or forever contract with no provision for reopening negotiations? As Rawls does not answer these questions it is difficult to take his contractual framework seriously.

Dworkin (1977, p. 153) raises another fundamental problem:

> A judgment of antecedent interest depends upon the circumstances under which the judgment is made, and, in particular, upon the knowledge available to the man making the

judgment. It might be in my antecedent interest to bet on a
certain horse at given odds before the starting gun, but not,
at least at the same odds, after he has stumbled on the first
turn. *The fact, therefore, that a particular choice is in my interest at a*
particular time, under conditions of great uncertainty, is not a good
argument for the fairness of enforcing that choice against me later
under conditions of much greater knowledge. [Italics added]

Dworkin is calling into grave doubt whether Rawls's painfully
tailored contract is binding upon the contractors. Is it prudent to
honor one's contracts? For ordinary contracts, fulfillment is often,
but certainly not invariably, the prudent policy. In the case of
Rawls's social contract, however, considerations of prudence
would call for virtually unanimous renunciation!

As Rawls acknowledges, no actual group has ever entered into
a contract under the conditions he assumes, or behaves *as if* it had.
His social contract is entirely hypothetical. According to Dworkin
(1977, pp. 150–1), however:

> If a group contracted in advance that disputes amongst
> them would be settled in a particular way, the fact of that
> contract would be a powerful argument that such disputes
> should be settled in that way when they do arise. The
> contract would be an argument in itself, independent of the
> force of the reasons that might have led different people to
> enter the contract. Ordinarily, for example, each of the
> parties supposes that a contract he signs is in his own interest;
> but if someone has made a mistake in calculating his self
> interest, the fact that he did contract is a strong reason for
> the fairness of holding him nevertheless to the bargain ...
> His [Rawls's] contract is hypothetical, and hypothetical
> contracts do not supply an independent argument for the
> fairness of enforcing their terms. A hypothetical contract is
> not simply a pale form of an actual contract, it is no contract
> at all.

If when he says that "hypothetical contracts do not supply an
independent argument for the fairness of enforcing their terms,"
Dworkin means that only *express*, as opposed to *cognitive* or

hypothetical, agreements are capable of arousing feelings of legitimate entitlements and indebtedness, I would be inclined to disagree (see further Dworkin, 1977, p. 177). Apparently, the legal rules of even a dictatorial state and customary practice are sometimes surrounded by powerful property feelings. Moreover, what I would have chosen matters to me even if I did not actually make the choice (see Raz, 1986, pp. 80–1). For the present purpose it seems sufficient to note one major difference between express and hypothetical contracts, of which Dworkin is well aware. The theorist is in a position to alter the content of a *hypothetical* agreement by manipulating his assumptions. This problem is also encountered in the law-and-economics literature when an actual legal relationship is presumed to be the outcome of an *as if* or *implicit* contract. As corporate law scholar Robert C. Clark (1985, p. 68) has pointed out: "The implicit-contracts form of reasoning is often indeterminate precisely because there is no consensus about which assumptions to use."

There is, however, ample reason to deny the appropriateness of the assumptions defining Rawls's "veil of ignorance." Rawls's (1971, p. 21) explanation of why individuals should abide by his hypothetical contract is weak and unconvincing: "The answer is that the conditions embodied in the description of the original position are ones that we do in fact accept. Or if we do not, then perhaps we can be persuaded to do so by philosophical reflection."

I submit that we do not accept Rawls's original position and cannot be persuaded to do so by arguments. The danger in Rawls's approach, economists Rowley and Peacock (1975, p. 143) warn, is that despite the logical deficiencies of this theory and the absence of supporting evidence "the policy implications are readily adoptable. In short, Rawls provides a spurious justification for egalitarianism." Rowley and Peacock's concern is reinforced by Melden's (1977, p. 105) observation that:

> For Rawls, only if the principles of justice that anyone would choose as a rational being for everyone else are embodied in the institutions of society, in which there are specific roles or offices for any particular person, will there be specific

constraints of moral obligation to which any individual is subject.

It is permissible to wonder, therefore, whether hidden within the velvet glove of prudence and hypothetical social contract lies the fist of forcible redistribution.

Notes

1 To deny that the poor have a *right* to objects produced by others is not, as Frank (1985, p. 124) charges, to "disregard" their plight.

2 This point is very well discussed by Nozick (1974, pp. 164–6); see also Suzumura (1983, pp. 189–90).

3 For undisguised examples of this kind of exercise, see Boadway and Bruce (1984, p. 177).

4 Harsanyi's (1985a, p. 49) suggestion that people should act so as to "maximize expected social utility" is implausible on both informational and psychological grounds.

5 For compact discussions of the von Neumann-Morgenstern axioms and the expected utility theorem, see Bonner (1986, pp. 161–5), Layard and Walters (1978, pp. 369–73), and Sen (1985a, pp. 192–3).

6 For useful discussions of Posner's theory, see Mercuro and Ryan (1984).

7 The definitions of fairness differ somewhat from one theorist to another (see Otsuki, 1980).

8 Baumol has never responded directly to Holcombe's criticism that it matters who produced an object (see Baumol, 1983b, p. 1161 and 1986, pp. 17, 40–1). In his recent book about *Superfairness*, Baumol (1986, pp. 11, 14) seeks to justify his redefinition of the word "fair" by posing the (allegedly) "intractable difficulties besetting the formulations of any unexceptionable criterion of fairness" against the fact that his "fairness theory *is* tractable . . . and can make good use of familiar analytic tools."

9 For useful discussions of Rawls's theory, see Blocker and Smith (1980), Boadway and Bruce (1984, pp. 181–4), Daniels (1975), A. H. Goldman (1980) and Suzumura (1983, pp. 156–67).

10 See Arrow (1973, pp. 256–7), Harsanyi (1976, pp. 44–5), Rowley and Peacock (1975, pp. 140–4), and Thurow (1975, pp. 29–32).

9

Alternative Economic Justice Rules (Concluded): Blame-freeness and Catastrophic Allocations

Economist Andrew Schotter's theory of justice, like the one advocated in this study, places *feelings* at center stage. He maintains that "an object distribution among the individuals in a society is just if no individual can blame any other individual for the actions he took in bringing that distribution about." Schotter (1985, p. 92) explains: "The most straightforward way to evaluate a person's behavior is to put oneself in his position and ask if you would have acted as he did under the circumstances. If the answer is yes, then you cannot blame him for his actions and in that sense his actions are justifiable." If all individuals answer "Yes, I would have acted as he did," the distribution of objects is blame-free and therefore economically just.

One may appreciate the value of Schotter's insight into the nature of justice, as I do, while rejecting his attempt to employ blame-freeness as the cutting edge for a policy of forcible redistribution. And this, it must be stated frankly, is Schotter's aim. At one point he seeks to soften this implication by maintaining that: "A rationally-based justice theory may not respect people's rights to keep *what the market gives them*" (Schotter, 1985, p. 98) [Italics added]. Schotter is here engaged in pure apologetics as can be seen immediately by substituting "what their efforts produce for them" for "what the market gives them". As Schotter is a feelings theorist it is surely appropriate to remind him that participants in the market *feel* that their rewards are earned not "given" (see

Chapter 3 and 4). Elsewhere, Schotter (1985, p. 97) eschews Aesopian language and broadens the range of blame-free redistribution far beyond reasonable bounds:

> The argument for income transfers is simple. The free market, by determining an *unequal* distribution of income (and possibly a corner solution) leads some fraction of the population to engage in crime as a rational response to their *plight*. If the activities they engage in are blame-free in the sense that all other agents in society would have done the same if they had been *reduced* to their circumstances, then the market has created a situation where blame-free thefts exist. [Italics added]

In existing and past societies the overwhelming majority of individuals would indeed blame a person who used force to acquire goods to which others were legitimately entitled solely because his income was below, even very much below, the social average.[1] This would be the case even if it were generally believed that "having low status may even impose measurable biochemical costs on people" (Frank, 1985, p. 121). The majority, I submit, would also blame the thief even if they thought he felt poor because he had less than other people (Frank, 1985, p. 126). The appendix on "Money and Happiness" argues that Frank and his theoretical predecessors have overestimated the importance of positional gains and losses. I would add that most of us would also blame a person who used force to remedy deprivations he had suffered, to use philosopher Joel Feinberg's (1970, p. 93) terms, "for no good reason," for example, his car was destroyed by a bolt of lightning.

Violence and social unrest results much more from the perception of exploitation than from inequality, poverty, and plain bad luck. It is moreover a myth that most of those who become criminals do so because the market "reduced" them to dire circumstances. For many if not most criminals crime simply pays better in money and psychic income than legitimate alternatives. Schotter (1985, p. 96) is surely mistaken in suggesting that any nontrivial portion of criminals are incapable of earning an honest living.

Thus, for example, the view of many leading social historians is that in the sixteenth and seventeenth centuries England suffered an upsurge of violence and a breakdown of law and order. Mcfarlane (1987, pp. 52–3) explains that:

> This is alleged by ... [one] school [of historians] to be the by-product of two features. First, there was the endemic brutality of a population ground down by poverty, perennial sickness and high mortality. This was exacerbated by the penetration of the new mode of production, capitalism, which destroyed the old community controls and undermined the moral order of a pre-capitalist society.

Yet when Macfarlane (1987, p. 62) considered the evidence of depositions and local documents in northern England, he found, quite simply, that:

> Crime was considered a short cut to greater wealth, rather than an attempt to stave off starvation ... It seems that clipping [of coins] and theft were merely thought to be easier ways to make money than other activities. The risks involved were worth taking and, as in other diversions, may have added to the pleasure. Such activities were bi-occupations: one could combine farming or blacksmithing or alehouse keeping with a little burglary or clipping, just as others would combine it with hunting or knitting stockings.

Only in catastrophic situations might theft be blame-free in Schotter's sense that other individuals would have done the same thing. Even then the thief might be blamed.

For example, according to Feinberg (1971, p. 93) a man with a large number of dependents deserves extra compensation. Yet those of us against whom he practised forcible "debt" collection would be inclined to blame him, unless of course they believed his mate(s) was capable of immaculate and involuntary conception. Robert Goodin (1985, p. 129) suggests that it is "surely absurd" to "stand idly by and watch people reap the bitter fruits of their own improvidence." "Absurd" in what sense? Goodin is entitled to *his* feelings, but are they typical? The issues are cogently posed by Don Brock (1982, p. 232):

> On any moral view that incorporates some right to determine the major directions of our own life on the basis of our own desires and values, it is plausible to argue that we have a responsibility for the forseeable and reasonably preventable consequences of the decisions we make in determining our life plan. "Responsibility for" not just in the causal sense, but in the sense that each must bear the consequences of his choices, and will have (at least within broad limits) no claim on others to relieve him of those consequences. This is necessary to distinguish cases in which a person through no fault of his own is in need of aid and others – as for example when he needs food to avert starvation in a famine resulting from unforseeable and unpreventable circumstances such as a long drought – from cases in which he is responsible for his plight–as for example when he lacks food supplies that he possessed and that would have sufficed, because he gambled and lost them or simply let them spoil. In the latter case, a right to aid that ould obtain in the former case has been forfeited.

If an individual were starving through no fault of his own the rest of us would not blame him for stealing a loaf of bread.

On second thought, questions arise even in this simple case. If our attitude is sincere, it would seem to be a corollary that we (nonstarving individuals) would be willing to give him the loaf as a loan or a gift. Would a nonstarving individual resist the attempt of a starving person to seize one of his loaves?

If not, the theft is really a gift or a loan. If the owner offered resistance despite the thief's starvation status, then either he blames the starving thief or he is psychologically capable of not blaming and still resisting his attacker. A resisting owner whose object was stolen might not be blamed by the rest of us, including even his starving attacker, for using force to recapture his loaf and to punish the thief. Blame-freeness might turn out to be a cyclic standard of economic justice.

In the best of circumstances blame-freeness is a tricky concept. Clearly its range of possible applicability is rather narrow. In the overwhelming majority of cases thieves are blamed. The main virtue of Schotter's approach is that it calls attention to the problem of *catastrophic emergency*.[2] Catastrophe, as Fried (1978, p. 10) points out, "*is a distinct concept just because it identifies the extreme situations in which usual categories of judgment (including that of right and wrong) do not apply*" (italics added). I would modify this description of catastrophe by substitution "categories of *feelings*" for Fried's "categories of judgment." In catastrophic situations it seems possible that survival "trumps" or "overrides" justice. That is, the rest of us will not blame the thief and he will not feel his action was *wrong*. More likely it will be felt by all that his action was wrong but *permissible* (see Griffin, 1986, p. 162). Fried (1978, p. 12) accurately reflects our property feelings, I believe, when he suggests that "so long as the consequences fall within a very broad range, the categorical norm [our rights principle] holds, no matter what the consequences."[3]

Sen (1985b, p. 6) probes this position as follows: "If disastrous consequences would be adequate to nullify any rights (even the most important ones), perhaps bad-but-not-so-disastrous consequences would be adequate to nullify other, less central rights." I am not sure which rights Sen would consider less central. However, in terms of the power of the underlying feelings, it is difficult to conceive of more central rights than that of producers to their objects (compare Thomson, 1986b, pp. 254–5). An individual who steals in "bad-but-not-so-disastrous" circumstances will be blamed – that is, his action will trigger moral indignation and a desire for punishment. This emotional response cannot be gainsaid by legalistic arguments.

Locke's proviso (see Chapter 2, Section 4) that an individual may acquire a "resource" just so long as there is "enough and as good" left over for others introduces an incongruous need-based *right* into a theory whose central thrust, it seems to me, is to ground rights in effort (see Bogart, 1985). The author may be forgiven for preferring a Lockean view in which the issue is not one of rights triggered by deprivation status, but of infringement of the rights of producers when the deprived cannot support themselves. In this case, however, it seems better to speak with J. S. Mill (1951, p. 79) of "laudable injustice" than with Schotter of "blame-free justice." Compassion and even a generalized revulsion for the misery of mankind are, after all, different feelings than moral indignation. Contrary to Sen's (1984b, p. 136) consequence sensitive analysis and his references to "failures of entitlement," a person has no more *right* to life at a producer's expense than he has to a "decent standard of living" or the amenities. This holds whether the producer eats beans or dines on the tongues of hummingbirds. Without feelings of legitimate entitlement there are no rights and without rights, no justice. It seems that even in catastrophic situations the infringement of legitimate entitlements is accompanied by a feeling of "moral disquiet" or "moral cost" (Slote, 1985, pp. 165–6). Thomson (1986b) speaks of such acts as leaving "moral traces." Obviously people will steal to survive. I very much doubt however, that our inborn feelings are really extinguished even in catastrophic situations. Theft may sometimes be permissible; it is never moral. Even an overwhelming interest in possessing an object does not bestow a right to that object. Welfare rights are "nonsense on stilts."

The welfare state must stand or fall on its philanthropic and pragmatic merits. I for one have long been convinced that citizens in affluent societies *desire* far more redistribution than is predictable on the basis of reasonable prudence alone (see Silver, 1980). It is in no way the intention of this study to suggest that the welfare state is theft written large. However, only confusion and intellectual mischief can result from attempts to smuggle altruism into our vision of society in the garb of rights and morality.[4]

Notes

1 Frank (1985, p.120) would perhaps object that in most cultures people are "taught" to be hostile to concerns about relative position.
2 Among the Bushmen, "should a family in extremity find . . . a cache

[of food or water] and use it they must trace the depositor and inform him lest he seek to avenge the theft" (Forde, 1963, pp. 29–30). Private necessity is everywhere only a conditional privilege.

Utilizing economics of law terminology we might speak of catastrophic emergency as a case of "market falure" leading to the substitution of one "transaction rule" for another or, more specifically, of the substitution of a "liability rule" calling for *ex post* compensation (usually set by a third party, for example, a court) for a "property rule" calling for the owner's *ex ante* consent (see Coleman and Kraus, 1986, and Davis, 1987, pp. 582–3). Gauthier (1986, p. 211) mistakenly believes that nonowners may *morally* choose a liability rule even when markets are intact. The same and no more can be said about Sen's (1982b) problem of "Ali and the Bashers."

3 A favorite extremist example involves murder by power of ownership: the owners of all drinkable water, all the land, or all of the food refuse to sell any to a particular individual.

4 For recent examples of this harmful tendency, see Frank (1985, Chapter 6, especially pp. 120–1) and Goodin (1985).

Summary and Concluding Observations

Moral or ethical words belong to the wider class of feelings words whose meaning is comprehended by means of feelings memory – that is, by recalling characteristic feelings. The meaning and proper usage of moral and other feelings words is learned by a process of linguistic inference. The meaning of the word "right," the key term in this study, is a kind of feeling of approval. To cope with the problem of economic justice it is essential to define property rights in a manner explicitly recognizing their emotive content, rather than with synonyms. Briefly stated, a property right is a complex of feelings of approval (or legitimate entitlement) with respect to an object. A complex of feelings because in addition to the feelings of the subject of the right, the feelings of the other members of the society must be taken into account. Property rights have a relational or social dimension. An object, this term being understood in a maximally general sense, to which this complex of feelings applies is property. Property rights must not be confounded, as they usually are, with powers over objects, legally based or otherwise. By thief is meant anyone or any group, including governments, who seeks power over an object to which another (the victim) is legitimately entitled by means of physical force, the threat of physical force, or by means of deceptive promises. Behavior of this kind transforms the victim's giving into taking.

The term property feelings refers to the moral sense of separation and personification of an object: "This is mine." The disposition to experience property feelings is actualized by various stimuli without reason or forethought. Moral judgments are objective in the sense that there is intersubjectivity of the feelings themselves as well as of the environmental scenarios capable of eliciting or triggering them. Moral goodness is not "out there," it is "in here." Emotionally and socially the most important and reliable trigger is the act of production. It is not, I repeat, the only stimulus and neither is it fail-safe. To be valuable, a theory of economic justice need not offer a solution to each and every problem.

What counts as productive activity varies from one society to another. In many if not most historical societies the shaman or priest who prays for rain triggers a right to a portion of the crop. This is not generally true in our own society. Culture matters. In all societies, however, production is, in emotional terms, a much broader activity than manufacturing. Natural objects are transformed into property by the acts of occupation (or possession) and improvement. The person who picks up an acorn is felt to have produced a new (relational) object. Lasting property rights to land, however, are triggered only if the occupant transmits labor signals of improvement to outsiders. Locke's peculiar proposition that one acquires property rights in natural objects by "mixing" one's labor with them represents a profound insight into the importance of what might be termed the creation of "texts of ownership." The basic problem with extremist objections to Locke's proposition such as philosopher Robert Nozick's (mixing of one's tomato juice with the sea), is that they fall outside the range of human experience and hence would probably fail to elicit appropriate emotional responses. The gaps in our *evolved* property feelings exposed by the occurrence of the truly novel must be filled by legal rule or social convention.

The cooperative production and exchange of objects raises more difficult problems than their individual manufacture or occupation improvement. Again, however, feelings are the relevant variable, not the rules of recursive systems on which Nozick relies. My working hypotheses are that: (a) individuals feel that they have produced the objects they acquire from others by means of exchange; and (b) a special application of hypothesis (a) with respect to cooperative production, individuals feel that they have produced the objects they previously agreed to accept from others in exchange for their services. As exchange requires transactors to expend effort in plan formulation and execution, it would certainly not be surprising if they and third parties emotionally experienced the manufacture of object X and its exchange, as operations in the production of Y, the desired object. Ultimately of course, these propositions need to be tested systematically against our empirical feelings. For the present it must suffice to report that, despite the undeniable gray areas and certain ambiguities, the above hypotheses do find support in introspection, casual observation, the analysis of language and ritual, ethnography, and the differential treatment of "naked" and "bargained-for" promises. Apparently, then, the elicitation of stable property rights does not require the exchanged objects to be deemed of comparable value. In addition it appears that no property right is violated merely by a discrepancy between the reward of a resource and the exchange value of is contribution to the value of output. Consideration of archaeological and historical evidence suggests also that Adam Smith knew whereof he spoke when he noted in mankind a certain "propensity to trade, barter, and exchange one thing for another." The implications of the psychology of property for public policy are monumental.

According to philosopher John Rawls and other prominent scholars (Arrow, Dworkin, Elster, Tinbergen), producers do not *deserve* their objects because they do not deserve their "endowments" of physical and mental characteristics, talents, and motivation. Nozick's attempt to defend the individualist position against Rawls failed because it was not grounded in a theory of the self. Human beings are incapable of reasoning away the natural events in us we call "choice," "self-reproach," and "pride in achievement." Despite Rawls's argument, each of us continues to feel strongly that the results of *his* attributes are *his* results. Rawls and his supporters have failed to distinguish between the logical fact that our actions are caused and the entirely emotional issue of our deserts.

It is quite true, of course, that a portion of the gain realized in a particular transaction is due to the broader network of social cooperation in which it is embedded. However, as social cooperation is equally produced (owned) by the cooperators, it is, contrary to the position of C. B. Macpherson and others, incapable of generating net claims of "society" against any subset of individuals. To charge a producer a "tax" or "immigration fee" merely for participation in society is theft (extortion), as he is the sole owner of his participation. On the other hand, as the individual does not have a property right (feeling of legitimate entitlement) in the structure of the economy, he cannot morally veto or demand compensation merely because he is harmed by new activities carried out by others. Violation of a person's rightful property powers harms him, but not all harms are violations of rightfully held objects. Most, indeed, are not.

In his rivalry with the thief the power of the producer is enhanced by his own moral indignation (and that of third parties) and the fear aversion and guilt felt by the thief. In ethological terms it is possible to speak in this connection of the "relative dominance" of ownership. *On the average right makes might.* The Hobbesian model of society championed by economist James M. Buchanan is not in tune with the real world in which objects are created by effort rather than simply "falling down." It is not true, moreover, as contractarians asserts, that political order must be antecedent to economic order. The *property institution*, by which is meant a reasonably tight connection between object production and object power, seems to be a common characteristic of markedly different societies, including stateless societies. Social ideas are powerful, however. The acceptance of certain ideas about the nature of socioeconomic relations may precipitate behavior apparently contrary to our arguments about property feelings. Upon further reflection we realize that such potent beliefs as "The Jew is a Thief" and Marx's "The Employer is a Thief," trade on the very property feelings they are intended to subvert.

It is not unreasonable to postulate an evolutionary origin for the innate moral feelings surrounding productive activity. The biological cost of being capable of experiencing these feelings appears to be modest compared to the resulting reproductive advantage. Perhaps the strongest evidence for an evolutionary origin is the manifestation of property-like behavior, including the "resident-wins" phenomenon, among nonhuman animals. While the theoretical arguments and supporting evidence are not conclusive, it seems reasonable to entertain as a working hypothesis a psychoevolutionary approach to emotions and, more specifically, to think of ethical behavior and awareness as products of biological evolution. More importantly, the surely built-in connection of moral indignation to theft provides an "Archemedian point" for evaluating the distribution of produced objects in society.

The universal feeling of approval is what makes it "good" or "right" for producers to have power over their objects. Goodness is intrinsically dispositional: there are no entailments relating good and feeling good. In this sense property rights triggered by production are natural rights. A rights principle – individuals ought to hold the objects they have produced; they ought not to be forcibly deprived of their objects – is put forward and grounded in species characteristics. Specifically, each normally formed person feels that a producer is legitimately entitled to his object and is outraged when a producer is forcibly deprived of his object. Our property feelings do not dictate our *actions* but they do dictate our *moral judgments*.

This rights principle is invulnerable to the so-called "open question argument" or "naturalistic fallacy" and, by recognizing that values *are* facts, it copes successfully with the "is-ought problem." Moreover, the universalizability criterion, vital for a moral rule, holds automatically instead of being problematic. On the other hand, contrary to the anonymity or symmetry assumptions encountered in the welfare economics literature, the identity of moral agents is crucial. In ranking alternative social states, producers are taken to be "intrinsically superior" to non-producers.

The foregoing analysis of property rights prepares a foundation for an endogenous, process-oriented rule of economic justice termed the congruence rule: The distribution of control over produced objects is just to the extent that control or power is congruent with right. The congruence rule does not dictate or predict the pursuit of unrestrained self-interest and does not preclude private charity, public welfare, and, in an uncertain world, schemes of mutual insurance. Even absolute equality of result is not precluded as an objective. Coerced contributions or participation are forbidden in a just socity, however. Only a major empirical study would permit a meaningful assessment of the relative shares of the "consent" and "theft" components in today's welfare states. The objective of the present study is, however, to establish the *theoretical* foundations of economic justice. To this end alternative rules of economic justice were evaluated in terms of whether they, like the congruence rule, respected the producer's natural right to his object.

In advocating the forcible redistribution of objects the standard utilitarian model fails to take account of all the relevant feelings: feelings of pleasure or happiness from consuming objects are heeded; the moral indignation of robbed producers (and third parties) is ignored along with the guilt feelings of the beneficiaries of theft. It is impossible to eliminate this bias by comparing the outrage of robbed producer A with the pleasure of theft beneficiary B. The reason is that moral indignation and happiness are qualitatively different feelings. (Alternatively viewed, moral indignation is lexicographically ordered relative to happiness.) Refinements of the standard utilitarian model which continue to assume (implicitly or explicitly) that utility numbers refer to an identifiable mental state (happiness or pleasure) are similarly flawed. Behaviorist or choice models avoid, at a cost, the incommensurability problem and they are in principle capable of taking account of property feelings, however.

Posner's wealth-maximization rule of economic justice has the advantages, relative to utilitarianism, of quantifiability and commensurability. Nevertheless, it is clearly unjust to assign an object produced by A to B merely because B values it more highly in terms of effective demand. The "fairness" theory of economists Baumol and Varian is attractive because it utilizes standard tools of economic analysis and, more importantly, permits the identification of a good distribution of objects without the necessity of an entire ordering of allocations, as is required in social choice theory. But the rule that objects produced by A (including even his labor) should be seized and turned over to B merely to realize an "envy-free" or "income-fair" distribution is not in the least "fair" and has nothing in common with justice.

The theoretical difficulties of Rawls's approach to justice are disguised by its attractive social contract superstructure. (The perennial appeal of social contract theories is itself a tribute to the power of property feelings.) His "original position" and "veil of ignorance" deny information to contractors that would improve their decisions without compromising their impartiality. Hypothetical or implicit contracts are in any event useful but dangerous tools of analysis. The danger arises because the theorist is in a position to shape the content of the agreement by manipulating assumptions about which there is no consensus. It follows, from the fact that there are no good reasons for Rawls's assumptions, that there is no good reason to suppose that prudent individuals would agree to maximize the payoff to the least fortunately placed member of society. Neither, it is important to note, is there any good reason to believe that any such agreement would be morally binding on the contracting parties.

Andrew Schotter's theory of "blame-free" justice, like the congruence rule, gives the central role to moral(?) feelings. However, in existing and past societies, contrary to Schotter's position, members would blame those who used force to acquire objects merely because their income was below, even much below, the social average. Inequality is not a blame-free justification for theft. Blame-freeness is in fact a tricky, possibly cyclic, standard whose range of applicability is narrow. The main and undoubted virtue of Schotter's theory is that it throws into sharp focus the problem of catastropic emergency. Perhaps, the moral rule calling for producers to hold their objects is categorical, not absolute. That is, the thief may not be blamed when circumstances are *felt*, that is, emotionally experienced, to be extreme. In a catastrophic emergency, survival may "trump" justice. Outside the very broad range in which our feelings demand justice it is better to speak with Mill of "laudable injustice" than with Schotter of "blame-free justice." Even in catastrophic conditions, violations of people's just deserts are accompanied by a feeling of moral disquiet.

Several final observations are in order. First, in view of the fact that the rules of economic justice surveyed in this work, with the possible exception of Rawls's (and, of course, congruence), required redistribution of objects, the reticence of the theorists with respect to the problem of *how*, or even *whether*, the mandated redistribution should be accomplished is intriguing, indeed remarkable (see Sen, 1987, pp. 37–8). One cannot help getting the impression that these are not the kinds of problems a reputable theorist and duly certified savant should discuss before his readers. Second, welfare economists who discuss economic justice without taking moral feelings into account are not treating the subject with the seriousness it merits and requires. They also risk assembling tractable, mathematically elegant moral monsters. Unfortunately, the view that ethics is an organic part of the general hedonistic theory of rational behavior seems to have gained ground among economists despite Sen's almost single-handed efforts. Sen (1982a, p. 28) has observed that the problem of incorporating rights into the evaluation of states of affairs has "typically met with absolute silence in welfare economics" notwithstanding the fact that fundamental issues of this kind "are, in fact, rather important for policy judgments and economic evaluation." This rather understated criticism of the hedonist presumption of much of the current work in welfare economics is decisive. In conclusion, I wish to fully agree with political scientist Robert McShea's (1979, p. 394) observation that: "The disappearance of value in objective, dehumanized thought does not represent a higher truth about the status of morality; it confirms the human nature thesis that morality has a biological rather than a metaphsical basis."

Appendix

Money and Happiness?: towards "Eudaimonology"*

Yew-Kwang Ng (1978) ends his provocative article on "Economic Growth and Social Welfare" with a plea "that more attention and more resources should be devoted to the study of happiness (Eudaimonology?) taking account of the objective, subjective, and institutional factors". What follows represents a modest step in this direction.

Does money buy happiness? Easterlin (1973) presents data and offers an interpretation to the effect that affluence is an illusion and our society is trapped on a "hedonic treadmill." He refers to a discrepancy in the findings of survey studies that relate income levels to happiness self-ratings. The latter ratings have taken two forms: the proportion of individuals who classify themselves as, say, "very happy," and the average value on a numerical (0 to 10) happiness scale. In cross-sections (given moment in time) for the United States and 19 other countries (developed and less developed) with different socioeconomic systems, the relationship between income level and the rating of personal happiness is positive. This finding, of course, suggests that money *does* "buy" happiness. On the other hand, two additional findings cited by Easterlin (1973) suggest it *does not*. First "richer countries are not typically happier than poorer ones" (1973, p. 7). Second, "in the United States, the average level of happiness in 1970 was not much different from that in the late 1940's, though average income ... could buy over 60 percent more" (1973, p. 7). However, the latter findings are far from conclusive.

In his technical paper Easterlin (1974) notes that there does appear to be a positive relationship among countries, but the impact of income on personal happiness is "much weaker" and less statistically reliable than exhibited in within country comparisons.[1] Later evidence from an ongoing survey study by the Gallup International Research Institutes provides more convincing evidence. Table 1 which summarizes data for 60 countries shows quite clearly that the proportion rating themselves "not too happy" is substantially lower in the more affluent nations of North America, Western Europe, and Australia. In table 2 nations are listed in descending order with respect to per capita income together with the sample percentage responding that they are "Highly satisfied with life as a whole". The impression of a positive relationship is confirmed by a value of 0.43 for Spearman's coefficient of rank correlation.[2]

Assuming, however, that the discrepancy noted by Easterlin is real, how should it be explained? Easterlin (1973, p. 8) argues quite reasonably that "people who live in richer times and places perceive their needs in more ambitious terms than those in poorer societies," and he goes on to conclude that the "upward shift in perceived needs" cancels the "positive effect of income growth on

Table 1 "Generally speaking, how happy would you say you are – very happy, fairly happy, or not too happy?"

	Very happy	*Fairly happy*	*Not too happy*
North America	40	51	8
Australia	37	57	6
Western Europe	20	60	18
Latin America	32	38	28
Africa	18	50	31
India and Japan	7	41	50

Source: George H. Gallup, "Human Needs and Satisfactions: A Global Survey," *Public Opinion Quarterly* (1976/77), Winter, Table 2, p. 465.

perceived well-being" (1973, p. 10).[3] Thus the "hedonic tread-mill." Gordon Tullock, in personal correspondence, has characterized this hypothesis as: "If everyone has a toothache it doesn't really hurt." Similarly, Cambell, Converse and Rodgers (1976, p. 208) assert: "Any doctrine that aspiration levels serve as perfect 'shock absorbers' to cope with change and maintain satisfactions at a constant level has implications which fly in the face of enormous amounts of individual and aggregative evidence."

I would agree that it is unreasonable to believe that the extent to which the desire for goods and services is satisfied depends *only* on the social environment and not at all upon the absolute level of consumption. Perhaps it is not *actual* but *reported* happiness that is sensitive to an individual's relative income position.[4]

How happy is "very happy?" Since an individual does not know his happiness "capacity," he cannot, as would be appropriate, report his happiness rating as: actual happiness/happiness capacity.[5] The best the individual can do at reasonable cost is to estimate the happiness of others by their consumption levels and, in effect, rate his happiness as own consumption/others' consumption. That is, when a higher income person reports himself to be "very happy" he means that he is *happier* (that is, consumes more)

Table 2 "Highly satisfied with life as a whole"

	%
United States	69
Denmark	67
West Germany	41
Belgium	51
France	26
Netherland	57
United Kingdom	50
Italy	17
Ireland	59

Source: *Public Opinion* (1978), July/August, p. 21

than his poorer time and place contemporaries.[6] According to the school of Epicurus in antiquity, perceived happiness is attainment/expectation. Again my reply is that since his happiness "capacity" is unknown, an individual estimates the happiness he "expects" by the consumption level of other persons. But none of this means that actual happiness will not rise when the individual's own consumption and the consumption of others rise in the same proportion.

Evidence running contrary to my hypothesis is provided by survey findings that Americans (usually by a ratio of 2 to 1) think of themselves as less happy than their predecessors of a generation ago.[7] But do such responses reflect actual satisfaction levels or, merely, the (casual) assumption that in earlier "simpler" times people were "more easily satisfied?" Do today's Americans confuse the *additional* (or marginal) satisfaction of a "crust of bread" for a hungry predecessor with the *total* satisfaction resulting from their own higher level of consumption? Support for the latter interpretations and for my hypothesis is provided by the survey finding that Americans reject the would-have-lived-then-rather-than-now option by a ratio of better than 2 to 1.[8]

Easterlin (1973, p. 10) believes his arguments point to the "uncomfortable conclusion" that we are "trapped in a material rat-race" in which "each person goes on, generation after generation, unaware of the self-defeating process in which he is caught up." I hope that this paper has not only advanced our understanding of happiness but has encouraged the reader to accept the more comfortable conclusion that when incomes generally increase people, on the average, feel better off.[9]

Notes

* Kyklos, 33(1) (1980), 157–60; it is reprinted here by kind permission of Kyklos-Verlag, Basel.
1 For 14 countries the rank order correlation between the rating of personal happiness (0 to 10 and a socioeconomic index, of which gross national product is one component, is positive and statistically significant at the 0.01 level (Cantril, 1965, pp. 193–4).

2 The coefficient manages to achieve statistical significance at the 0.15 level on a one-tailed test.

3 Easterlin's (1973) argument bears a family resemblence to Ng's (1978) problem of aspiration levels with respect to "Harrod-Hirsch positional goods" and to Scitovsky's (1976, p. 137) notion of "addiction": "Many comforts are satisfying at first, but soon become routine and taken for granted. Consumer demand for them remains undiminished, but the original motivation, the desire for additional satisfaction, is replaced by a new and very different motivation of wishing to avoid the pain and frustration of giving up a habit to which one has grown accustomed." Again, Inglehart (1977, pp. 38–4) believes that it is *changes* in experiences that really matter so that "for the long run, it appears that human beings can be about equally happy with a modest as a lavish standard of material consumption." Finally, Mishan (1977, p. 69) suggests that "in a perfectly air-conditioned habitation ... there can be no anticipating the cool of the evening, no slaking one's thirst with a cold drink or immersing oneself in a stream ... Thus, material abundance, plus the priority given to physical comfort, may act to reduce the experience of pleasure."

4 This may be what Ng (1978, pp. 584–5) has in mind when he refers to difficulties of comparability in happiness ratings.

5 An alternative would be to report

$$\frac{\text{actual happiness}}{\text{maximum prior happiness}}$$

but with the passage of time it becomes extremely difficult to recapture the intensity of past sensations.

6 This argument can be presented in a more formal way. According to Duesenberry (1967) a given individual's utility index (U_i) is a function of his own consumption (C_j) deflated by the weighted average of the consumption of other persons ($Sa_{ij}C_j$) about whose consumption the individual has some knowledge (or, what comes to the same thing, by some sort of standard consumption package). Since the maximum value for a given individual's utility index (U_{im}) is not known the individual cannot report his happiness rating as U_i/U_m. Instead the individual estimates the happiness of others by their consumption level and rates his own happiness as $C_i/Sa_{ij}C_j$. But U_i will rise when C_i and $Sa_{ij}C_j$ rise in the same proportion.

7 See Rescher (1972, pp. 44–7).

8 See Rescher (1972, pp.46–7).

9 Readers interested in the relationship between money and happiness would do well to consult the ongoing research of the Leyden University Income Evaluation Project, for example, Kapteyn, Van Praag, and Van Herwaarden (1978). Layard (1980) is also recommended.

References

Ackerman, Bruce (1980): *Social Justice in the Liberal State*. New Haven, CT: Yale University Press.

Alchian, Armen A. (1979): "Some Implications of Recognition of Property Right Transaction Costs." In Karl Brunner (ed.), *Economics and Social Institutions*. Boston, MA: Martinus Nijhoff.

Alchian, Armen A. and William R. Allen (1964): *University Economics*, 1st edn. Belmont, CA: Wadsworth.

Alchian, Armen A. and Harold Demsetz (1972): "Production, Information Costs, and Economic Organization." *American Economic Review*, 62, 777–95.

Alexander, Richard D. (1987): *The Biology of Moral Systems*. New York: de Gruyter.

Andreades, A. M. (1933): *A History of Greek Public Finance*, vol. I. Cambridge, MA: Harvard University Press.

Appleby, Joyce Oldham (1978): *Economic Thought and Ideology in Seventeenth-Century England*. Princeton, NJ: Princeton University Press.

Arneson, Richard J. (1987): "Locke Versus Hobbes in Gauthier's Ethics." *Inquiry*, 30, 295–316.

Arrow, Kenneth J. (1973): "Some Ordinalist-Utilitarian Notes on Rawls' Theory of Justice." *Journal of Philosophy*, 70, 245–63.

Arrow, Kenneth J. (1974): *The Limits of Organization*. New York: Norton.

Arrow, Kenneth J. (1978): "A Cautious Case for Socialism." *Dissent*, 25, 472–80.

Ault, David E. and Gilbert L. Rutman (1979): "The Development of Individual Rights to Property in Tribal Africa." *Journal of Law and Economics*, 77, 163–82.

Auster, Richard D. and Morris Silver (1979): *The State as a Firm: Economic Forces in Political Development*. Boston, MA: Martinus Nijhoff.

Averill, James R. (1982): *Anger and Aggression: An Essay on Emotions*. Heidelberg/Berlin: Springer-Verlag.

Baden-Powell, B. H. (1899): *The Origin and Growth of Village Communities in India*. New York: Scribner's Sons.

Baechler, Jean (1980): "Liberty, Property, and Equality." in J. R. Pennock and J. W. Chapman (eds), *Property Nomos XXII*. New York: New York University Press.

Banfield, Edward C. (1974): *The Unheavenly City Revisited*. Boston, MA: Little Brown.

Barash, David P. (1982): *Sociobiology and Behavior*, 2nd edn. New York: Elsevier.

Barnett, Randy E. (1986): "A Consent Theory of Contract." *Columbia Law Review*, 86, 269–321.

Basu, Kaushik (1986): "One Kind of Power." *Oxford Economic Papers*, 38, 259–82.

Baumol, William J. (1982): "Applied Fairness Theory and Rationing Policy." *American Economic Review*, 72, 639–51.

Baumol, William J. (1983a): "Marx and the Iron Law of Wages." *American Economic Review*, 73, 303–8.

Baumol, William J. (1983b): "Applied Fairness Theory: Reply." *American Economic Review*, 73, 1161–2.

Baumol, William J. (1986): *Superfairness: Applications and Theory*, Cambridge, MA: MIT Press.

Beaglehole, Ernest (1932): *Property: A Study in Social Psychology*. New York: Macmillan.

Becker, Lawrence C. (1973): *On Justifying Moral Judgments*. New York: Humanities.

Becker, Lawrence C. (1977): *Property Rights: Philosophic Foundations*, London: Routledge and Kegan Paul.

Beitz, Charles R. (1986): "Review of Amartya Sen, *Resources, Values and Development*." *Economics and Philosophy*, 2, 282–91.

Bentham, Jeremy (1970): *An Introduction to the Principles of Morals and Legislation*, H. L. A. Hart (ed.). London: Athlone.

Benveniste, Emile (1973): *Indo-European Language and Society*, Elizabeth Palmer (trans.). Coral Gables, FL: University of Miami Press.

Berger, Fred (1984): *Happiness, Justice, and Freedom: The Moral and Political Philosophy of John Stuart Mill*. Berkeley, CA: University of California Press.

Berghe, Pierre L. van den (1975): *Man in Society: A Biosocial View*. New York: Elsevier.

Berlev, Oleg D. (1987): "A Social Experiment in Nubia During the Years 9–17 of Sesostris I." In Marvin A. Powell (ed.), *Labor in the Ancient Near East*. New Haven, CT: American Oriental Society, 143–57.

Berns, Walter (1979): "For Capital Punishment." *Harper's*, 15–20 April.

Bishop, Charles A. (1974): *The Northern Ojibwa and the Fur Trade*. Toronto: Holt, Rinehart, and Winston.

Blanshard, Brand (1966): *Reason and Goodness*. London: Allen & Unwin.

Block, Walter (1987): "Trading Money for Silence." In Gerard Radnitzky and Peter Bernholz (eds), *Economic Imperialism: The Economic Approach Applied Outside the Field of Economics*. New York: Paragon House, 157–217.

Blocker, H. Gene and Elizabeth H. Smith (eds) (1980): *John Rawls' Theory of Social Justice: An Introduction*. Athens, OH: Ohio University Press.

Bodenheimer, Edgar (1974): *Jurisprudence: The Philosophy and Method of the Law*, rev. edn. Cambridge MA: Harvard University Press.

Bogart, J. H. (1985): "Lockean Provisos and State of Nature Theories." *Ethics*, 95, 828–36.

Boissonnade, P. (1964): *Life and Work in Medieval France*. New York: Harper & Row.

Bonner, John (1986): *Introduction to the Theory of Social Choice*. Baltimore: Johns Hopkins University Press.

Boulding, Kenneth E. (1973): *The Economy of Love and Fear: A Preface to Grants Economics*. Belmont, CA: Belmont.

Box, Hilary O. (1984): *Primate Behavior and Social Ecology*. London: Chapman & Hall.

Boyd, David J. (1985): "The Commercialisation of Ritual in the Eastern Highlands of Papua New Guinea." *Man*, 20, 325–40.

Brandt, Richard B. (1979): *A Theory of the Good and the Right*. Oxford: Oxford University Press.

Brennan, Geoffrey and James M. Buchanan (1985): *The Reason of Rules: Constitutional Political Economy*. Cambridge: Cambridge University Press.

Brittain, John A. (1978): *Inheritance and the Inequality of Material Wealth*. Washington, DC: The Brookings Institution.

Boadway, Robin W. and Neil Bruce (1984): *Welfare Economics*. Oxford: Blackwell.

Brock, Dan W. (1982): "Utilitarianism and Aiding Others." In H. B. Miller and W. H. Williams (eds), *The Limits of Utilitarianism*. Minneapolis, MN: University of Minnesota Press, 225–41.

Buchanan, Allen E. (1985): *Ethics, Efficiency, and the Market*. Totowa, NJ: Rowman & Allanheld.

Buchanan, Allen E. (1987): "Marx, Morality, and History: An Assessment of Recent Analytical Work on Marx." *Ethics*, 98, 104–36.

Buchanan, James M. (1975): *The Limits of Liberty: Between Anarchy and Leviathan*. Chicago, IL: University of Chicago Press.

Buchanan, James M. (1977): *Freedom in Constitutional Contract: Perspectives of a Political Economist*. College Station: Texas A & M University Press.

Calabresi, Guido and A. Douglas Melamed (1983): "Property Rules, Liability Rules, and Inalienability: One View of the Cathedral." In M. Kuperberg and C. Beitz (eds). *Law, Economics, and Philosophy: A Critical Introduction, with Application to the Law of Torts*. Totowa, NJ: Rowman & Allanheld, 41–80.

Callahan, Joan (1987): "On Harming the Dead." *Ethics*, 97, 341–52.

Campbell, Angus, Philip E. Converse, and Willard L. Rogers (1976): *The Quality of American Life: Perceptions, Evaluations, and Satisfactions*. New York: Russell Sage.

Campbell, Donald T. (1976): "On the Conflicts Between Biological and Social Evolution and Between Psychology and Moral Tradition." *Zygon*, 1, 167–208.

Cantril, Hadley (1965): *The Pattern of Human Concerns*. New Brunswick, NJ: Rutgers University Press.

Cashdan, Elizabeth (1983): "Territoriality Among Human Foragers: Ecological Models and an Application to Four Bushmen Groups." *Current Anthropology*, February, 47–55.

Cashdan, Elizabeth (1986): "Competition Between Foragers and Food-Producers on the Bottletli River, Botswana." *Africa*, 3, 299–318.

Castorina, Camile P. (1980): "Review." *Journal of Economic Literature*, 18, 131–3.

Chatorian, Sandra (1986): "Tort Remedies for Breach of Contract: The Expansion of the Tortious Breach of the Implied Covenant of Good Faith Dealing in the Commercial Realm." *Columbia Law Review*, 86, 377–406.

Cheyne, J. A. (1977): "Communication, Affect, and Social Behavior." In L. Krames P. Plines, and T. Alloway (eds), *Advances in the Study of Communication and Affect*. New York: Plenum, 129–53.

Chomsky, Noam (1980): *Rules and Representations*. New York: Columbia University Press.

Christman, John (1986): "Can Ownership be Justified by Natural Rights." *Philosophy and Public Affairs*, 15, 156–77.

Clark, Robert C. (1985): "Agency Costs Versus Fiduciary Duties." In John W. Pratt and Richard J. Zeckhauser (eds), *Principals and Agents: The Structure of Business*. Boston, MA: Harvard University Press, 55–79.

Cloninger, C. R. and I. I. Gottesman (1987): "Genetic and Environmental Factors in Antisocial Behavior Disorders." In S. A. Mednick, T. E. Moffitt, and S. A. Stack (eds), *The Causes of Crime: New Biological Approaches*. Cambridge: Cambridge University Press.

Coase, Ronald L. (1982): The Problem of Social Cost." *Journal of Law and Economics*, 3, 1–44.

Cohen, G. A. (1978): *Karl Marx's Theory of History*. Princeton, NJ: Princeton University Press.

Cohen, G. A. (1986a): "Peter Mew on Justice and Capitalism." *Inquiry*, 29, 315–23.

Cohen, G. A. (1986b): "Self-Ownership, World-Ownership, and Equality." In Frank S. Lucash (ed.), *Justice and Equality Here and Now*. Ithaca, NY: Cornell University Press, 108–35.

Cohen, Ronald L. (1982): "Perceiving Justice: An Attributional Perspective." In Jerald Greenberg and Ronald L. Cohen (eds), *Equity and Justice in Social Behavior*. New York: Academic Press, 119–60.

Coleman, Jules L. and Jody Kraus (1986): "Rethinking the Theory of Legal Rights." *Yale Law Journal*, 95, 1335–71.

Cooley, Charles H. (1964): *Human Nature and the Social Order*. New York: Scribner.

Coulanges, Numa Denis Fustel de (1980): *The Ancient City*. Baltimore: Johns Hopkins University Press.

Cronon, William (1983): *Changes in the Land: Indians, Colonists, and the Ecology of New England*. New York: Hill and Wang.

Damon, Frederick H. (1980): "The Kula and Generalized Exchange: Considering Some Uncommon Aspects of the Elementary Structures of Kinship." *Man*, 15, 169–92.

Daniels, Norman (ed.) (1975): *Reading Rawls: Critical Studies on Rawls' A Theory of Justice*. New York: Basic Books.

Davis, Michael (1986): "Harm and Retribution." *Philosophy and Public Affairs*, 15, 236–66.

Davis, Michael (1987): "Nozick's Argument *for* the Legitimacy of the

Welfare State." *Ethics*, 97, 576–94.

Dawkins, Richard (1976): *The Selfish Gene*. Oxford: Oxford University Press.

Dawson, John P. (1980): *Gifts and Promises: Continental and American Law Compared*. New Haven, CT: Yale University Press.

Demsetz, Harold (1967): "Towards a Theory of Property Rights." *American Economic Review*, 57, 347–59.

Demsetz, Harold (1979): "Ethics and Efficiency in Property Rights Systems." In Mario J. Rizzo (ed.), *Time, Uncertainty, and Equilibrium*. Lexington, MA: Lexington, 97–116.

Dentan, Robert Knox (1968): *The Semai: A Nonviolent People of Malaya*. New York: Rinehart and Winston.

Denzin, Norman K. (1984): *On Understanding Emotion*. San Francisco, CA: Jossey-Bass.

Dick, Everett (1970): *The Lure of the Land: A Social History of the Public Lands from Articles of Confederation to the New Deal*. Lincoln, NB: University of Nebraska Press.

Diósdi, Gyorgy (1970): *Ownership in Ancient and Preclassical Roman Law*. Budapest: Akadémiai Kiadó.

Donahue, Charles Jr. (1980): "The Future of the Concept of Property Predicted from its Past." In J. R. Pennock and J. W. Chapman (eds), *Property, Nomos XXII*. New York: New York University Press, 26–68.

Dowling, John M. (1968): "Individual Ownership and the Sharing of Game in Hunting Societies." *American Anthropologist*, 70, 502–7.

Duesenbery, James (1967): *Income, Saving, and the Theory of Consumer Behavior*. Cambridge, MA: Harvard University Press.

Durkheim, Emile (1958): *Professional Ethics and Civic Morals*, Cornelia Brostsfield (trans.). Westport, CT: Greenwood.

Durrenberger, E. Paul and Gísli Pálsson (1987): "Ownership at Sea: Fishing Territories and Access to Sea Resources." *American Ethnologist*, 14, 508–22.

Dutton, H. I. (1984): *The Patent System and Inventive Activity During the Industrial Revolution, 1750–1852*. Manchester: Manchester University Press.

Dworkin, Ronald (1977): *Taking Rights Seriously*. Cambridge: Cambridge University Press.

Dworkin, Ronald (1980): "Is Wealth a Value?" *Journal of Legal Studies*, 9, 191–226.

Dworkin, Ronald (1985): *A Matter of Principle*. Cambridge: Cambridge University Press.

Easterlin, Richard A. (1973): "Does Money Buy Happiness." *Public Interest*, 30, 3–10.

Easterlin, Richard (1974): "Does Economic Growth Improve the Human Lot: Some Empirical Evidence." In Paul A. David and Melvin W. Reder (eds). *Nations and Households in Economic Growth*. New York: Academic Press, 89–125.

Eibl-Eibesfeldt, Iraneus (1979): *The Biology of Peace and War: Men, Animals, and Aggression*. New York: Viking.

Ellis, Lee (1986): "Evolution and the Nonlegal Equivalent of Aggressive Criminal Behavior." *Aggressive Behavior*, 12, 57–71.

Elster, Jon (1985): *Making Sense of Marx*. Cambridge: Cambridge University Press.

Epstein, Richard A. (1979): "Possession as the Root of Title." *Georgia Law Review*, 13, 1221–43.

Epstein, Richard A. (1980): "A Taste for Privacy? Evolution and the Emergence of a Naturalistic Ethic." *Journal of Legal Studies*, 9, 665–81.

Epstein, Richard A. (1985): *Takings: Private Property and the Power of Eminent Domain*. Cambridge: Cambridge University Press.

Etzioni, Amitai (1986): "The Case for a Multiple-Utility Conception." *Economics and Philosphy*, 2, 159–83.

Falls, J. Bruce (1977): "Bird Songs and Territorial Behavior." In L. Krames, P. Pliner, and T. Alloway (eds), *Advances in the Study of Communication and Affect*. New York: Plenun 61–89.

Feinberg, Joel (1970): *Doing and Deserving: Essay in the Theory of Responsibility*. Princeton, NJ: Princeton University Press.

Femia, Joseph V. (1985): "Marxism and Radical Democracy." *Inquiry*, 28, 293–319.

Ferguson, Adam (1966): *An Essay on the History of Civil Society*, Duncan Forbes (ed.). Edinburgh: Edinburgh University Press.

Firth, Raymond (1965): *Primitive Polynesian Economy*. London: Routledge and Kegan Paul.

Firth, Raymond (1967): *The Work of the Gods in Tikopia*. London: Athlone Press.

Fischer, Henry George (1961a): "The Nubian Mercenaries of Gebelein During the First Intermediate Period." *Kush*, 9, 44–80.

Fischer, Henry George (1961b): "Notes on the Mo'alla Inscriptions and some Contemporaneous Texts." *Wiener Zeitschrift für die Kunde des Morgenlandes*, 57, 59–77.

Fishbane, Michael (1985): *Biblical Interpretation in Ancient Israel*. Oxford: Oxford University Press.

Forbes, Duncan (1975): *Hume's Philosophical Politics.* Cambridge: Cambridge University Press.

Forde, C. Daryll (1963): *Habitat, Economy, and Society: A Geographic Introduction to Ethnology.* New York: Dutton.

Frank, Robert H. (1985): *Choosing the Right Pond: Human Behavior and the Quest for Status.* New York: Oxford University Press.

Frank, Robert H. (1987): "If *Homo Economicus* Could Choose His Own Utility Function Would He Want One with a Conscience?" *American Economic Review.* 77, 593–604.

Fredlund, Melvin C. (1976): "Wolves, Chimps, and Demsetz." *Economic Inquiry.* 14, 279–90.

Freedman, David Noel (1981): "Temple Without Hands." In A. Biran (ed.), *Temples and High Places in Biblical Times.* Jerusalem: Nelson Glueck School of Biblical Archaeology, 21–9.

Fressola, Anthony (1981): "Liberty and Property: Reflections on the Right of Appropriation in the State of Nature," *American Philosophical Quarterly*, 18, 315–22.

Frey, R. G. (1980): *Interests and Rights: The Case Against Animals*, Oxford: Oxford University Press.

Fried, Charles (1978): *Right and Wrong.* Cambridge, MA: Harvard University Press.

Fried, Charles (1980): "The Laws of Change: The Cunning of Reason in Moral and Legal History." *Journal of Legal Studies*, 9, 335–53.

Fried, Charles (1981): *Contract as Promise: A Theory of Contractual Obligation.* Cambridge, MA: Harvard University Press.

Friedman, Milton (1962): *Capitalism and Freedom.* Chicago, IL: University of Chicago Press.

Galston, William A. (1980): *Justice and the Human Good.* Chicago, IL: University of Chicago Press.

Gardiner, Alan H. (1933): "The Dakhleh Stela." *Journal of Egyptian Archaeology*, 19, 19–30.

Gauthier, David (1982): "On the Refutation of Utilitarianism." In H. B. Miller and W. H. Williams (eds). *The Limits of Utilitarianism.* Minneapolis: University of Minnesola, 145–63.

Gauthier, David (1986): *Morals by Agreement.* Oxford: Oxford University Press.

Gernet, Louis (1981): *The Anthropology of Ancient Greece*, John Hamilton, S. J. and Blaise Nagy (trans.). Baltimore: Johns Hopkins University Press.

Gewirth, Alan (1978): *Reason and Morality.* Chicago, IL: University of

Chicago Press.

Gewirth, Alan (1985): "Economic Justice: Concepts and Criteria." In Kenneth Kipnis and Diana T. Myers (eds), *Economic Justice*. Totowa, NJ: Rowman & Allanheld, 7–32.

Gibbard, Allan (1976): "Natural Property Rights." *Nous*, 10, 77–86.

Gibbard, Allan (1985): "What's Morally Special About Free Exchange?" In E. F. Paul, J. Paul, and F. J. Miller (eds), *Ethics and Economics*. Oxford: Blackwell for the Social Philosophy Center, Bowling Green State University, 20–8.

Gide, Charles and Charles Rist (1913): *A History of Economic Doctrines*, 2nd edn. Boston, MA: Heath.

Glick, Thomas F. (1979): *Islamic and Christian Spain in the Early Middle Ages*. Princeton, NJ: Princeton University Press.

Goetz, Charles J. And Robert E. Scott (1980) "Enforcing Promises: An Examination of the Basis of Contract." *Yale Law Journal*, 89, 1261–1322.

Goldman, Alan H. (1979): *Justice and Reverse Discrimination*. Princeton, NJ: Princeton University Press.

Goldman, Alan H. (1980): "Responses to Rawls from the Political Right." In H. K. Blocker and E. H. Smith (eds.), *Justice. An Introduction*. Athens, OH: Ohio University Press, 431–62.

Goldman, Holly Smith (1980): "Rawls and Utilitarianism." In H. C. Blocker and E. H. Smith (eds), *John Rawls' Theory of Social Justice: An Introduction*. Athens, OH: Ohio University Press, 346–94.

Goldstein, Irwin (1985): "Communication and Mental Events." *American Philosophical Quarterly*, 22, 331–8.

Goodin, Robert E. (1985): *Protecting the Vulnerable: A Reanalysis of Our Social Responsibilities*. Chicago, IL: University of Chicago Press.

Gordon, Scott (1976): "The New Contractarians." *Journal of Political Economy*, 84, 573–90.

Gouldner, Alvin W. (1985): *Against Fragmentation: The Origins of Marxism and the Sociology of the Intellectuals*. New York: Oxford University Press.

Green, Philip (1981): *The Pursuit of Inequality*. New York: Pantheon.

Greenberg, Jerald (1984): "On the Apocryphal Nature of Inequity Distress." In Robert Folger (ed.), *The Sense of Injustice: Social Psychological Perspectives*. New York: Plenum, 167–86.

Greenberg, Martin S. (1980): "A Theory of Indebtedness." In K. J. Gergen, M. P. Greenberg, and R. H. Willis (eds), *Social Exchange: Advances in Theory and Research*. New York: Plenum, 3–26.

Greene, Kenneth V. (1973): "Inheritance Unjustified?" *Journal of Law and Economics*, 16, 417–19.

Gregory, C. A. (1980): "Gifts to Men and Gifts to God: Gift Exchange and Capital Accumulation in Contemporary Papua." *Man*, 15, 626–52.

Griffin, James (1986): *Well-Being: Its Meaning, Measurement, and Moral Importance*. Oxford: Oxford University Press.

Grossman, Lawrence S. (1984): *Peasants, Subsistence Ecology, and Development in the Highlands of Papua New Guinea*. Princeton, NJ: Princeton University Press.

Gutmann, Amy (1980): *Liberal Equality*. Cambridge: Cambridge University Press.

Habermas, Jürgen (1975): *Legitimation Crisis*. Boston, MA: Beacon.

Hägerström, Axel (1953): *Inquiries Into the Nature of Law and Morals*. Stockholm: Almquist and Wiksell.

Hahn, Frank (1982): "On Some Difficulties of the Utilitarian Economist." In A. Sen and B. Williams (eds), *Utilitarianism and Beyond*. Cambridge: Cambridge University Press, 187–98.

Hapgood, Fred (1979): *Why Males Exist: An Inquiry into the Evolution of Sex*. New York: Morrow.

Harako, Reizo (1981): "The Cultural Ecology of Hunting Behavior Among Mbuti Pygmies in the Ituri Forest, Zaire." In R. S. O Harding and C. Teleki (eds), *Omniverous Primates: Gathering and Hunting in Human Evolution*. New York: Columbia University Press, 499–555.

Harding, Robert S. O. (1975): "Meat-Eating and Hunting in Baboons." In Russell H. Tuttle (ed.), *Socioecology and Psychology of Primates*. The Hague: Mouton, 245–57.

Hare, R. M. (1952): *The Language of Morals*, London: Oxford University Press.

Hare, R. M. (1975): "Rawls' Theory of Justice." In N. Daniels (ed.), *Reading Rawls, Critical Studies on Rawls' A Theory of Justice*. New York: Basic Books, 81–107.

Hare, R. M. (1981): *Moral Thinking: Its Levels, Method, and Point*. Oxford: Oxford University Press.

Hare, R. M. (1982): "Utility and Rights: Comment of David Lyons's Essay." In J. R. Pennock and J. W. Chapman (eds.), *Ethics, Economics, and the Law, Nomos XXIV*. New York: New York University Press, 148–57.

Hare, R. M. (1985): "Ontology in Ethics." In Ted Honderich (ed.), *Morality and Objectivity: A Tribute to J. L. Mackie*. London: Routledge and Kegan Paul, 39–53.

Harper-Fender, Ann (1981): "Discouraging the Use of a Common Resource: The Crees of Saskatchewan." *Journal of Economic History*, 41,

163–70.

Harris, Richard J. (1983): "Pinning Down the Equity Formula." In David M. Messick and Karen S. Cook (eds), *Equity Theory: Psychological and Sociological Perspectives.* New York: Praeger, 207–41.

Harsanyi, John C. (1976): *Essays on Ethics, Social Behavior, and Scientific Explanation.* Dordrecht: Reidel.

Harsanyi, John C. (1977): *Rational Behavior and Bargaining Equilibrium in Games and Social Situations.* Cambridge: Cambridge University Press.

Harsanyi, John C. (1982): "Morality and the Theory of Rational Behavior." In A. Sen and B. Williams (eds.), *Utilitarianism and Beyond.* Cambridge: Cambridge University Press, 39–62.

Harsanyi, John C. (1985a): "Does Reason Tell Us What Moral Code To Follow and Indeed, to Follow Any Moral Code at All?" *Ethico,* 96, 42–55.

Harsanyi, John C. (1985b): "Rule Utilitarianism, Equality, and Justice." In E. F. Paul, J. Paul and F. J. Miller Jr. (eds), *Ethics and Economics.* Oxford: Blackwell for the Social Philosophy Center, Bowling Green State University, 115–27.

Harsanyi, John C. (1987): 'Review of *Morals by Agreement,* David Gauthier." *Economics and Philosophy,* 3, 339–51.

Hart, John A. (1978): "From Subsistence to Market: A Case Study of the Mbuti Net Hunters." *Human Ecology,* 6, 325–53.

Hatch, Elvin (1983): *Culture and Morality: The Relativity of Values in Anthropology.* New York: Columbia University Press.

Hawkins, J. D. and A. Morpurgo-Davies (1982): "Buying and Selling in Hieroglyphic Luwian." In Johann Tischler (ed.), *Serta Indogermanica.* Innsbruck: Institut für Sprachwissenschaft der Universität Innsbruck, 91–105.

Hayek, F. A. (1960): *The Constitution of Liberty.* Chicago, IL: University of Chicago Press.

Hazard, Geoffrey C. Jr. (1965): "Rationing Justice." *Journal of Law and Economics,* 8, 1–10.

Hegel, G. F. (1942): *Philosophy of Right.* London: Oxford University Press.

Herlihy, D. (1960): "The Carolingian Mansus." *Economic History Review,* 13, 79–89.

Herskovits, Melville J. (1952): *Economic Anthropology: The Economic Life of Primitive People.* New York: Norton.

Herzog, Don (1985): *Without Foundations: Justification in Political Theory.* Ithaca, NY: Cornell University Press.

Hirshleifer, Jack (1977): "Economics from a Biological Viewpoint."

Journal of Law and Economics, 20, 1–52.

Hirshleifer, Jack (1978): "Natural Economy Versus Political Economy." *Journal of Social and Biological Structures*, 1, 319–37.

Hirshleifer, Jack (1985) "The Expanding Domain of Economics." *American Economic Review*, 75, December, 53–68.

Hobbes, Thomas (1962): *Leviathan: Or the Matter, Form, and Power of a Commonwealth Ecclesiastical and Civil*, Michael Oakeshott (ed.), Richard S. Peters (introd.), London: Macmillan.

Hoebel, E. Adamson (1961): *The Law of Primitive Man: A Study in Comparative Legal Dynamics*. Cambridge, MA: Harvard University Press.

Hoekema, David A. (1986): *Rights and Wrongs: Coercion, Punishment and the State*. Cronburg, NJ: Associated University Presses.

Hogan, Robert and Nicholas P. Emler (1981): "Retributive Justice." In Melvin J. Lerner and Sally C. Lerner (eds). *The Justice Motive in Social Behavior: Adapting to Times of Scarcity and Change*. New York: Plenum, 125–43.

Hohfeld, Wesley Newcomb (1919): *Fundamental Legal Conceptions*. New Haven, CT: Yale University Press.

Holcombe Randall C. (1983): "Applied Fairness Theory: Comment." *American Economic Review*, 73, 1153–6.

Holmberg, Allan R. (1969): *Nomads of the Long Bow: The Siriono of Eastern Bolivia*. Garden City, NY: Natural History Press.

Hudson, W. D. (1967): *Ethical Intuitionism*. London: Macmillan.

Hudson, W. D. (1970): *Modern Moral Philosophy*. Garden City, NY: Doubleday.

Hudson, W. D. (1980): *A Century of Moral Philosophy*. New York: St Martin's Press.

Hume, David (1948): *Hume's Moral and Political Philosophy*, Henry D. Aiken (ed.). New York: Hafner.

Husami, Ziyad I. (1978): "Marx on Distributive Justice." *Philosophy and Public Affairs*, 8, 27–64.

Inglehart, Ronald (1977): *The Silent Revolution: Changing Values and Political Styles Among Western Publics*. Princeton, NJ: Princeton University Press.

Ingold, Tim (1980): *Hunters, Pastoralists, and Ranchers: Reindeer Economies and Their Transformations*. Cambridge: Cambridge University Press.

Ingold, Tim (1987): *The Appropriation of Nature: Essays on Human Ecology and Social Relations*. Iowa City, IA: University of Iowa Press.

Irani, K. D. (1981): "Values and Rights Underlying Social Justice." In R. L. Braham (ed.), *Social Justice*. Boston, MA: Martinus Nijhoff,

29–44.

Irani, K. D. (1983): "Understanding Emotions." In K. D. Irani and G. E. Myers (eds), *Emotion: Philosophical Studies*. New York: Haven, 1–18.

Isaac, Glynn Ll. (1978): "Food-Sharing and Human Evolution: Archaeological Evidence from the Plio-Pleistocene of East Africa." *Journal of Anthropological Research*, 34, 311–25.

Isaac, Glynn Ll. (1983): "Aspects of Human Evolution." In D. S. Bendall (ed.), *Evolution: From Molecules to Men*. Cambridge: Cambridge University Press, 509–43.

Isaac, Glynn Ll. and Diana C. Crader (1981): "To What Extent Were Early Hominids Carnivorous?: An Archaeological Perspective." In R. S. O. Harding and G. Teleki (eds), *Omniverous Primates: Gathering and Hunting in Human Evolution*. New York: Columbia University Press.

Jennings, Francis (1984): *The Ambiguous Iroquois Empire*. New York: Norton.

Kant, Immanuel (1952): *The Science of Right*. Chicago, IL: Encyclopaedia Brittanica, 395–458.

Kapteyn, Arie, Bernard M. S. Van Praag, and Floor G. Van Herwaarden (1978): "Individual Welfare Functions and Social Reference Spaces." *Economics Letters*, 1, 173–7.

Kirzner, Israel M. (1979): *Perception, Opportunity, and Profit*. Chicago, IL: University of Chicago Press.

Klevorick, Alvin K. (1985): "Legal Theory and the Economic Analysis of Torts and Crimes." *Columbia Law Review*, 85, 905–20.

Klopfer, Peter H. (1969): *Habitats and Territories: A Study of the Use of Space by Animals*. New York: Basic Books.

Kluegel, James R. and Eliot R. Smith (1986): *Beliefs About Inequality: American's View of What Is and What Ought to Be*. New York: de Gruyter.

Krebs, J. R. and N. B. Davies (1981): *An Introduction to Behavioral Ecology*. Sunderland, MA: Sinauer Associates.

Kronman, Anthony T. (1980a): "Wealth Maximization as a Normative Value." *Journal of Legal Studies*, 9, 227–42.

Kronman, Anthony T. (1980b): "Contract Law and Distributive Justice." *Yale Law Journal*, 89, 472–511.

Kronman, Anthony T. (1981): "Talent Pooling." In J. R. Pennock and J. W. Chapman (eds), *Human Rights, Nomos XXIII*. New York: New York University Press, 58–79.

Kumar, Dharma (1985): "Private Property in Asia? The Case of Medieval South India." *Comparative Studies in Society and History*, 27, 340–66.

Kummer, H. (1973): "Dominance Versus Possession: An Experiment on Hamadryas Baboons." In E. W. Menzel Jr. (ed.), *Precultural Primate Behavior*, Basel: Karger, 226–31.

Kummer, H. (1980): "Analogs of Morality Among Nonhuman Primates." In Gunther S. Stent (ed.), *Morality as a Biological Phenomenon*, rev. edn, Berkeley, CA: University of California Press, 31–47.

Kurland, Jeffrey A. and Stephen J. Beckerman (1985): "Optimal Foraging and Hominid Evolution: Labor and Reciprocity." *American Anthropologist*, 87, 73–93.

Lawick-Goodall, Jane van (1971): *In the Shadow of Man*. Boston, MA: Houghton Mifflin.

Layard, P. R. C. and A. A. Walters (1978): *Microeconomic Theory*, New York: McGraw-Hill.

Layard, R. (1980): "Human Satisfactions and Public Policy." *Economic Journal*, 90, 737–50.

Lemos, Ramon M. (1986): *Rights, Goods, and Democracy*, Newark, DE: University of Delaware Press.

Lerner, Melvin J. (1977): "The Justice Motive: Some Hypotheses as to its Origins and Forms." *Journal of Personality*, 4, 1–52.

Letourneau, Charles (1900): *Property: Its Origin and Development*, New York: Scribner's Sons.

Leventhal, Gerald S. (1980): "What Should Be Done with Equity Theory." In K. I. Gergen, M. S. Greenberg, and R. H. Willis (eds), *Social Exchange: Advances in Theory and Research*, 27–55.

Levy, Ernst (1951): *West German Vulgar Law: The Law of Property*. Philadelphia, PA American Philosophical Society.

Levy, Robert I. (1984): "Emotion, Knowing, and Culture." In Richard A. Shweder and Robert A. Levine (eds). *Culture Theory: Essays on Mind. Self, and Emotion*. Cambridge: Cambridge University Press, 214–37.

Lindert, Peter H. and Jeffrey G. Williamson (1983): "English Workers' Living Standards During the Industrial Revolution: A New Look." *Economic History Review*, 36, 1–25.

Linton, Ralph (1933): *The Tanala: A Hill Tribe of Madâgascar*. Chicago, IL: Field Museum of Natural History.

Linton, Ralph (1952): "Universal Ethical Principles: An Anthropological View." In Ruth Nanda Anshen (ed.), *Moral Principles in Action*. New York: Harper & Row, 645–60.

Locke, John (1952): *The Second Treatise of Government*, Thomas P. Reardon (ed.). Indianapolis, IN: Bobbs-Merill.

Locke, John (1959): *An Essay Concerning Human Understanding*, Alexander Campbell (ed.). New York: Fraser.

Lomasky, Loren E. (1987): *Persons, Rights, and the Moral Community*. New York: Oxford University Press.

Lorenz, Konrad (1987): *The Waning of Humaneness*, Robert Warren Kickert (trans.). Boston, MA: Little, Brown.

Lowie, Robert H. (1920): *Primitive Socity*. New York: Harper.

Lukes, Steven (1985): *Marxism and Morality*, Oxford University Press.

Lumsden, Charles J. and Edward O. Wilson (1983): *Promethean Fire: Reflections on the Origins of Mind*. Cambridge: Cambridge University Press.

Lyons, David (1975): "Nature and Soundness of the Contract and Coherence Arguments." In N. Daniels, *Reading Rawls; Critical Studies on Rawls' A Theory of Justice*. New York: Basic Books, 141–67.

Lyons, David (1982): "Utility and Rights" In J. R. Pennock and J. W. Chapman, (eds). *Ethics, Economics, and the Law:* Nomos XXIV. New York: New York University Press, 107–38.

Lyons, William (1980): *Emotion*. Cambridge: Cambridge University Press.

McCloskey, Herbert and John Zaller (1984): *The American Ethos: Public Attitudes Toward Capitalism and Democracy*, Cambridge, MA: Harvard University Press for the Twentieth Century Fund.

McDowell, John (1985): "Values and Secondary Qualities." In T. Honderich (ed.), *Morality and Objectivity; A Tribute to J. L. Mackie*. London: Routledge & Kegan Paul, 110–29.

Macfarlane, Alan (1987): *The Culture of Capitalism*. Oxford: Blackwell.

McGinn, Colin (1979): "Evolution, Animals, and the Basis of Morality," *Inquiry*, 22, 81–99.

McGinn, Colin (183): *The Subjective View: Secondary Qualities and Indexical Thoughts*, Oxford: Oxford University Press.

Mackie, J. L. (1977): *Ethics: Inventing Right and Wrong*, New York: Penguin.

McMurtry, John (1978): *The Structure of Marx's World View*. Princeton, NJ: Princeton University Press.

Macpherson, C. B. (1962): *The Political Economy of Possessive Individualism: Hobbes to Locke*, London: Oxford University Press.

Macpherson, C. B. (1978): "Liberal-Democracy and Property." In C. B. Macpherson (ed.), *Property: Mainstream and Critical Positions*. Toronto: University of Toronto Press, 199–207.

McShea, Robert J. (1978): "Biology and Ethics." *Ethics*, 88, 139–49.

McShea, Robert J. (1979): "Human Nature and Ethical Theory." *Philosophy and Phenomenological Research*, 39, 386–401.

Maher, Gerry (1986): "Natural Justice as Fairness." In Neil MacCormick and Peter Birks (eds), *The Legal Mind*. Oxford: Oxford University Press, 103–20.

Malul, Meir (1985): "The *bukannum*-Clause-Relinquishment of Rights by Previous Right Holder," *Zeitschrift für Assyriologie und Vorderasiatische Archaologie*, 75, 66–77.

Marshall, Lorna (1976): *The !Kung of Nyae Nyae*. Cambridge, MA: Harvard University Press.

Martin, Calvin (1978): *Keepers of the Game: Indian-Animal Relationships and the Fur Trade*. Berkeley, CA: University of Calfornia Press.

Marx, Karl (1965): *Pre-Capitalist Economic Formations*, E. J. Hobsbawn (ed. and introd.), Jack Cohen (trans.). New York: International Publishers.

Mednick, Sarnoff A., William F. Gabrielli Jr., and Barry Hutchings (1987): "Genetic Factors in the Etiology of Criminal Behavior." In S. A. Mednick, T. E. Moffitt, and S. A. Stack (eds), *The Causes of Crime: New Biological Approaches*. Cambridge: Cambridge University Press, 74–91.

Melden, A. I. (1977): *Rights and Persons*. Berkeley, CA: University of California Press.

Mercuro, Nicholas and Timothy P. Ryan (1984): *Law, Economics, and Public Policy*. Greenwich, CT: JAI Press.

Midgley, Mary (1979): *Beast and Man: The Roots of Human Nature*. Ithaca, NY: Cornell University Press.

Mill, John Stuart (1951): "Utilitarianism." In A. D. Lindsay (introd.), *Utilitarianism, Liberty, and Representative Government*. New York: Dutton, 1–80.

Mill, John Stuart (1965): *Principles of Political Economy: With Some of Their Applications to Social Philosophy*, John M. Robson (ed.). Toronto: University of Toronto Press.

Miller, Jeanine (1985): *The Vision of the Cosmic Order in the Vedas*. London: Routledge & Kegan Paul.

Miller, Richard W. (1981): "Rights and Reality." *Philosophical Review*, 90, 383–407.

Minogue, Kenneth (1985): *Alien Powers: The Pure Theory of Ideology*. New York: St, Martin's Press.

Mirrlees, J. A. (1982): "The Economic Uses of Utilitarianism." In A. Sen and B. Williams (eds), *Utilitarianism and Beyond*. Cambridge, UK:

Cambridge University Press, 63–84.

Mishan, E. J. (1977): *The Economic Growth Debate: An Assessment*. London: Allen & Unwin.

Mishan, E. J. (1981): *Introduction to Normative Economics*. New York: Oxford University Press.

Moore, Barrington Jr. (1978): *Injustice: The Social Bases of Obedience and Revolt*. White Plains, NY: Sharpe.

Moore, G. E. (1965): *Ethics*. New York: Oxford University Press.

Mueller, Dennis C. (1986): "Rational Egoism Versus Adaptive Egoism as Fundamental Postualates for a Descriptive Theory of Human Behavior." *Public Choice*, 51, 3–23.

Muffs, Yochanan (1969): *Studies in the Aramaic Legal Papyri from Elephantine*. Leiden: Brill.

Mumy, Gene E. (1987): "What Does Nozick's Minimal State Do?" *Economics and Philosophy*, 3, 275–305.

Myrdal, Gunnar (1961): *The Political Element in the Development of Economic Theory*. Cambridge, MA: Harvard University Press.

Nader, Ralph, Mark Green, and Joel Seligman (1976): *Constitutionalizing the Corporation: The Case for Federal Chartering of Giant Corporations*. Washington, DC: Corporate Accountability Research Group.

Nagel, Thomas (1975): "Libertarianism Without Foundations." *Yale Law Journal*, 85, 136–49.

Nagel, Thomas (1979): *Mortal Questions*. London: Cambridge University Press.

Neale, Walter C. (1985): "Property in Land as Cultural Imperialism: or, Why Ethocentrical Ideas Won't Work in India and Afica." *Journal of Economic Issues*, 19, 951–8.

Newcomb, Simon (1886): *Principles of Political Economy*. New York: Harper.

Ng, Yew-Kwang (1978): "Economic Growth and Social Welfare: The Need for a Complete Study of Happiness." *Kyklos*, Fasc. 4, 575–87.

Nielson, Kai (1982): "Capitalism, Socialism, and Justice." In Tom Regan and Donald Van Veer (eds), *And Justice for All*. Totowa, NJ: Rowan and Allenheld, 264–86.

Norton, David L. (1977): "Individualism and Productive Justice." *Ethics*, 87, 113–25.

Nozick, Robert (1974): *Anarchy, State, and Utopia*. New York: Basic Books.

O'Driscoll, Gerald P. Jr. (1980): "Justice, Efficiency, and the Economic Analysis of Law: A Comment on Fried." *Journal of Legal Studies*, 9, 355–66.

Okun, Arthur M. (1975): *Equality and Efficiency: The Big Tradeoff.* Washington, DC: Brookings Institution.

Olivecrona, Karl (1971): *Law as Fact,* 2nd. edn. London: Stevens.

Olivecrona, Karl (1974): "Locke's Theory of Appropriation." *Philosophical Quarterly,* 24, 220–34.

Otsuki, Mikiro (1980): "On Distribution According to Labour–A Concept of Fairness." *Review of Economic Studies,* 47, 945–58.

Painter, Sidney (1951): *The Rise of the Feudal Monarchy.* Ithaca, NY: Cornell University Press.

Palmer, L. R. (1963): *The Interpretation of Mycenaean Greek Texts.* London: Oxford University Press.

Parringham, R. E. (1982): *The Human Primate.* Oxford: Freeman.

Parry, Jonathan (1986): *"The Gift,* The Indian Gift and The 'Indian Gift'. " *Man,* 21, 453–73.

Partridge, Ernest (1981): "Posthumous Interests and Posthumous Respect." *Ethics,* 91, 243–64.

Paul, Ellen Frankel (1987): *Property Rights and Eminent Domain.* New Brunswick, NJ: Transaction Books.

Paul, Shalom M. (1969): "Sargon's Administrative Diction in II Kings 17:27." *Journal of Biblical Literature,* 88, 73–4.

Pazner, Elisha A. and David Schmeidler (1972): "Decentralization and the Role of Money in Socialist Economies." *Technical Report no. 8,* Institute of Economic Research, Tel Aviv University, September.

Pazner, Elisha and David Schmeidler (1974): "A Difficulty in the Concept of Fairness". *Review of Economic Studies,* 41, 441–3.

Perlman, Harvey S. (1982): "Interference with Contract and Other Economic Expectancies: A Clash of Tort and Contract Doctrine." *University of Chicago Law Review,* 49, 61–129.

Phelps, Edmund S. (1973): "Introduction" in Phelps (ed.), *Economic Justice.* Harmondsworth: Penguin, pp. 9–31.

Phillips, Derek L. (1979): *Equality, Justice and Rectification: An Exploration in Normative Sociology.* London: Academic Press.

Phillips, Derek L. (1986): *Toward a Just Social Order.* Princeton, NJ: Princeton University Press.

Plutchik, Robert (1980): "A General Psychoevolutionary Theory of Emotion." In Robert Plutchik and Henry Kellerman (eds.), *Emotion: Theory, Research, and Experience,* Vol. I. New York: Academic Press 3–33.

Plutchik, Robert (1983): "Emotions in Early Development: A Psychoevolutionary Approach." In Robert Plutchik and Henry Kellerman (eds.), *Emotion: Theory, Research, and Experience,* Vol. II. New York:

Academic Press, 221–57.

Pollock, John L. (1986): "A Theory of Moral Reasoning." *Ethics*, 96, pp. 506–23.

Polotsky, Hans Jakob (1930): "The Stela of Heka-Yeb." *Journal of Egyptian Archaeology*, 16, pp. 194–9.

Posner, Richard A. (1979): "Utilitarianism, Economics, and Legal Theory." *Journal of Legal Studies*, pp. 119–21.

Posner, Richard A. (1981): *The Economics of Justice*. Cambridge, MA: Harvard University Press.

Posner, Richard A. (1985): "An Economic Theory of the Criminal Law." *Columbia Law Review*, 85, pp. 1193–231.

Pospisil, Leopold (1963): *Kapauku Papuan Economy*. New Haven, CT: Department of Anthropology, Yale University.

Potts, Richard (1984): "Home Bases and Early Hominids." *American Scientist*, 72, 338–47.

Pryor, Frederic L. (1981): "A Survey of the Economic Systems of Wild Chimpanzees and Baboons." *Journal of Economic Issues*, 15, 33–59.

Pugh, George Edgin (1977): *The Biological Origin of Human Values*. New York: Basic Books.

Puhvel, Jaan (1987): *Comparative Mythology*. Baltimore: Johns Hopkins University Press.

Rawls, John (1971): *A Theory of Justice*. Cambridge, MA: Harvard University Press.

Rawls, John (1980): "Representation of Freedom and Equality." *Journal of Philosophy*, 77, 535–59.

Raz, Joseph (1986): *The Morality of Freedom*. Oxford: Oxford University Press.

Reeve, Andrew (1986): *Property*. Atlantic Highlands, NJ: Humanities Press International.

Reid, John Phillip (1970): *A Law of Blood: The Primitive Law of the Cherokee Nation*. New York: New York University Press.

Reiman, Jeffrey (1981): "The Fallacy of Libertarian Capitalism." *Ethics*, 92, 85–95.

Reimer, John E. (1982): "Exploitation, Alternatives, and Socialism." *Economic Journal*, 92, 87–107.

Renteln, Alison Dundes (1988): "Relativism and the Search for Human Rights." *American Anthropologist*, 90, 56–72.

Rescher, Nicholas (1972): *Welfare*. Pittsburgh, PA: University of Pittsburgh Press.

Roemer, John E. (1982): "Exploitation, Alternatives, and Socialism." *Economic Journal*, 92, 87–107.

Rose, Carol M. (1985): "Possession as the Origin of Property." *University of Chicago Law Review*, 52, 73–88.

Rowley, Charles and Alan T. Peacock (1975): *Welfare Economics: A Liberal Restatement.* New York: Wiley.

Runciman, W. C. (1978): "Processes, End-States, and Social Justice." *Philosophical Quarterly*, 28, 37–45.

Ruse, Michael (1986): "Evolutionary Ethics: A Phoenix Arisen." *Zygon*, 21, 95–112.

Ruse, Michael and Edward O. Wilson (1986): "Moral Philosophy as Applied Science." *Philosophy*, 61, 173–92.

Ryan, Alan (1983): "Property, Liberty, and *On Liberty*." In A. Phillips Griffiths (ed.), *Of Liberty: Royal Institute of Philosophy Lecture Series: Supplement of Philosophy*, 1983. Cambridge: Cambridge University Press, 217–31.

Samuelson, Paul A. (1957): "Intertemporal Price Equilibrium: A Prologue to the Theory of Speculation." *Weltwirtschaftliches Archiv*, 79, 181–221.

Samuelson, Paul A. (1985): "Modes of Thought in Economics and Biology." *American Economic Review*, 75, 166–72.

Sandel, Michael J. (1982): *Liberalism and the Limits of Justice.* Cambridge: Cambridge University Press.

Santos Granero, Fernando (1986): "Power, Ideology and the Ritual of Production in Lowland South America." *Man*, 21, 657–79.

Scanlon, T. M. (1982): "Contractualism and Utilitarianism." In A. Sen and B. Williams (eds), *Utilitarianism and Beyond*. Cambridge: Cambridge University Press, 103–20.

Schilcher, Florian von and Neil Tennant (1984): *Philosophy, Evolution, and Human Nature.* London: Routledge & Kegan Paul.

Schmid, A. Allan (1978): *Property, Power, and Public Choice: An Inquiry Into Law and Economics.* New York: Praeger.

Schneider, Harold K. (1979): *Livestock and Equality in East Africa: The Economic Basis for Social Structure.* Bloomington, IN: Indiana University Press.

Schotter, Andrew (1985): *Free Market Economics: A Critical Appraisal.* New York: St Martin's Press.

Scitovsky, Tibor (1976): *The Joyless Economy.* New York: Oxford University Press.

Scott, James C. (1976): *The Moral Economy of the Peasant.* New Haven, CT: Yale University Press.

Scott, John Paul (1958): *Aggression.* Chicago, IL: University of Chicago Press.

Selbourne, David (1984): *Against Socialist Illusion: A Radical Argument.* New York: Schocken.

Sen, Amartya (1970): "The Impossibility of a Paretian Liberal." *Journal of Political Economy*, 78, 152–7.

Sen, Amartya (1982a): *Choice, Welfare, and Measurement.* Cambridge, MA: MIT Press.

Sen, Amartya (1982b): "Rights and Agency." *Philosophy and Public Affairs*, 11, 1–39.

Sen Amartya (1984a): "Ethical Issues in Income Distribution: National and International." In Amartya Sen, *Resources, Values, and Development.* Cambridge, MN: Harvard University Press, 277–306.

Sen, Amartya (1984b): "Rights and Capabilities." In T. Honderich (ed.), *Morality and Objectivity: A Tribute to J. L. Mackie.* London: Routledge & Kegan Paul, 130–44.

Sen, Amartya (1985a): "Well-being, Agency, and Freedom: The Dewey Lectures, 1984." *Journal of Philosophy*, 82, 169–221.

Sen, Amartya (1985b): "The Moral Standing of the Market." In E. F. Paul, J. Paul, and F. J. Miller Jr. (eds), Ethics and Economics, Oxford: Blackwell for the Social Philosophy Center, Bowling Green State University.

Sen, Amartya (1985c): *Commodities and Capabilities.* Amsterdam: North-Holland.

Sen, Amartya (1987): *On Ethics and Economics*, Oxford: Blackwell.

Sencerz, Stefan (1986): "Moral Intuitions and Justification in Ethics." *Philosophical Studies*, 50, 79–95.

Service, Elman R. (1979): *The Hunters*, 2nd. edn. Englewood Cliffs, NJ: Prentice-Hall.

Sher, George (1979): "Effort, Ability, and Personal Desert." *Philosophy and Public Affairs*, 8, 361–96.

Silver, Morris (1980): *Affluence, Altruism, and Atrophy: The Decline of Welfare States*, New York: New York University Press.

Silver, Morris (1981): "Men, Monkeys, and Morals: A Property Rights Theory of Social Justice." In R. L. Braham (ed.), *Social Justice.* Boston, MA: Martinus Nijhoff, 121–44.

Silver, Morris (1983): *Prophets and Markets: The Political Economy of Ancient Israel.* Boston, MA: Kluwer-Nijhoff.

Silver, Morris (1984): "Marxian Surplus Value, Enforcement, and Entrepreneurship." In Morris Silver, *Enterprise and the Scope of the Firm: The Role of Vertical Integration.* Oxford: Blackwell/Robertson, 139–46.

Silver, Morris (1985): *Economic Structures of the Ancient Near East.* Beckenham: Croom Helm.

Simpson, A. W. B. (1961): *An Introduction to the History of Land Law*. London: Oxford University Press.

Singer, Peter (1981): *The Expanding Circle: Ethics and Sociobiology*. New York: Farrar, Strauss, and Giroux.

Sinha, D. P. (1972): "The Birhors." In M. G. Bicchieri (ed.), *Hunters and Gatherers Today*. New York: Holt, Rinehart, and Winston, 371–403.

Slote, Michael A. (1977): "The Morality of Wealth." In William Aiken and Hugh LaFollette (eds), *World Hunger and Moral Obligation*. Englewood Cliffs, NJ: Prentice-Hall, 134–47.

Slote, Michael (1985): "Utilitarianism, Moral Dilemmas, and Moral Cost." *American Philosophic Quarterly*, 22, 161–8.

Smith, Adam (1976): *An Inquiry into the Nature and Causes of the Wealth of Nations*, Edwin Cannan (ed.). Chicago, IL: University of Chicago Press.

Smith, W. Robertson (1956): *The Religion of the Semites*. New York: Macmillan.

Solomon, Robert C. (1976): *The Passions*. Garden City, NY: Doubleday.

Sperry, Roger (1983): *Science and Moral Priority: Merging Mind, Brain, and Human Values*. New York: Columbia University Press.

Steiner, Hillel (1977): "The Natural Right to the Means of Production." *Philosophical Quarterly*, 27, 48–54.

Stevenson, Charles L. (1944): *Ethics and Language*. New Haven, CT: Yale University Press.

Strawson, P. F. (1974): *Freedom and Resentment and Other Essays*. London: Macmillan.

Strongman, K. T. (1978): *The Psychology of Emotion*, 2nd edn. New York: Wiley.

Sugden, Robert (1986): *The Economics of Rights, Co-operation and Welfare*. Oxford: Blackwell.

Sumner, L. W. (1981): "Rights Denaturalized." In R. G. Frey (ed.), *Utility and Rights*. Minneapolis, MN: University of Minnesota Press, 20–41.

Suzumura, Kotaro (1983): *Rational Choice, Collective Decisions, and Social Welfare*. Cambridge: Cambrdige University Press.

Tanner, Nancy Makepiece (1981): *On Becoming Human: A Model of the Transition from Ape to Human and the Reconstruction of Early Human Social Life*. Cambridge: Cambridge University Press.

Tapper, Richard (1979): *Pasture and Politics: Economics, Conflict, and Ritual Among Shahsevan Nomads of Northwestern Iran*. London: Academic Press.

Teleki, Geza (1973): *The Predatory Behavior of Wild Chimpanzees*, Lewisburg, PA: Bucknell University Press.

Teleki, Geza (1975): "Primate Subsistence Patterns: Collector-Predators and Gatherer-Hunters." *Journal of Human Evolution*, 4, 125–84.

Teleki, Geza (1981): "The Omnivorous Diet and Eclectic Feeding Habits of Chimpanzees in Gombe National Park, Tanzania." In R. S. O. Harding and G. Teleki (eds.), *Omnivorous Primates: Gathering and Hunting in Human Evolution.* New York: Columbia University Press, 303–43.

Tennant, Neil (1983): "Evolutionary v. Evolved Ethica." *Philosophy*, 58, 289–302.

Testart, Alan (1987): "Game-Sharing Systems and Kinship Systems Among Hunter-Gatherers." *Man*, 22, 287–304.

Thistle, Paul C. (1986): *Indian-European Trade Relations in the Lower Saskatchewan River Region to 1840.* Winnipeg: University of Manitoba Press.

Thomson, Judith Jarvis (1973): "Preferential Hiring." *Philosophy and Public Affairs*, 2, 364–84.

Thomson, Judith Jarvis (1986a): "The Right to Privacy." In J. J. Thomson, *Rights, Restitution, and Risk: Essays in Moral Theory.* Cambridge, MA Harvard University Press, 116–34.

Thomson, Judith Jarvis (1986b): *Rights, Restitution, and Risk: Essays in Moral Theory.* Cambridge, MA: Harvard University Press.

Thorp, John (1980): *Free Will: A Defence Against Neurophysiological Determinism.* London: Routledge and Kegan Paul.

Thurow, Lester (1973): "Towards a Definition of Economic Justice." *Public Interest*, 31, 56–80.

Thurow, Lester (1975): *Generating Inequality: Mechanisms of Distribution in the U. S. Economy.* New York: Basic Books.

Tiger, Lionel (1975): "Somatic Factors and Social Behaviors." In Robin Fox (ed.), *Biosocial Anthropology.* London: Malaby, 115–32.

Timmons, Mark (1987): "Foundationalism and the Structure of Ethical Justification." *Ethics*, 97, 595–609.

Tinbergen, Jan (1978): "Equitable Distribution: Definition, Measurement, Feasibility." In Wilhelm Krelle and Anthony F. Shorroches (eds.), *Personal Income Distribution.* Amsterdam: North-Holland, 35–50.

Torii, M. (1975): "Possession by Non-Human Primates." In S. Kondo et al (eds.), *Contemporary Primatology.* Basel: Karger, 310–14.

Tribe, Lawrence H. (1985): "Compensation, Contract, and Capital: Preserving the Distribution of Wealth." In Lawrence H. Tribe, *Constitutional Choices.* Cambridge, MA: Harvard University Press, 165–87.

Trivers, R. L. (1985): *Social Evolution*. Menlo Park, CA: Cummings.

Tullock, Gordon (1971): "Inheritance Justified." *Journal of Law and Economics*, 14, 465–74.

Turnbull, Colin M. (1972): *The Mountain People*. New York: Simon and Shuster.

Umbeck, John (1981): "Might Makes Rights: A Theory of the Formation and Initial Distribution of Property Rights." *Economic Inquiry*, 19, 37–59.

Unger, Roberto Mangabeira (1986): *The Critical Legal Studies Movement*. Cambridge, MA: Harvard University Press.

Urmson, J. O. (1986): *The Emotive Theory of Ethics*. London: Hutchinson University Library.

Van Praag, Bernard M. S. (1976): "The Individual Welfare Function of Income and its Offspring." In J. S. Cramer *et al* (eds), *Relevance and Precision*. Sansom: North-Holland, 263–93.

Van de Veer, Donald (1973): "Marx's View of Justice." *Philosophy and Phenomenological Research*, 33, 366–86.

Varian, Hal R. (1974): "Equity, Envy, and Efficiency." *Journal of Economic Theory*, 9, 63–91.

Varian, Hal R. (1978): *Microeconomic Analysis*. New York: Norton.

Varian, Hal R. (1985): "Dworkin on Equality of Resources." *Economics and Philosophy*, 1, 110–25.

Vernant, Jean Pierre (1983): *Myth and Thought Among the Greeks*. London: Routledge & Kegan Paul.

Vinogradoff, Paul (1929): *Roman Law in Medieval Europe*, 2nd edn. London: Oxford University Press.

Walster, Elaine, C. William Walster, and Ellen Berscheid (1978): *Equity: Theory and Research*. Boston, MA: Allyn and Bacon.

Ward, Harry M. (1975): *Statism in Plymouth Colony*. Port Washington, New York: Kennjkat Press.

Watkins, Calvert (1970): "Studies in Indo-European Legal Language, Institutions, and Mythology." in George Cardona, Henry M. Hoenigswald, and Alfred Senn (eds), *Indo-European and Indo-Europeans*. Philadelphia, PA: University of Pennsylvania Press, 321–54.

Weldon, Jeremy (1983): "Two Worries about Mixing One's Labour." *Philosophical Quarterly*, 33, 37–44.

Wellman, Carl (1961): *The Language of Ethics*. Cambridge, MA: Harvard University Press.

Wellman, Carl (1985): *A Theory of Rights: Persons Under Laws, Institutions, and Morals*. Totowa, NJ: Rowman & Allanheld.

Wesson, Robert C. (1976): *Why Marxism? The Continuing Success of a Failed Theory*. New York: Basic Books.

Westermarck, Edward (1926): *The Origin and Development of the Moral Ideas*. 2nd. edn. London: Macmillan.

Westermarck, Edward (1932): *Ethical Relativity*. New York: Harcourt, Brace.

White, Richard (1983): *The Roots of Dependency: Subsistence, Environment, and Social Change among the choctaws, Pawnees, and Navajos*. Lincoln, NB: University of Nebraska Press.

Wierzbicka, Anna (1986): 'Human Emotions: Universal or Culture-Specific?" *American Anthropologist*, 88, 584–94.

Wilson, Edward (1978): *On Human Nature*. Cambridge, MA: Harvard University Press.

Wilson, James Q. and Richard J. Herrnstein (1985): *Crime and Human Nature*. New York: Simon and Shuster.

Wolfson, Dirk J. (1985): "Criteria in Engineering Social Justics." In Guy Terny and A. J. Gulyer (eds), *Public Finance and Social Policy*. Detroit, MI: Wayne State University Press, 185–96.

Wood, Allen W. (1981): *Karl Marx*. London: Routledge & Kegan Paul.

Wriglesworth, John L. (1985): "Respecting Individual Rights in Social Choice." *Oxford Economic Papers*, 37, 100–17.

Wyatt, Nicolas (1988): "When Adam Delved: The Meaning of Genesis III: 23." *Vetus Testamentum*, 38, 117–22.

Yablon, Charles M. (1987): "Arguing About Rights." *Michigan Law Review*, 85, 871–94.

Yasukawa, Ken (1984): "Animals Make the Most of the Home-field Advantage." In Georgina Ferry (ed.), *The Understanding of Animals*. Oxford: Blackwell and New Scientist, 182–9.

Index